CONNECTING
GOALS
TO IMPACTS
AND OUTCOMES

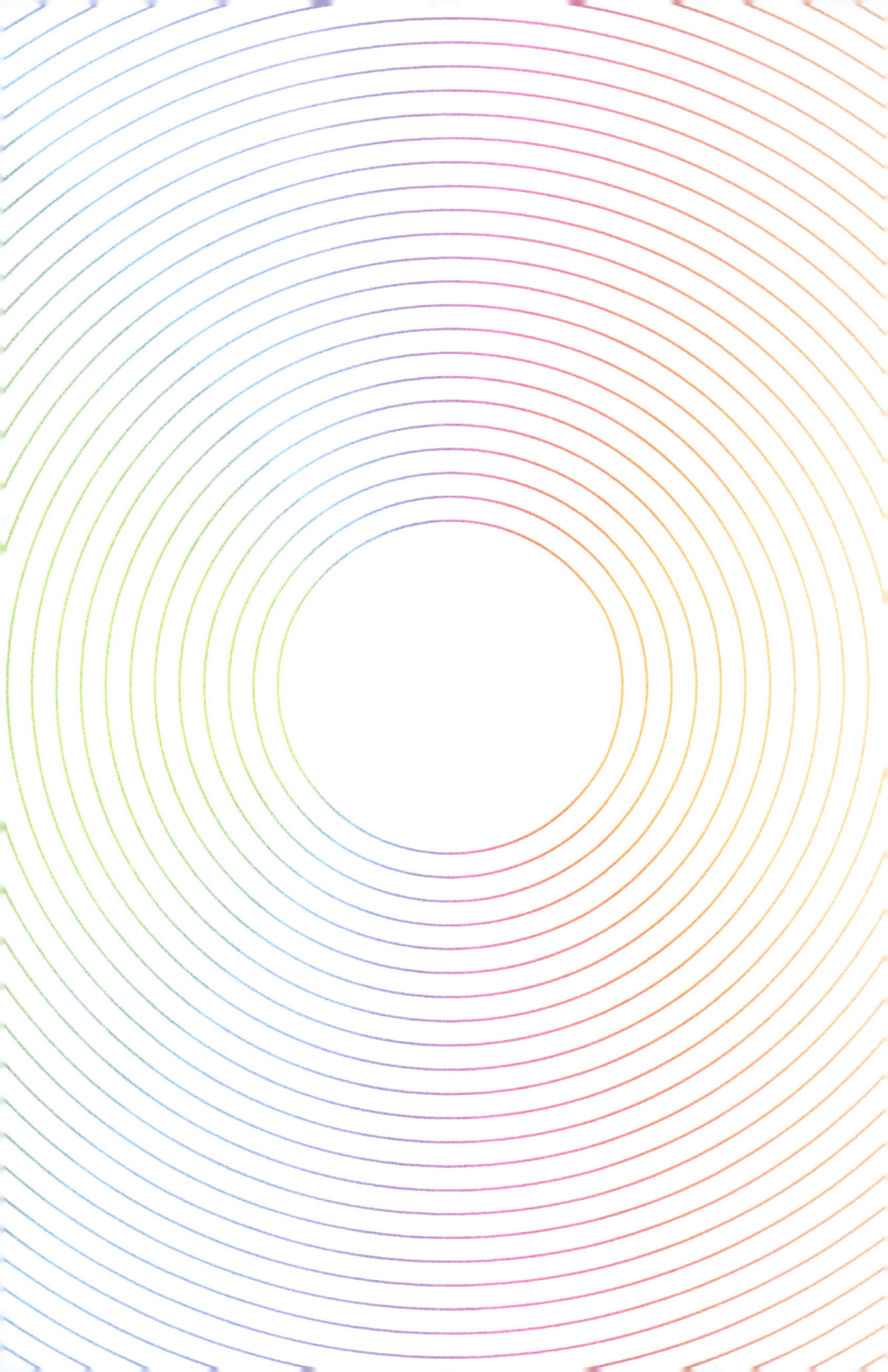

Harnessing Structured Conversations
for Customer-Driven Value Delivery

CONNECTING GOALS TO IMPACTS AND OUTCOMES

Claude Hanhart & Rachel Collins

Connecting Goals to Impacts and Outcomes: Harnessing Structured Conversations for Customer-Driven Value Delivery

Copyright © 2026 by Claude Hanhart & Rachel Collins

Published in the United States by Structured Conversations Press
www.structured-conversations.com

Paperback: 979-8-218-92188-0
eBook: 979-8-218-92189-7

Cover Design by Designs Guru Studio
Book Design by Molly Mortimer, Mayfly book design

Library of Congress Catalog Number: 2026901765
First Printing: 2026

Claude

For my wife and parents,
who always supported me in pursuing my dreams.

Rachel

For Claude,
who believed in me enough to ask me to co-author this book!

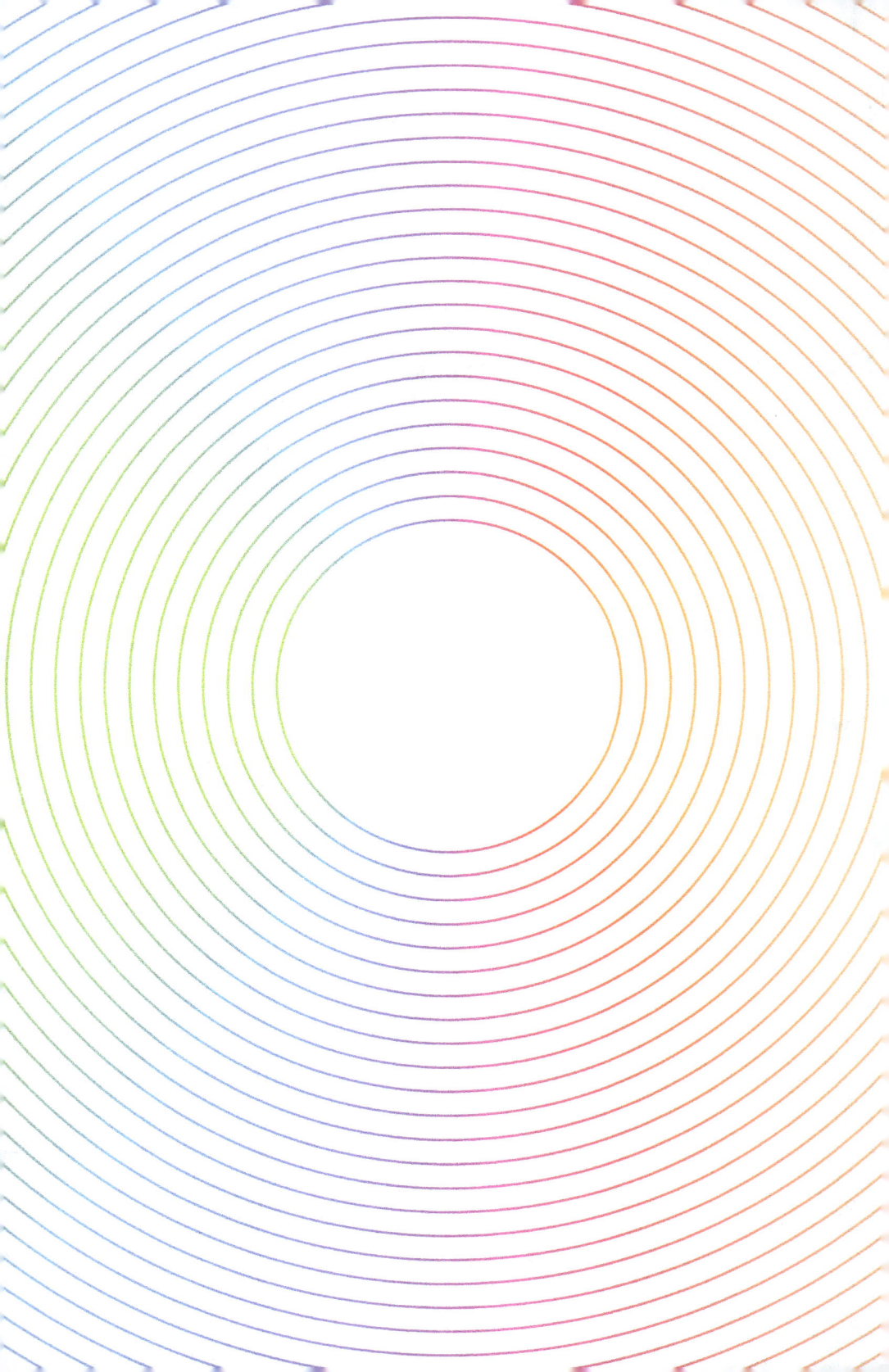

Contents

PART 1: FOUNDATIONS

PART 2: MAPPING FOR ALIGNMENT

PART 3: CRAFTING DELIVERABLES

Preface

There's a gap between what product teams build and what customers actually need. It's not a problem of talent or effort—it's a problem of communication. Teams work hard, hold countless meetings, and ship features on schedule, yet somehow miss the mark on creating real value.

Years ago, we experienced this firsthand while leading an ambitious product effort. Despite everyone's best intentions and genuine commitment, the initiative slowly unraveled. In the post-mortem, we realized the core issue wasn't technical or strategic—it was conversational. We had no reliable way to ensure that when we talked about goals, requirements, or success, we were all talking about the same thing.

That realization became the foundation for this book.

Structured Conversations aren't about adding bureaucracy or rigid processes. They're lightweight, practical techniques that help teams communicate with precision and align around shared outcomes. The central insight is simple but powerful: the quality of our conversations determines the quality of our results.

Take **VERB + NOUN**—a cornerstone technique that transforms how teams write goals and requirements. Instead of saying "customer experience improvement" (vague and unmeasurable), you write "increase customer retention by 10%" (specific and actionable). The difference seems small, but the impact is profound. VERB + NOUN syntax forces clarity about what action you're taking and what you're acting upon. It eliminates ambiguity and creates shared understanding across product, design, and engineering teams.

This clarity ripples through everything: sharper user stories, better prioritization decisions, measurable outcomes everyone can track. When combined with visual techniques like Empathy Mapping and Impact Mapping, VERB + NOUN becomes part of a comprehensive strategy for turning fuzzy conversations into focused action.

The techniques in this book have been tested across diverse contexts: tech startups and enterprise transformations, financial services and government initiatives, small teams and large organizations. Each technique is designed to be immediately useful—no special training required.

This book is for you if:

- You're tired of debating what "done" really means
- You want your team guided by purpose, not just productivity
- You believe great products start with shared understanding

The chapters can be read in any order. Each introduces a specific technique for adding focus and clarity to your work. You can't always control how products get built or delivered, but you can choose how clearly you communicate what you're building and why.

That choice—starting with something as simple as VERB + NOUN syntax—is the first step toward better outcomes.

Why This Book?

You've been in that meeting. The one where everyone nods enthusiastically about "improving customer experience" or "increasing customer engagement," but when you walk out, nobody can actually explain what those words mean or how you'll know if you've succeeded.

Three months later, your team ships a feature that took weeks to build and . . . crickets. Customers don't use it. Stakeholders ask uncomfortable questions. Someone inevitably says, "I thought we were building something different."

These moments aren't caused by bad intentions or lazy thinking. They're caused by something much more fundamental: the way we talk about our work. When our conversations lack structure and precision, our outcomes follow suit.

Structured Conversations is a practical approach to fixing this problem. It's a toolkit of visual mapping techniques and language patterns that help teams align around shared goals, surface hidden assumptions, and deliver real value to customers.

Over 15 years of working in technology and financial services, we've applied these techniques across startups and enterprises, product teams and executive committees, urgent bug fixes and multi-year initiatives. The core insight is deceptively simple: **the quality of your conversations determines the quality of your results.**

These techniques will help you:

- Articulate clear, executable goals before diving into solutions
- Align stakeholders around a shared vision and common language
- Surface assumptions and risks early, before they become expensive mistakes
- Connect daily work to your highest priorities
- Build transparency and momentum across development teams

While many of these techniques have roots in Agile practices, they're flexible enough to apply beyond software development. Whether you're leading a marketing campaign, planning a product roadmap, or aligning executive strategy, these techniques bridge the gap between good intentions and measurable outcomes.

Challenges You'll Recognize

If you've worked in product development for any length of time, these scenarios probably sound familiar:

- Meetings that end without clear next steps or owners
- Features that solve problems nobody actually has
- Quiet team members with valuable insights who never get heard

- Brainstorming sessions that generate lots of ideas but no decisions
- Teams that stay busy but make little progress toward meaningful outcomes
- Stakeholders who ask for one thing but expect something completely different

These aren't character flaws or organizational failures—they're communication problems. Structured Conversations make it easier for everyone to be heard, for priorities to be clear, and for energy to flow toward actual value creation.

The Two Pillars: Syntax and Mapping

Structured Conversations are built on two complementary approaches:

Syntax: The Language of Clarity. Simple rules for writing goals and requirements that eliminate ambiguity. The foundation is **VERB + NOUN**—a pattern that forces specificity about what action you're taking and what you're acting upon.

- **Instead of**: Customer experience improvement
- **Write**: Reduce checkout abandonment by 15%

The difference seems small, but the impact is profound. VERB + NOUN syntax creates shared understanding about exactly what success looks like and how you'll measure it.

Mapping: Making the Invisible Visible. Visual canvases like impact maps, customer journey maps, and empathy maps help teams see relationships, dependencies, and priorities that are hard to discuss in linear conversation.

These aren't just pretty pictures—they're thinking techniques that help teams discover insights they'd miss in traditional planning meetings.

Together, syntax and mapping create a chain of clarity that connects:

- **Goals:** Your high-level vision
- **Objectives:** Specific, measurable steps toward that vision
- **Impacts:** The changes your work will create
- **Outcomes:** Concrete value for customers and business

When these elements align, everything you do becomes intentional and measurable.

Templates

The techniques in this book work best when they're visual and collaborative. That's why we've created free downloadable templates at **structured-conversations.com** that you can use immediately with your team.

These templates aren't meant to replace conversation— they're designed to guide it. They help you capture insights, surface disagreements, and turn discoveries into actionable next steps.

Who This Book Is For

The book is for anyone responsible for turning ideas into value:

- **Leaders.** Learn how to align teams around strategy and vision without micromanaging execution.
- **Product Managers.** Master the language and techniques for defining customer-centric success.

- **Marketers & Analysts.** Connect initiatives to quantifiable business outcomes.
- **Team Leads:** Facilitate collaboration across silos and ensure every voice contributes.
- **Engineers and Designers.** Understand how your daily work connects to customer value and business goals.

Whether you're planning features, setting strategy, or just trying to run better meetings, Structured Conversations will help you convert good intentions into measurable results.

How This Book Is Organized

The book is structured as a guided journey through the foundations and key techniques of Structured Conversations.

Early chapters focus on the fundamentals: why Structured Conversations matter, how language patterns shape thinking, and how visual canvases transform team alignment.

Later chapters dive into specific techniques, each building on previous concepts as shown in the Structured Conversations Navigation Wheel (Fig. 1). You can read them in order for the full progression, or jump to specific techniques that address your current challenges.

Each chapter includes:

- Clear learning objectives and key takeaways
- Step-by-step guidance for practical application
- Real examples that bring techniques to life
- References to free templates you can download and use immediately
- "Try This Right Now" sections for immediate experimentation

This structure gives you both a comprehensive approach and modular techniques you can apply individually based on your team's needs.

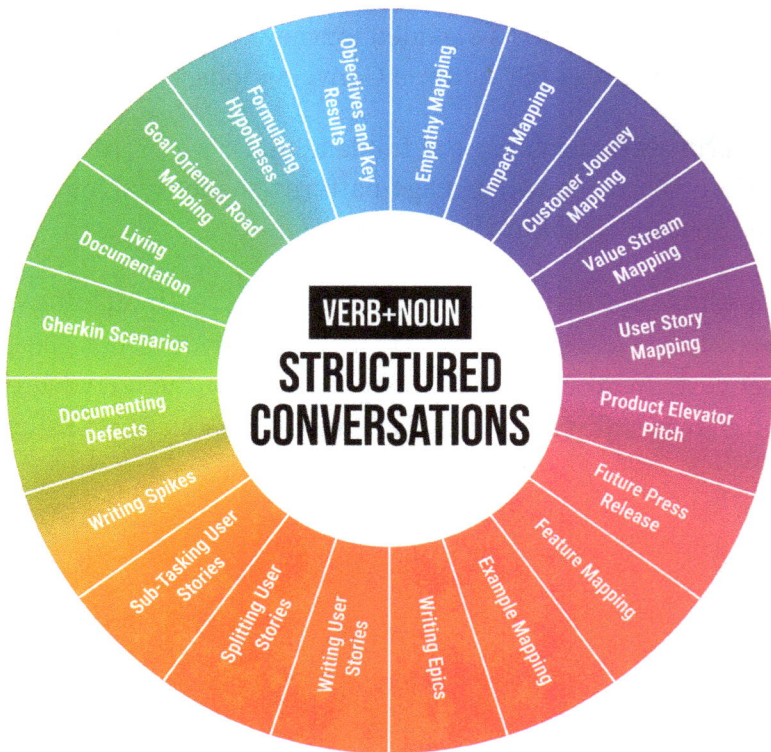

Fig. 1: Structured Conversations Navigation Wheel

Your Journey Starts Now

The way we talk determines the value we create. Every conversation is an opportunity to move from vague to specific, from assumptions to evidence, from good intentions to measurable outcomes.

You don't need organizational change or special training to start. You can begin with your very next conversation by asking one simple question: "What specific customer behavior are we trying to change?"

That question—and the structured conversation that follows—is the first step toward building products and services that actually matter to the people who use them.

Let's begin.

The Structured Conversations Manifesto

Better communication leads to better results. The *Structured Conversations Manifesto* guides teams to connect goals to customer value with plain language and visualizations.

Our Vision: Better Results Through Structured Conversations

We believe:

Clear, purposeful language surpasses ambiguous demands.

Shared understanding eclipses solo perspectives.

Impacts and Outcomes eclipse mere outputs and checklists.

Continuous visual mapping surpasses static documentation.

Intentional syntax surpasses accidental semantics.

Guiding Principles

Clear language sparks action. Concise expressions concentrate teams.

Visual maps show the path. Exposing gaps enhances choices.

Every story is a conversation. User stories harmonize on customer requirements.

Outcomes define success. Quantifiable achievements matter foremost.

Small changes, big impact. Precise words reshape priorities.

This isn't yet another framework – it's a way to talk, align, and act with intention.

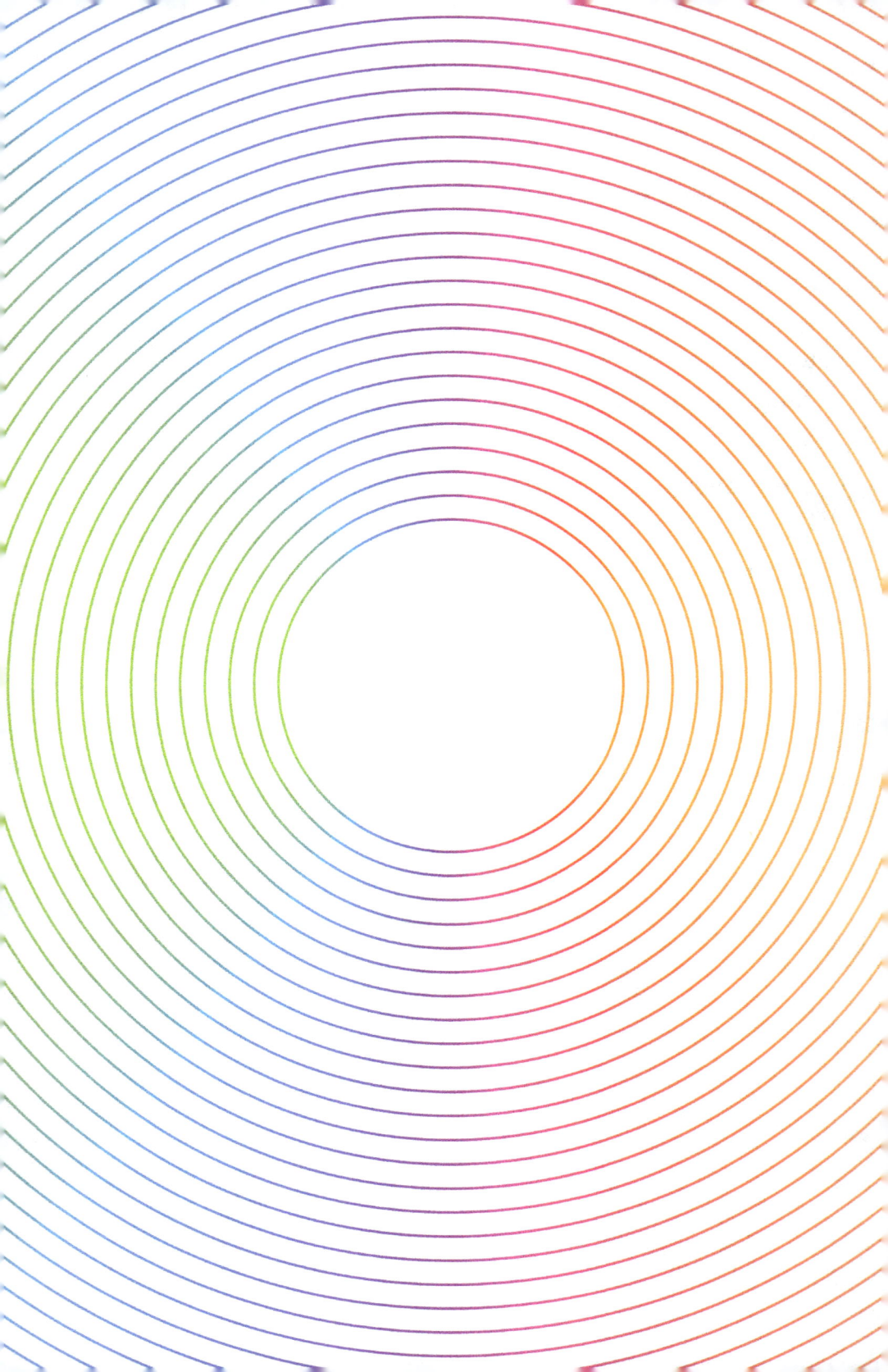

PART 1

FOUNDATIONS

CHAPTER 1

Structured Conversations

Building the Foundation for Clear Outcomes

What You'll Learn

- Why many product failures trace back to communication problems, not technical ones
- How three simple elements can transform your team's ability to align and deliver value
- The practical foundation you need to start having clearer, more productive conversations today

The Meeting That Broke Everything

The restaurant app team was excited about their Q3 planning session. They'd blocked out two full days to align on priorities, define success metrics, and leave with a clear roadmap everyone felt good about.

By 10 AM, things were already going sideways.

The CEO kicked things off by saying they needed to "dramatically improve customer experience" to hit their growth targets. Everyone nodded—who could argue with better customer experience?

Sarah the developer interpreted this as fixing the app's performance issues. Page load times were terrible, and she'd been getting complaints from customer support. Mike the designer heard it as improving the visual design and user interface flow. The app looked dated compared to competitors. Jessica the product manager assumed it meant building features customers had been requesting—loyalty programs, order tracking, social sharing.

Two hours in, they were debating whether to prioritize a complete UI redesign, a technical performance overhaul, or a roadmap full of new features. Everyone was passionate about their interpretation. Everyone had data supporting their approach. And everyone was getting frustrated that the others "weren't listening" to the obvious priority.

By lunch, they'd accomplished nothing except agreeing that customer experience was important—something they'd all believed when they walked in that morning.

Sound familiar? This scenario plays out in conference rooms and Zoom meetings every day. Smart, well-intentioned people who want to build great products, trapped in conversations that generate heat without creating light.

The problem wasn't the people or their priorities. The problem was the conversation itself.

Where This Fits

This chapter introduces the foundation that makes every other technique in this book possible. Before you can run effective Empathy

Mapping sessions (Chapter 5) or write clear user stories (Chapter 15), you need to understand why structured conversations matter and how they work.

Think of this as installing the operating system that will run all your future product conversations.

What Are Structured Conversations?

Structured Conversations are a set of language patterns and visual techniques that help teams create shared understanding and move from scattered discussion to focused action.

They're not rigid rules or complex processes. Think of them more like a GPS for team communication—techniques that help you navigate from fuzzy intentions to specific, measurable outcomes.

Here's what makes them different from typical team discussions:

They force specificity. Instead of "Customer experience improvement," you end up with "reduce checkout abandonment by 15% in Q2."

They make assumptions visible. Instead of everyone nodding at vague goals while imagining different things, you surface and discuss the differences explicitly.

They connect daily work to customer value. Instead of building features because they seem important, you build them because they drive specific customer behaviors you want to influence.

They create shared vocabulary. Instead of each function speaking its own language, everyone uses the same techniques to describe problems and solutions.

The Three Elements That Make It Work

Structured Conversations harness three complementary elements:

Syntax: The Language of Precision. Syntax is about using specific language patterns that eliminate ambiguity. The foundation is simple constructs like **VERB + NOUN** that force clarity about what action you're taking and what you're acting upon.

- **Instead of**: We need to improve engagement
- **Use**: Increase daily active users by 20%

The difference seems small, but it changes everything. The first version leaves room for five different interpretations. The second version means exactly one thing to everyone who hears it.

Mapping: Making the Invisible Visible. Mapping means using visual techniques to organize ideas, surface relationships, and identify gaps that are hard to see in linear conversation.

An impact map, for example, doesn't just list features you might build—it shows how those features connect to specific customer behaviors and business outcomes. An empathy map doesn't just describe your customers—it reveals insights about their motivations that inform what you should build.

These aren't just pretty pictures. They're thinking techniques that help teams discover insights they'd miss in traditional planning meetings.

Dialogue: The Safe Space for Hard Conversations. Dialogue is the process that brings syntax and mapping to life. It's creating an environment where people with different perspectives can contribute their insights without fear of judgment or dismissal.

This isn't about being nice or avoiding conflict. It's about channeling disagreement into productive discussion that leads to better decisions.

Together, these three elements create a system for turning good intentions into measurable outcomes. This aligns with research from Douglas Squirrel and Jeffrey Fredrick in *Agile Conversations* (2020), which shows that teams with structured communication patterns consistently outperform those that rely on ad-hoc discussions.

Why Many Product Conversations Fail

Before diving into solutions, let's understand the problem. Many product conversations fail for predictable reasons:

Vague language that sounds meaningful but isn't. Words like "engagement," "experience," and "quality" feel important but mean different things to different people.

Hidden assumptions that never get surfaced. Everyone brings their own mental model of the customer, the problem, and the solution. These models rarely align, but teams don't discover the misalignment until much later.

Focus on outputs instead of outcomes. Teams discuss what to build rather than what change they want to create in customer behavior.

No shared strategy for making decisions. When priorities conflict, teams resort to politics, opinion, or whoever speaks loudest rather than objective criteria.

Linear thinking about complex problems. Product development involves relationships, dependencies, and feedback loops that are hard to understand in traditional discussion formats.

Structured Conversations address each of these problems systematically.

How Structured Conversations Transform Teams

When teams master structured conversations, several things change:

Planning becomes faster and more accurate. Instead of spending days debating interpretations of vague goals, teams quickly align around specific, measurable objectives.

Disagreements become productive. Instead of arguing about opinions, teams discuss evidence, assumptions, and trade-offs against shared success criteria.

New team members contribute faster. Instead of months learning tribal knowledge, new hires can read clear documentation that explains why decisions were made and how success is measured.

Customer value becomes the default filter. Instead of building features because they seem cool or competitors have them, every conversation starts with "how does this help our customers accomplish their goals?"

Stakeholder conversations improve. Instead of defending decisions with "trust us, we know our customers," teams can point to specific research, clear hypotheses, and measurable outcomes.

Work becomes more meaningful. When everyone understands how their daily tasks connect to customer outcomes and business results, the work feels purposeful instead of arbitrary.

Real Example: How Structure Changed Everything

Let's go back to our restaurant app team and see how structured conversation techniques transformed their Q3 planning:

Before (**Traditional Approach**). Goal: Dramatically improve customer experience. Result: Three different interpretations, no clear direction, frustrated team.

After (**Structured Conversation**). Goal: Become the preferred choice for busy families' weeknight dinners.

Impact Mapping Session. Identified that busy parents' biggest pain point wasn't app performance or visual design—it was decision fatigue during the 5-7 PM dinner rush.

Specific Goals:

- Reduce average order time for repeat customers to under 90 seconds
- Increase Monday-Thursday order frequency for families by 25%
- Achieve 90% satisfaction score for weeknight ordering experience

Aligned Understanding. Everyone now knew they were optimizing for speed and convenience during specific time periods for a specific customer segment, not just "better experience" in general.

This clarity transformed their next three months. Instead of three teams working on three different interpretations of "customer experience," they had one team working toward three specific, measurable outcomes.

Starting Your Journey

You don't need to implement everything at once. Here are three simple ways to start having more structured conversations today:

1. Use VERB + NOUN for goals. Next time someone proposes a vague objective like "Customer engagement improvement," ask "what specific customer behavior are we trying to change?" Keep asking until you get to something like "increase daily app use by 30%."

2. Make assumptions explicit. When discussing solutions, ask "what would have to be true for this to work?" Write those assumptions down and discuss whether they're actually true.

3. Start with customer value. Before jumping into features or solutions, spend five minutes discussing "what customer problem are we trying to solve?" and "how will we know if we've solved it?"

These small changes will immediately improve the quality of your team's conversations.

Applications Across Your Work

Structured Conversations aren't just for product teams. The same principles apply across different contexts:

Strategy sessions. Aligning leadership around specific, measurable outcomes instead of aspirational vision statements.

Product planning. Defining initiatives that connect clearly to customer behavior changes and business results.

Sprint planning. Writing user stories that specify not just what to build, but why it matters to customers.

Customer research. Mapping user journeys to identify specific opportunities for improvement.

Stakeholder alignment. Creating visual artifacts that help everyone understand priorities and trade-offs.

The techniques scale from quick team discussions to major strategic initiatives.

What's Coming Next

The rest of this book dives deep into specific techniques that make structured conversations practical and powerful:

VERB + NOUN syntax (Chapter 2) for writing goals that actually guide decisions.

Empathy Mapping (Chapter 5) for understanding customer motivations.

Impact Mapping (Chapter 6) for connecting features to business outcomes.

Customer Journey Mapping (Chapter 7) for designing seamless customer experiences.

Value Stream Mapping (Chapter 8) for optimizing the flow of value.

User Story Mapping (Chapter 9) for planning product development that serves real customer needs.

Product Elevator Pitch (Chapter 10) for telling your product's story compellingly.

Future Press Release (Chapter 11) for painting a vision of customer success.

Feature Mapping (Chapter 12) for creating actionable acceptance criteria fast.

Example Mapping (Chapter 13) for bringing users stories to life with concrete examples.

Writing Epics (Chapter 14) for framing strategic initiatives for maximum impact.

Writing User Stories (Chapter 15) for capturing the atomic unit of getting stuff done.

Splitting User Stories (Chapter 16) for breaking work into deliverable pieces.

Writing Spikes (Chapter 17) for tackling uncertainty with focused research.

Sub-Tasking User Stories (Chapter 18) for tactical planning that ensures delivery.

Documenting Defects (Chapter 19) for ensuring clarity that enables swift resolution.

Writing Gherkin Scenarios (Chapter 20) for defining behavior with clarity and automation.

Living Documentation (Chapter 21) for creating documentation that actually tells the truth.

Goal-Oriented Roadmapping (Chapter 22) for charting a path to customer value.

Formulating Hypotheses (Chapter 23) for validating ideas that drive impactful outcomes.

Objectives and Key Results (OKRs) (Chapter 24) for aligning team work with organizational goals.

Each technique builds on the foundation we've established here: using precise language and visual thinking to create shared understanding and drive better outcomes.

You can read the chapters in order for the complete journey, or jump to specific techniques that address your team's current challenges.

Your Next Conversation

The transformation starts with your very next conversation. Whether it's a sprint planning meeting, a stakeholder discussion, or a casual chat about priorities, you can begin applying these techniques immediately.

Ask yourself: Is this conversation moving us toward shared understanding and specific outcomes? Or are we talking past each other while nodding at vague concepts?

That awareness—and the commitment to do something about it—is the first step toward building products that actually matter to the people who use them.

What's Next

Chapter 2 explores the **VERB + NOUN** syntax in detail. You'll learn how this simple language pattern eliminates ambiguity, guides decision-making, and creates the foundation for every other structured conversation technique in this book.

VERB + NOUN

The Syntax of Clarity

What You'll Learn

- Why two simple words can eliminate confusion in your product conversations
- How VERB + NOUN transforms vague ideas into actionable goals that teams can actually execute
- A practical approach for writing requirements that mean the same thing to everyone who reads them

The Hour-Long Debate About Nothing

The restaurant app team was deep into their sprint planning when they hit a roadblock that would consume the rest of their morning.

"We need to prioritize account management optimization options this sprint," announced Jessica the product manager, pulling up a backlog item that had been sitting there for weeks.

Sarah the developer squinted at her screen. "What exactly does that mean? Are we talking about changing how customers log in? Updating profile settings? Something with password recovery?"

Mike the designer chimed in: "I thought it meant redesigning the account dashboard. The UI is pretty outdated and customers complain about finding things."

"Actually," said Alex from customer support, "most of our tickets are about people wanting to change their delivery preferences but not being able to find where to do it. Maybe it's about that?"

Jessica looked at the backlog item description: "Improve account management options to enhance customer experience and reduce support burden." Helpful?

An hour later, they were still debating what "account management optimization options" actually meant. Each person had a reasonable interpretation. Each interpretation would require different work, different timelines, and different success metrics. And none of them were wrong—the requirement was just too vague to be useful.

This is exactly why our Structured Conversations Manifesto says *"Clear language sparks action."* But unclear language does the opposite—it sparks endless debate about what we're supposed to be doing instead of actually doing it.

Where this Fits

VERB + NOUN is the foundation of every other technique in this book. Before you can run effective Empathy Mapping sessions (Chapter 5) or write compelling user stories (Chapter 15), you need to master the basic syntax that eliminates ambiguity from your product conversations.

Think of this chapter as learning the grammar that makes all your future structured conversations possible.

Why Language Choices Matter More Than You Think

Let's be honest about something: product teams can be terrible at naming things. We create backlog items like "Customer experience enhancements" and "Performance optimization initiative" and "Customer engagement improvements"—then wonder why nobody can agree on what to work on first.

These aren't just bad names—they're conversation killers. When your goals are vague, every discussion becomes a debate about interpretation instead of a focused conversation about execution.

Here's what happens when teams use fuzzy language:

Planning takes forever. Instead of quickly aligning on what to build, teams spend hours clarifying what vague requirements actually mean.

Everyone builds different things. Developers, designers, and product managers all interpret ambiguous goals differently, leading to misaligned work.

Success becomes unmeasurable. If you can't define what you're trying to accomplish precisely, you can't tell if you've accomplished it.

Stakeholder conversations get frustrating. Executives ask "what are we building?" and get answers like "customer engagement optimization" that don't actually answer the question.

New team members stay confused longer. Unclear requirements create tribal knowledge that takes months to decode.

The root cause isn't bad intentions or poor planning skills—it's linguistic imprecision. And linguistic imprecision has a linguistic solution.

The Power of Two Words

VERB + NOUN is the simplest pattern that eliminates ambiguity: start with a verb that signals intent, add a noun that defines the target, and you have a structure that means exactly one thing to everyone who reads it.

This pattern isn't new to product work. Anthony W. Ulwick established similar thinking in his 2016 book *Jobs To Be Done: Theory to Practice*, where he defines job statements with the format: verb + object of the verb (noun) + contextual clarifier. As Ulwick writes, "A job statement always begins with a verb and is followed by the object of the verb (a noun)." His example—"listen to music while on the go"—shows how this verb-noun structure creates clarity, with the contextual clarifier ("while on the go") adding necessary specificity.

We've adapted this principle for writing product requirements and backlog items. Instead of "Account management optimization options," you might write:

- **Update** delivery preferences
- **Enable** password reset
- **Delete** saved payment methods

Each of these phrases tells you exactly what action to take and exactly what you're acting upon. No interpretation required.

The magic isn't in the individual words—it's in the constraint. When you force yourself to use VERB + NOUN, you can't hide behind vague concepts. You have to be specific about what you're actually trying to accomplish.

How VERB + NOUN Changes Everything

This simple syntax pattern transforms your product conversations in several ways:

Sparks immediate action. Verbs are action words. When your goals start with verbs, they naturally push toward execution instead of endless discussion.

Focuses team energy. Nouns identify exactly what you're working on. Instead of broad concepts like "customer experience," you're focused on specific things like "checkout flow" or "search results."

Makes testing obvious. When your goal is "reduce page load time," everyone knows how to measure success. When your goal is "improve performance," nobody does.

Reduces assumptions. Vague language lets people fill in gaps with their own interpretations. Precise language eliminates most of those gaps.

Enables better estimation. Teams can accurately estimate "add shopping cart persistence" much more easily than "enhance e-commerce functionality."

Real Example: From Confusion to Clarity

Let's go back to our restaurant app team and see how VERB + NOUN transformed their "Account management optimization options" debate:

Original (confusing): Account management optimization options

VERB + NOUN breakdown:

- **Update** delivery preferences
- **Enable** notification settings
- **Delete** saved payment methods
- **Add** order history filters

Suddenly, what seemed like one big, vague initiative became four specific, actionable items. The team could now:

- Prioritize which item to tackle first based on customer impact
- Estimate each item independently
- Assign clear ownership for each piece
- Define specific success criteria for each action
- Track progress meaningfully

The hour-long debate became a 10-minute prioritization discussion.

Breaking Down "Noun Piles"

One of the biggest sources of confusion in product work is what we call "noun piles"—strings of nouns that sound important but don't actually specify what you're supposed to do.

Common noun pile offenders:

- Notification center redesign
- Customer experience enhancement
- Data analytics dashboard optimization
- Mobile performance improvement initiative

Each of these could mean dozens of different things. VERB + NOUN forces you to unpack the pile:

Notification center redesign becomes:

- **Reorganize** notification categories
- **Update** visual styling
- **Add** filtering options
- **Enable** bulk actions

Customer experience enhancement becomes:

- **Reduce** checkout steps
- **Improve** search accuracy
- **Speed up** page loading
- **Automate** return label generation

Data analytics dashboard optimization becomes:

- **Consolidate** key metrics onto single view
- **Automate** data refresh intervals
- **Customize** widget arrangements
- **Export** reports in multiple formats

Mobile performance improvement initiative becomes:

- **Reduce** app startup time
- **Compress** image file sizes
- **Cache** frequently accessed data
- **Eliminate** unnecessary network calls

Notice how the noun pile version leaves everything open to interpretation, while the VERB + NOUN versions give teams concrete work to do.

A Curated Verb Toolkit

Teams should develop their own curated verb toolkit tailored to their specific domain and customer needs. While the foundation of clear, actionable verbs remains consistent, the most effective vocabulary varies significantly across different products, industries, and customer contexts.

Not all verbs are created equal for product work. Here's a foundational list of action verbs that work well for writing clear, actionable goals:

Creation & Modification. Add, Create, Build, Generate, Produce, Develop, Design, Write, Edit, Update, Modify, Delete, Remove, Replace.

Access & Navigation. View, Display, Show, Search, Find, Filter, Sort, Browse, Navigate, Open, Close, Download, Upload, Import, Export.

Configuration & Control. Configure, Set, Adjust, Enable, Disable, Toggle, Reset, Customize, Personalize, Control, Manage.

Interaction & Communication. Send, Receive, Share, Notify, Alert, Remind, Subscribe, Unsubscribe, Comment, Rate, Review, Recommend.

Analysis & Reporting. Track, Monitor, Measure, Analyze, Report, Calculate, Compare, Visualize, Summarize.

Security & Validation. Authenticate, Authorize, Verify, Validate, Approve, Reject, Encrypt, Decrypt, Secure, Protect.

Examples in action:

- **Create** order confirmation (instead of "Order processing enhancement")
- **Filter** search results (instead of "Search experience optimization")
- **Enable** two-factor authentication (instead of "Security improvements")
- **Track** delivery status (instead of "Logistics visibility initiative")

This list serves as a starting point, but teams should expand and refine it based on their specific context. A healthcare team might prioritize verbs like "diagnose," "treat," or "monitor," while a financial services team might focus on "transfer," "reconcile," or "audit."

The key is choosing verbs that specify exactly what action you want customers or systems to take within your particular domain.

Connecting Individual Actions to Strategic Goals

VERB + NOUN isn't just about writing better backlog items—it's about creating a chain of clarity that connects daily work to strategic outcomes.

Here's an example:

Strategic Goal: Increase customer retention by 20%

Impact: Reduce checkout abandonment

Outcome: 15% more completed purchases

User Story: Enable one-click checkout

Each level gets more specific, but they're all connected. The user story clearly serves the outcome, which drives the impact, which helps achieve the strategic goal.

This chain ensures that every VERB + NOUN item in your backlog connects to something that matters to customers and the business.

Try This Right Now

Look at your backlog and find the three most confusing or vague items. They probably contain noun piles or abstract concepts.

For each item, ask yourself:

1. What specific action do we want customers to take?
2. What specific thing are we changing or improving?
3. How would we explain this to someone who's never seen our product?

Then rewrite each item using VERB + NOUN format. Share the before and after versions with your team and ask: "Does this make our intent clearer?"

You'll probably discover that some of your "single" backlog items are actually multiple different actions that should be separate user stories.

Common VERB + NOUN Mistakes (And How to Avoid Them)

Mistake 1: Using weak or vague verbs.

- **Bad**: Improve checkout flow
- **Good**: Reduce checkout steps

Strong verbs specify exactly what kind of change you're making.

Mistake 2: Multiple actions in one phrase.

- **Bad**: Update and redesign user profile
- **Good**: Update profile information + Redesign profile layout

One action per user story keeps things focused and estimable.

Mistake 3: Abstract nouns that don't specify targets.

- **Bad**: Enhance usability
- **Good**: Collapse navigation menu subcategories

Concrete nouns tell you exactly what part of the product you're changing.

Mistake 4: Hidden complexity in simple phrases.

- **Bad**: Add reporting (could mean anything from a single chart to a full analytics suite)
- **Good**: Generate weekly sales report

Be specific enough that the scope is clear.

Making VERB + NOUN a Team Habit

To make this a natural part of how your team works:

Use it in backlog refinement. When someone proposes a new item, ask: "What's the verb? What's the noun?" Keep refining until you get to clear actions.

Apply it to goals at every level. Use VERB + NOUN for user stories, sprint goals, quarterly objectives, and strategic initiatives.

Make it visible. Put VERB + NOUN examples on your meeting room walls or team documentation to reinforce the pattern.

Practice in daily conversations. When someone says "we need better performance," ask "do you mean reduce page load time or increase server uptime?"

Connect to acceptance criteria. Your VERB + NOUN user story should make it obvious how you'll test that it's working.

One team we worked with has a simple rule: if you can't write it as VERB + NOUN, you don't understand it well enough to build it yet.

The Ripple Effect

Here's what happens when teams master VERB + NOUN syntax: conversations get faster, estimation gets more accurate, and everyone spends less time confused about what they're supposed to be working on.

But the real benefit is that it forces clarity of thought. You can't write clear VERB + NOUN requirements unless you clearly understand what you're trying to accomplish. The discipline of precise language leads to precise thinking, which leads to precise execution.

Teams that master this simple pattern find themselves naturally asking better questions: "What specific customer behavior are we trying to change?" "What exactly will be different when this is done?" "How will we know if it's working?"

Those questions lead to better products.

What's Next

Chapter 3 builds on VERB + NOUN to explore broader **syntax patterns** that help you articulate goals, behaviors, and outcomes throughout the product lifecycle. You'll learn how to extend this foundation of clarity to every type of product conversation.

The goal isn't just better backlog items—it's transforming how your entire team thinks and talks about the work you do together.

Syntax

The Grammar of Aligned Thinking

What You'll Learn

- How simple sentence templates can eliminate confusion in your product planning
- Why teams that master syntax patterns ship features faster and with less rework
- A toolkit of proven patterns you can start using in your next planning meeting

The Sprint Planning Session From Hell

The restaurant app team thought they were having a productive sprint planning session. Everyone was engaged, ideas were flowing, and they'd filled their backlog with what seemed like clear, actionable work:

- Improve the order process
- Better payment experience
- Enhanced user notifications
- Optimized delivery tracking

Three days into the sprint, chaos erupted.

Sarah the developer had been "improving the order process" by optimizing database queries to speed up order submission. Mike the designer had been working on "better payment experience" by redesigning the entire checkout flow. Jessica the product manager expected "enhanced user notifications" to mean building a new preferences center, but the team had been updating push notification styling.

When they demoed their work, nothing fit together. Sarah's backend optimizations didn't connect to Mike's new UI. Jessica's expected notification features didn't exist. The "optimized delivery tracking" turned out to be three different interpretations: real-time GPS updates, SMS notifications, and a redesigned tracking page.

They'd all been working hard on reasonable interpretations of reasonable-sounding goals. But "reasonable" isn't enough when you're building software. You need to be precise.

This is exactly why our Structured Conversations Manifesto emphasizes *"Intentional syntax surpasses accidental semantics."* When your language is intentionally structured, everyone interprets it the same way. When it's accidentally vague, everyone fills in the gaps with their own assumptions.

Where This Fits

You've mastered VERB + NOUN syntax from Chapter 2, which gives you the foundation for writing clear, actionable goals. Now you need to expand that foundation with syntax patterns—proven templates for different types of product conversations.

Think of this chapter as learning the complete grammar that will make every mapping session (Chapters 5-9) and planning conversation (Chapters 10-24) more productive and aligned.

Why Many Teams Wing It (And Why That's Expensive)

Many product teams approach writing requirements, user stories, and goals the same way they approach writing emails—they just start typing and hope it makes sense. Sometimes it works out. Often it doesn't.

Here's what happens when teams don't have structured approaches to writing requirements:

Every conversation becomes a negotiation about meaning. Instead of quickly aligning on what to build, teams spend time debating what vague requirements actually mean.

Different roles develop different vocabularies. Designers talk about "customer experience improvements," developers talk about "performance optimizations," and product managers talk about "feature enhancements"—but they're often describing the same work in incompatible ways.

Context gets lost over time. When someone writes "improve checkout flow" without structure, the reasoning behind that goal disappears. Six months later, nobody remembers what problem they were trying to solve.

Handoffs become translation exercises. Business requirements get "translated" into technical specifications, which get "translated" into design mockups, which get "translated" into user stories. Each translation introduces new opportunities for misunderstanding.

Testing becomes guesswork. How do you test whether you've achieved "better customer experience"? You can't, because the goal isn't specific enough to be testable.

Syntax patterns solve these problems by giving teams a shared vocabulary and structure for different types of product conversations.

What Makes a Syntax Pattern Powerful

A good syntax pattern is like a recipe—it's a simple template that consistently produces good results when you follow it. Daniel Stillman argues in *Good Talk* (2020) that the structure of our conversations determines their outcomes, and syntax patterns provide exactly this kind of intentional conversational structure for product work.

The best patterns share several characteristics:

They force specificity. You can't complete the template without being clear about what you're trying to accomplish.

They're memorable. Teams can learn them quickly and apply them without constantly referencing documentation.

They work across contexts. The same pattern works whether you're planning features, writing acceptance criteria, or setting strategic goals.

They connect to outcomes. Each pattern naturally leads you to think about how you'll measure success.

They reveal assumptions. The act of filling in the template surfaces beliefs and expectations that need to be discussed.

The Essential Syntax Pattern Toolkit

Here are the core syntax patterns that can assist in transforming how teams communicate about product work:

Traditional User Story

Format: As a [user type], I want to [action], so that [benefit]

Purpose: Defines customer-facing functionality from the user's perspective

Example: As a busy parent, I want to reorder my last meal, so that I can skip menu browsing during dinner rush

Hypothesis Statement

Format: We believe that [action] will result in [outcome]. We'll know we're right when [measurable signal]

Purpose: Tests assumptions before committing resources

Example: We believe that adding one-tap reordering will result in more frequent orders. We'll know we're right when repeat customers order 25% more often

Job Story

Format: When [situation], I want to [motivation], so I can [expected outcome]

Purpose: Captures the context and motivation behind customer needs

Example: When I'm ordering dinner after a long workday, I want to quickly reorder a meal my family enjoyed, so I can avoid decision fatigue

Feature Definition

Format: [Action] [object] [qualifier]

Purpose: Describes system-level functionality clearly

Example: Log order errors to operations dashboard for real-time monitoring

Event-Based Trigger

Format: When [trigger event], [system] should [response]

Purpose: Models system behavior and business rules

Example: When an order is 10 minutes late, the system should send an update notification to the customer

Constraint-Based Story

Format: Even when [limitation], I want to [action], so that [benefit]

Purpose: Addresses edge cases and challenging customer contexts

Example: Even when my internet connection is slow, I want to place an order, so that I can still get food delivered

Choosing the Right Pattern for the Job

Different situations call for different syntax patterns. Here's how to choose:

Use Traditional User Stories when you're defining customer-facing features and want to emphasize customer value.

Use Hypothesis Statements when you're testing assumptions about customer behavior or business outcomes.

Use Job Stories when you need to understand the context and motivation behind customer needs, especially for complex decision-making scenarios.

Use Feature Definitions when you're describing technical functionality or system behavior that doesn't directly involve customer interaction.

Use Event-Based Triggers when you're modeling business rules, automated processes, or system responses to specific conditions.

Use Constraint-Based Stories when you're addressing edge cases, accessibility needs, or challenging customer environments.

Real Example: Transforming the Chaos

Let's go back to our restaurant app team and see how syntax patterns could have prevented their sprint planning disaster:

Original (confusing): Improve the order process

Using different syntax patterns:

- **User Story:** As a returning customer, I want to reorder my previous meal, so that I can skip browsing when I'm in a hurry
- **Hypothesis:** We believe that reducing order steps from 7 to 3 will result in higher conversion. We'll know we're right when checkout abandonment drops by 20%
- **Feature Definition:** Cache customer preferences to enable one-click reordering
- **Event Trigger:** When a customer views their order history, the system should display a 'Reorder' button for previous orders

Each pattern reveals different aspects of the same general goal, and each one gives the team specific, actionable direction.

Original (confusing): Enhanced user notifications

Using syntax patterns:

- **Job Story:** When my order is running late, I want to receive proactive updates, so I can adjust my plans accordingly
- **Constraint Story:** Even when I have notifications disabled, I want to receive order status updates, so that I stay informed about delivery timing
- **Event Trigger:** When an order is 5 minutes late, the system should send an SMS update to the customer

Now instead of three different interpretations, the team has clear, aligned work.

Applying Syntax Patterns Across the Product Lifecycle

Syntax patterns work across every phase of product development:

Strategy Phase. Use hypothesis statements to frame strategic bets:

- We believe that focusing on family customers will result in higher lifetime value. We'll know we're right when average order frequency increases by 30%

Planning Phase. Use user stories and job stories to define features:

- As a restaurant owner, I want to update my menu in real-time, so that customers only see available items

Development Phase. Use feature definitions and event triggers for technical specifications:

- Update inventory counts when orders are placed to maintain accurate availability

Testing Phase. Use constraint stories to cover edge cases:

- Even when the restaurant is closed, I want to schedule orders for tomorrow, so that I can plan ahead

Validation Phase. Use hypothesis statements to design experiments:

- We believe that showing estimated delivery times will reduce customer anxiety. We'll know we're right when support tickets about delivery timing drop by 90%

Try This Right Now

Look at your backlog and find three items that feel vague or open to interpretation. For each item:

1. Identify what type of work it represents (customer-facing feature, technical improvement, business rule, etc.)

2. Choose the appropriate syntax pattern for that type of work

3. Rewrite the item using the pattern

4. Ask yourself: Does this make the intent clearer? Would a new team member understand what to build?

Share the before and after versions with your team. You'll probably discover that some of your "single" backlog items are actually multiple different requirements that should be separate user stories.

Common Syntax Pattern Mistakes (And How to Avoid Them)

Mistake 1: Using the wrong pattern for the job. Using user story format for technical debt or system improvements creates awkward, unnatural language that doesn't help anyone.

Mistake 2: Filling in templates mechanically without thinking. Just because you follow the format doesn't mean the content is clear. As a customer, I want to use the system, so that it works follows user story syntax but says nothing useful.

Mistake 3: Making patterns too complex. Simple patterns work better than comprehensive ones. If your template requires a paragraph to fill out, it's probably too complex.

Mistake 4: Not connecting patterns to outcomes. Every syntax pattern should help you understand how you'll measure success. If you can't tell whether you've achieved the goal, the pattern isn't working.

Making Syntax Patterns a Team Habit

To make syntax patterns a natural part of your workflow:

Start with one pattern. Don't try to implement all patterns at once. Pick the one that addresses your biggest current pain point and master it first.

Make templates visible. Put syntax pattern examples on meeting room walls or in shared documents so people can reference them easily.

Practice in backlog refinement. When someone proposes a vague requirement, ask "which syntax pattern would make this clearer?"

Connect patterns to roles. Product managers might use hypothesis statements, designers might prefer job stories, developers might use feature definitions—but everyone should understand all patterns.

Review and iterate. Look at patterns that aren't working for your team and adapt them. The goal is clarity, not rigid adherence to templates.

One team we worked with has a simple rule: if you can't write it using one of their chosen syntax patterns, you don't understand it well enough to build it yet.

The Compound Effect of Clear Communication

When teams master syntax patterns, something interesting happens: they start thinking more clearly about their work before they start doing it.

The discipline of filling out structured templates forces product conversations to become more specific, more testable, and more connected to customer value. Teams spend less time confused about what they're building and more time focused on building the right things well.

Most importantly, syntax patterns create a shared language that spans roles and teams over time. New team members can read old requirements and understand the reasoning behind decisions. Stakeholders can follow product logic without getting lost in technical details. Everyone speaks the same language about what success looks like.

What's Next

Chapters 4-9 put syntax into action through **visual mapping techniques**. You'll learn how to use empathy maps, impact maps, customer journey maps, and other visual techniques to organize the clear thinking that syntax patterns create.

The combination of structured language and visual thinking is where the real magic happens—turning scattered conversations into aligned action that delivers measurable customer value.

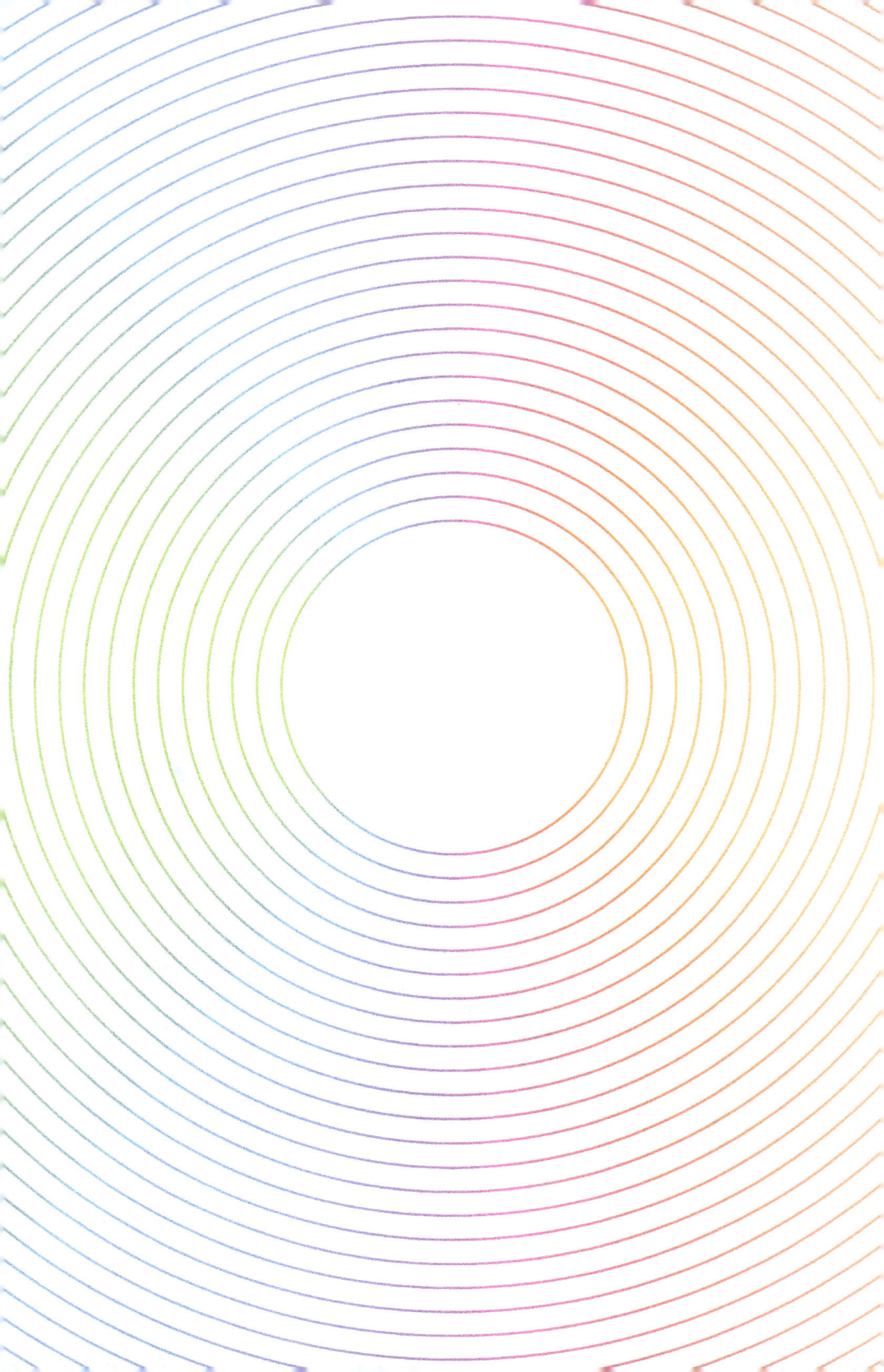

PART 2

MAPPING FOR ALIGNMENT

CHAPTER 4

Are We All on the Same Map?

Visualizing Alignment

What You'll Learn

- Why smart teams with good intentions end up building completely different things (and how visual maps prevent this)
- How five simple mapping techniques can transform scattered conversations into focused action
- The practical foundation you need before diving into specific mapping techniques in Chapters 5-9

The Strategy Meeting That Fooled Everyone

The restaurant app team left their Q2 strategy session feeling great. They'd spent three hours discussing priorities, debating options, and ultimately aligning around a clear goal: "dramatically improve the experience to drive customer retention."

Everyone nodded enthusiastically. The CEO was excited about the business impact. The product manager felt confident about the direction. The designers were already brainstorming improvements. The developers were ready to optimize whatever needed optimizing.

Three months later, the results were in. Customer retention hadn't improved. If anything, it had gotten slightly worse.

In the post-mortem, the painful truth emerged. Everyone had been working toward "improved customer experience," but they'd all been working on completely different things:

- Product had built a loyalty rewards program because research showed customers wanted "more value for frequent ordering"
- Design had redesigned the entire menu interface because customer testing revealed "navigation confusion"
- Engineering had optimized image loading and database queries because performance metrics showed "slow app responsiveness"
- Customer support had created new help documentation because tickets often mentioned "not knowing how to use features"

Each initiative was reasonable. Each addressed real customer feedback. Each improved some aspect of "customer experience." But together, they created a scattered, unfocused product that didn't meaningfully solve any customer's core problems.

The team had been rowing hard in the same general direction, but they were all on different maps of what "customer experience" meant.

This is exactly why our Structured Conversations Manifesto says "*Visual maps show the path.*" But you need to make sure everyone's looking at the same map.

Where This Fits

You've learned structured syntax patterns (Chapters 2-3) that help teams write clear, specific goals. Now you need visual techniques that help teams align around those goals and see how all the pieces fit together.

This chapter introduces the concept of mapping—using visual techniques to organize thinking, surface assumptions, and create shared understanding. It's the foundation you need before diving into specific mapping techniques in Chapters 5-9.

Why Words Alone Aren't Enough

Even with perfect syntax and crystal-clear language, teams still struggle with alignment. That's because product development involves complex relationships between customers, features, outcomes, and constraints that are hard to understand in linear conversation.

Consider the phrase "improve checkout conversion." Using VERB + NOUN syntax, you might refine this to "reduce checkout abandonment by 15%." That's much clearer, but it still leaves critical questions unanswered:

- What specific steps in checkout are causing abandonment?
- Which customer segments are most affected?
- How does checkout abandonment connect to broader business goals?
- What other features or changes might be needed to achieve the goal?
- Which improvements should we prioritize if we can't do everything?

These relationships are hard to see in words alone. They become obvious when you visualize them.

How Your Brain Processes Information

Different people absorb and process information in fundamentally different ways. Some people are verbal processors—they understand concepts through language, lists, and sequential explanations. Others are visual processors—they need to see patterns, relationships, and spatial arrangements to fully grasp complex ideas.

Most product teams are mixed groups of verbal and visual thinkers:

- **Product Managers** often think in terms of metrics and outcomes (verbal)
- **Designers** naturally think in terms of flows and experiences (visual)
- **Developers** think in terms of systems and logic (mixed)
- **Executives** think in terms of strategy and goals (verbal)

When teams rely only on verbal communication—meetings, documents, bullet points—they're essentially asking half the team to translate everything into their less-preferred thinking mode. This creates friction, misunderstanding, and fatigue.

Visual maps provide a common language that works for both verbal and visual thinkers. They make abstract relationships concrete and turn complex systems into understandable patterns.

As scientist Temple Grandin explains in *Visual Thinking* (2022), some minds naturally organize information through images rather than language: *"The world didn't come to me through syntax and grammar. It came through images."*

What Makes a Map Actually Useful

Not all visual techniques are created equal. The most effective maps for product teams share several characteristics:

They organize complexity without oversimplifying. Good maps help you see patterns in complex information without losing important nuances.

They reveal relationships. The spatial arrangement shows how different elements connect to each other in ways that lists and paragraphs can't.

They surface assumptions. The act of placing ideas on a map forces you to be explicit about beliefs and dependencies that usually stay hidden.

They guide decisions. A well-constructed map doesn't just organize information—it helps you see what's most important and what to do next.

They're collaborative. The best maps are created together, with different perspectives contributing to a shared understanding.

They evolve. Maps aren't static documents—they're thinking tools that get updated as you learn more.

The Five Maps That Transform Product Teams

The upcoming chapters dive deep into five specific mapping techniques that address different aspects of product development. Here's a preview of what each map helps you accomplish:

Empathy Mapping (Chapter 5): Understanding Your Customer's Inner World

What it does. Organizes customer research into what people think, feel, see, say, and do.

When to use it. When you need to deeply understand customer motivations and pain points.

Example. Mapping busy parents' dinner-ordering experience to understand why they abandon checkout.

Impact Mapping (Chapter 6): Connecting Deliverables to Business Goals

What it does. Visually connects business objectives to customer behaviors to product deliverables.

When to use it. When you need to ensure your roadmap actually drives the outcomes you care about.

Example. Mapping how simplified reordering connects to increased customer retention.

Customer Journey Mapping (Chapter 7): Seeing the Complete Experience

What it does. Charts the customer's experience across all touchpoints and interactions.

When to use it. When you need to optimize the end-to-end customer experience.

Example. Mapping the complete food ordering journey to identify friction points.

Value Stream Mapping (Chapter 8): Optimizing How Work Gets Done

What it does. Visualizes your internal processes to identify bottlenecks and waste.

When to use it. When you need to improve how your team delivers value.

Example. Mapping the feature development process to reduce time from idea to customer value.

User Story Mapping (Chapter 9): Building Customer-Centric Backlogs

What it does. Organizes user stories into a visual narrative of customer activities.

When to use it. When you need to prioritize features and plan releases around customer value.

Example. Mapping the restaurant ordering experience to plan which features to build first.

Each of these mapping techniques builds on the VERB + NOUN foundation from Chapter 2, addressing different questions and serving different purposes, but they all share the same goal: turning fuzzy conversations into clear, shared understanding.

Real Example: How Mapping Changed Everything

Let's see how visual mapping could have transformed our restaurant app team's scattered Q2 efforts:

Before (Words Only). Goal: Dramatically improve the experience to drive customer retention. Result: Four different interpretations, scattered effort, no meaningful impact.

After (Visual Mapping). The team starts with an impact map to connect retention goals to specific customer behaviors:

- Business goal: Increase customer retention by 25%
- Target customers: Busy families ordering weeknight dinners
- Desired behavior change: Order more frequently (3x per month → 5x per month)
- Key insight: Retention drops because ordering takes too long during dinner rush

This leads to **Customer Journey Mapping** the weeknight ordering experience:

- Discovery: Parents spend 5-7 minutes browsing menus while kids get impatient
- Pain point: Decision fatigue at 6 PM when everyone's hungry and tired
- Opportunity: Enable quick reordering of family favorites

Which informs **Empathy Mapping** of busy parents:

- Think: I just want dinner handled quickly
- Feel: Stressed, overwhelmed, pressed for time
- See: Too many menu options, kids getting cranky
- Do: Browse randomly, second-guess choices, sometimes abandon order

This creates a clear, shared understanding that guides all work toward the same outcome: making weeknight ordering effortless for busy families.

Now instead of four different interpretations of "customer experience," the team has one focused direction supported by visual evidence.

Starting Your Mapping Journey

You don't need to master all five mapping techniques at once. Here's how to start:

Pick one pain point. Choose a specific problem your team is facing—unclear priorities, misaligned stakeholders, customer confusion, whatever feels most urgent.

Choose the right map. Each mapping technique addresses different types of problems:

- Not sure what customers really want? → Empathy Mapping
- Features don't seem to drive business results? → Impact Mapping
- Customer experience feels disconnected? → Customer Journey Mapping
- Internal processes are slow or wasteful? → Value Stream Mapping
- Backlog feels random and unfocused? → User Story Mapping

Start simple. Don't worry about perfect facilitation or beautiful visuals. Grab a whiteboard (or digital equivalent) and start sketching with your team.

Make it collaborative. The real value comes from creating maps together, not from having one person make them and present them to others.

Connect to action. Every mapping session should end with clear next steps informed by what you discovered.

Try This Right Now

Think about a current challenge your team is facing—something where you're not sure everyone is aligned or where the path forward isn't clear.

Spend 20 minutes sketching a simple visual representation:

- Put the main goal or problem in the center
- Add the key players (customers, team members, stakeholders) around it
- Draw connections between different elements
- Mark areas where you're not sure how things connect

Share your sketch with a teammate and ask: "Does this match how you see the problem? What's missing? What connections am I not seeing?"

You'll probably discover that the act of visualizing reveals assumptions and questions you hadn't considered.

When Mapping Becomes Addictive

Teams that start using visual mapping techniques often become enthusiastic converts. Once you experience the clarity that comes from seeing complex relationships laid out visually, going back to purely verbal planning feels frustrating and inefficient.

Here's what typically happens:

- **Week 1:** "This feels like extra work, but I guess we'll try it"
- **Week 3:** "Oh, I see how this helps us align faster"
- **Week 6:** "Can we map this out?" becomes the default response to confusion
- **Month 3:** "How did we ever plan anything without maps?"

The techniques become natural extensions of how teams think and communicate about their work.

Common Mapping Mistakes to Avoid

Mistake 1: Making maps too complex. Simple, rough maps that everyone understands beat beautiful, detailed maps that confuse people.

Mistake 2: Creating maps in isolation. Maps created by one person and presented to others miss the alignment benefits of collaborative creation.

Mistake 3: Treating maps as permanent documentation. Maps are thinking tools that should evolve as you learn. Don't get attached to outdated versions.

Mistake 4: Mapping for the sake of mapping. Every mapping session should have a clear purpose and lead to actionable insights or decisions.

Mistake 5: Not connecting maps to daily work. If your maps don't influence sprint planning, feature prioritization, or other regular decisions, they're just expensive wallpaper.

Building Your Mapping Toolkit

As you work through Chapters 5-9, you'll build proficiency with each mapping technique. But the real power comes from combining them:

- Use **Empathy Maps** to understand customer motivations
- Use **Impact Maps** to connect those motivations to business goals
- Use **Customer Journey Maps** to see the complete customer experience
- Use **Value Stream Maps** to optimize how you deliver improvements
- Use **Story Maps** to organize your backlog around customer value

Each map informs and improves the others, creating a comprehensive view of your customers, your product, and your development process.

What's Next

Chapter 5 dives into **Empathy Mapping**—the foundation for understanding your customers' thoughts, feelings, and motivations. You'll learn how to organize customer research into actionable insights that guide every other mapping technique.

Before you can build the right product, you need to deeply understand the people you're building it for. That understanding starts with seeing the world through their eyes.

CHAPTER 5:

Empathy Mapping

Seeing Through Your Customer's Eyes

What You'll Learn

- How empathy maps help teams see what customers think, feel, and need
- A simple process to create empathy maps that drive customer-focused decisions
- Best practices for using empathy maps to align teams and ignite innovation

When Assumptions Go Spectacularly Wrong

The restaurant app team was absolutely pumped about their latest creation. They'd spent months perfecting these gorgeous animated menus—smooth transitions, playful micro-interactions, the works. This was going to be their "wow" moment, the thing that made their app unforgettable.

Launch day came, and the reactions started pouring in. But instead of the delighted customer videos they'd imagined, they got a flood of confused and frustrated messages. "I can't find anything!" "Why can't I just see a simple list?" "This takes forever to load!"

Turns out, their beautiful swipe-through carousel design buried popular items three screens deep. The artistic category animations meant customers had to wait through transitions just to browse. And those elaborate expanding card effects that looked stunning in their demos? They made it impossible to quickly scan the menu—each item required a tap to reveal the price and description.

What felt innovative to the team felt broken to their customers.

Here's the thing that stings: all of this was totally preventable. If they'd just taken a moment to truly walk in their customers' shoes, these pain points would have been obvious from day one.

This is exactly why our Structured Conversations Manifesto says "*Visual maps show the path.*" Instead of building based on what we think customers want, we can actually step into their world and see what they really need. When we truly empathize with customers, we can confidently say: We see your world, and we're building for it.

That's what Empathy Mapping is all about—bringing customer thoughts, feelings, and daily realities into sharp focus so teams can spot both the pain points and the opportunities everyone else is missing.

Where This Fits

Empathy Mapping becomes your new starting point for making any product decision. Instead of beginning with "What should we build?" you start with "Who are we building for, and what's their world really like?"

Once you've got that foundation, it naturally flows into Impact Mapping (Chapter 6), where you'll connect those customer needs to business outcomes, and Customer Journey Mapping (Chapter 7), where you'll map their entire experience from start to finish.

Why Empathy Mapping Matters

Look, "customer-centricity" gets thrown around a lot, but many teams are still making decisions based on gut feelings and assumptions. Empathy maps change that by helping you:

Get inside your customers' heads and understand what actually drives their decisions (spoiler: it's usually not what you think).

Spot real pain points before you waste months building solutions for problems that don't exist.

Align your team around actual customer needs instead of whoever talks loudest in meetings.

Here's a real example: An e-commerce team discovered through Empathy Mapping that customers were genuinely anxious about return policies—not just annoyed, but actually worried about getting stuck with stuff they didn't want. So they created a prominent "Easy Returns" banner right on product pages. Cart abandonment dropped significantly because they addressed a real fear, not just a surface complaint.

The magic happens when you stop assuming and start seeing. As Microsoft's CEO Satya Nadella (2018, 2019, 2021) puts it, **empathy drives innovation**. When you truly understand your customers' world, you build things that actually fit into it.

What Is an Empathy Map?

An empathy map (Fig. 2) is a simple visual technique that captures what's really going on in your customers' world. It's organized into sections:

Who. The specific person you're mapping (not "customers" but "Sarah, the busy parent")

What. Their actual goals they're trying to accomplish

See. What their environment looks like—the apps, ads, chaos around them

Say. Direct quotes from them about their situation or frustrations

Do. Their current behaviors and daily routines

Hear. What others around them are saying—friends, family, coworkers

Think & Feel. The emotions, anxieties, desires driving their decisions

The key difference from personas? Empathy maps focus on right-now insights from real interactions, not theoretical demographic profiles. They're immediately actionable because they're grounded in actual customer reality.

See Fig. 1 (Navigation Wheel) for where empathy maps fit into Structured Conversations.

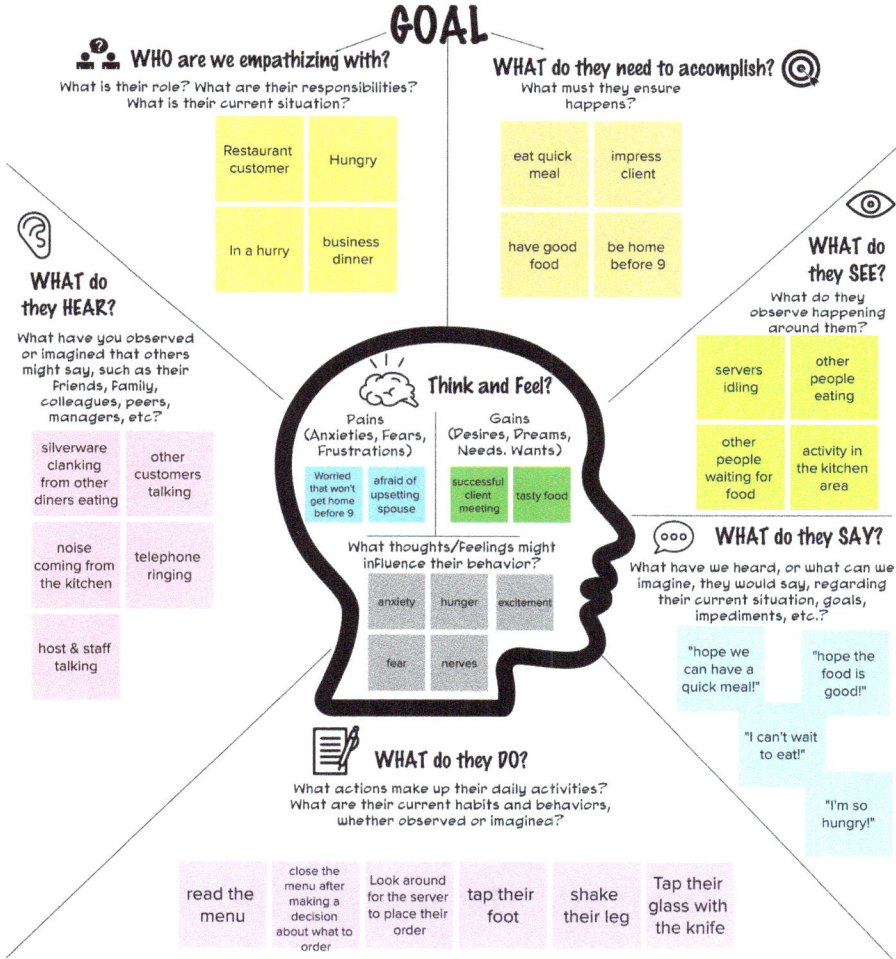

Fig. 2: Empathy Mapping Template (Gray, 2017)

How to Build an Empathy Map (Step by Step)

Download our free template from structured-conversations.com to follow along:

1. **Start with Who.** Get specific. "Sarah, 35, busy parent who uses our restaurant app" beats "working mothers" every time.

2. **Capture What they're trying to accomplish.** Real goals like "Order dinner in under 5 minutes" or "Feed family without breaking budget."

3. **Note what they See in their environment.** The cluttered interface, competing apps, distracting ads, chaotic kitchen—all the stuff competing for their attention.

4. **Record what they Say.** Actual quotes from customer interviews, support tickets, reviews. "This menu is way too complicated!" tells you more than any survey.

5. **Observe what they Do.** Current behaviors like "Scrolls through menu, abandons if it takes too long" or "Calls restaurant directly instead of using app."

6. **Listen to what they Hear.** Kids asking "What's for dinner?" Friends recommending different apps. Online reviews. All the voices influencing their decisions.

7. **Uncover what they Think.** Inner thoughts like "I just need something fast" or "This better not mess up my order."

8. **Feel their emotions.** Both the pains (frustrated by delays, worried about cost) and gains (relieved when something works smoothly).

Real Example: Restaurant App Empathy Map

- **Who.** Sarah, 35, busy parent trying to get dinner sorted after work
- **What.** Order dinner in under 5 minutes while managing evening chaos
- **See.** Cluttered app interface, kids homework spread everywhere, competing food delivery ads
- **Say.** "Why is this so hard to navigate? I just want to reorder what we had last week!"
- **Do.** Scrolls through endless menu options, abandons if app is slow, often just calls the restaurant directly
- **Hear.** Kids complaining they're hungry, husband asking "What's the plan for dinner?", friend mentioning how easy DoorDash is
- **Think.** "I just need food fast—why is this taking forever?"
- **Feel.** Frustrated by complexity, stressed about time, relieved when something actually works

This exercise led the team to completely rethink their approach. Instead of adding more features, they focused on making reordering dead simple. The result? Significant reduction in order time and way happier customers.

Making Empathy Mapping Work in Real Life

Empathy maps aren't just a nice-to-have exercise. Here's how to weave them into your actual workflow:

User research. Start discovery work with Empathy Mapping to ground everything in real customer needs, not assumptions.

Backlog refinement. Use insights to write user stories that actually reflect how people think and feel. "As a stressed parent" hits different than "As a customer."

Design reviews. Test whether your proposed solutions address real pain points or just theoretical problems.

Stakeholder alignment. Share empathy maps to get everyone seeing through the same lens instead of arguing from different assumptions.

One retail team used Empathy Mapping and discovered customers weren't just annoyed by their checkout process—they were genuinely confused about whether their order went through. The team simplified the confirmation flow and saw a nice bump in completed purchases.

Try This Right Now

In your next backlog refinement session, pick a specific customer and try this 20-minute exercise:

1. Draw out the empathy map sections on a whiteboard

2. Add 3-5 real insights per section (no generic stuff like "wants good value")

3. Summarize the 2-3 biggest pains and gains you uncovered

4. Ask the team: What surprised you? What does this change about our priorities?

The magic happens in those surprises—the moments when you realize you've been solving the wrong problem.

Making Empathy a Team Habit

To make this stick beyond one-off workshops:

Start every product cycle with customers. Kick off each sprint or project by refreshing your empathy maps with current insights.

Make it collaborative. Get product, design, and engineering in the room together. Different perspectives reveal different insights.

Keep them current. Update your empathy maps when you get new customer feedback, analytics insights, or support tickets.

Connect to action. Translate those empathy insights into clear goals using the VERB + NOUN syntax (like "Simplify checkout process" or "Reduce menu complexity").

During one backlog refinement, a team's Empathy Mapping revealed that customers were way more anxious about delivery timing than they were about food photos. So instead of spending time on better food photography, they prioritized real-time delivery tracking. That's the power of starting with empathy.

What's Next

In Chapter 6, we'll dive into **Impact Mapping** which builds directly on these empathy insights. You'll learn how to connect what you've discovered about customer needs to measurable business outcomes, keeping your whole team focused on delivering real value instead of just shipping features.

Impact Mapping

Connecting Goals to Deliverables Through Behavioral Change

What You'll Learn

- How impact maps connect business goals to deliverables by identifying key actors and the behavioral changes needed
- A straightforward process for building impact maps that align teams
- Best practices for using impact maps to prioritize deliverables that actually move the needle toward your goals

The Strategy Session That Led Nowhere

The restaurant app team was pumped about their mission to "boost customer engagement." Everyone was nodding along in meetings, sleeves rolled up, ready to make it happen. The CEO was excited about the metrics. The product manager felt confident about the direction. The designers were already sketching ideas.

Three months later, when they launched their solution, it was a complete faceplant.

They'd built this elaborate gamified rewards system that left customers scratching their heads. "Why do I need points to order food?" Meanwhile, their shiny new menu redesign looked gorgeous in screenshots but somehow made it harder for people to actually find what they wanted to eat.

Sound familiar? Here's what went wrong: they had a destination but no map to get there. They never connected their big picture goal ("boost engagement") to what customers actually needed to do differently (order more frequently, spend less time browsing, come back sooner).

The team had been rowing hard, but they were rowing in circles.

This is exactly why we need Impact Mapping. As our Structured Conversations Manifesto puts it: *Visual maps show the path*." Impact Mapping ensures every deliverable you build actually moves the needle on real behavior changes that drive your goals.

Where This Fits

You just finished digging into customer needs with Empathy Mapping (Chapter 5). Now Impact Mapping helps you figure out what to build based on those insights. Think of it as the bridge between understanding your customers and mapping their entire journey (which we'll cover in Chapter 7).

This technique builds directly on the empathy insights you've gathered and connects them to measurable business outcomes your team can work toward.

Why Impact Mapping Matters

Impact Mapping is basically strategic planning that doesn't suck. It's a lightweight visual technique that connects what you're building to the changes you're trying to create, while making all your assumptions crystal clear. Gojko Adzic pioneered this approach back in 2012, and it's become essential for teams who want to build deliverables that actually matter.

Here's what it does for your team:

Finds the shortest path to impact by helping you spot which deliverables are most likely to actually work. No more throwing deliverables at the wall to see what sticks.

Keeps you focused on outcomes instead of falling in love with features. (We've all been there—spending weeks perfecting something customers don't actually want.)

Helps you prioritize work that makes a real difference instead of just keeping busy.

Spots problems before they're expensive by surfacing gaps in your logic before you start building.

Here's a real example: A retail team was trying to increase repeat purchases. Instead of guessing what might work, they used an impact map and realized their biggest opportunity was fixing their clunky checkout process. They focused their efforts there first. Result? Cart abandonment dropped by 30% and repeat purchases went up by 18%.

The magic happens when you stop building features and start driving behavior changes.

What Is an Impact Map?

An impact map (Fig. 3) is a diagram that answers four questions in order:

Why? What's the business goal? (Like "Increase order volume by 10%").

Who? Which people (actors) can actually influence whether you hit that goal? (Customers, staff, partners).

How? What would these people need to do differently? (Place more orders, process orders faster).

What? What could you build to make those behavior changes more likely? (Simplify menu navigation, add reorder button).

The key difference from your typical roadmap? Traditional roadmaps obsess over timelines and features. Impact maps obsess over the behavioral changes that actually move your business forward.

You're not just building stuff—you're influencing how people behave in ways that create value for them and for your business.

See Fig. 1 (Navigation Wheel) for how Impact Mapping fits into Structured Conversations.

Impact Mapping

"The shortest path to the goal." - Gojko Adzic

Purpose: To link business objectives to actors (users or personas) who can influence those goals, to impacts, deliverables/outcomes, and user stories to be developed by product teams.

Audience: Software Delivery Teams, in collaboration with Product Managers/ Owners and other Stakeholders, can all contribute to this activity in order to create user stories that will ultimately contribute toward organizational objectives.

Process Steps:
1. Choose the **organizational objectives** that your product team can affect. Not every organizational objective may be affected by your team, and this is OK!
2. Determine which of your **personas**, or users, can impact these goals. There could be more than one.
3. Describe the **impact** or experience that you want each persona or user to have.
4. Describe a high-level outcome, or **deliverable**, that your product team will create.
5. Write your **user story** in a way that accounts for the user, impact, and deliverable that will ultimately connect back to the organizational objective.

Objectives	Personas/ Users	Impacts
Deliverables / Outcomes	User Stories	

Impact Mapping

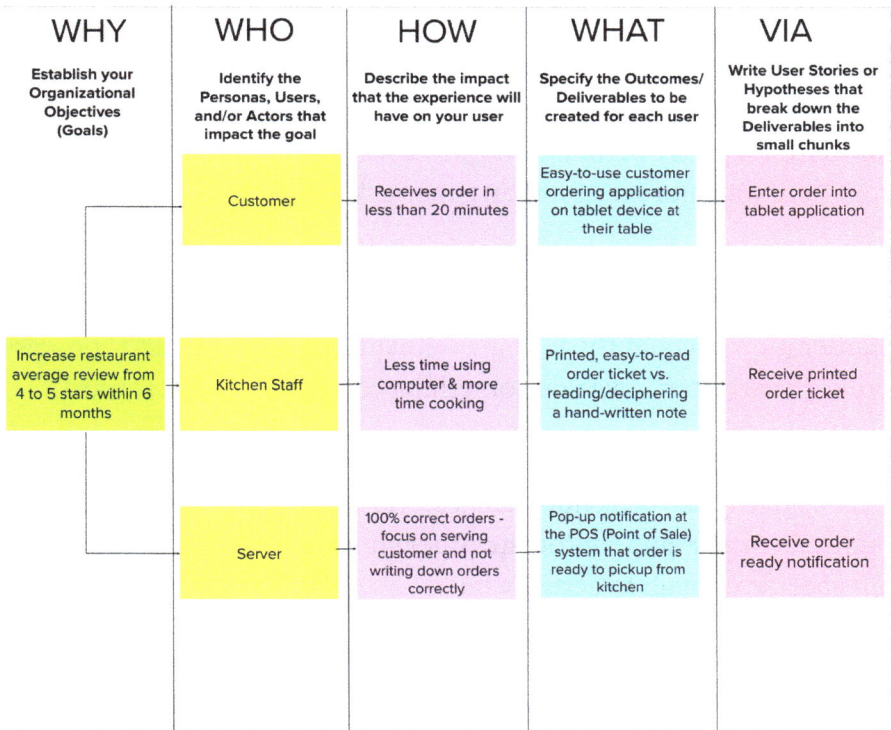

WHY	WHO	HOW	WHAT	VIA
Establish your Organizational Objectives (Goals)	Identify the Personas, Users, and/or Actors that impact the goal	Describe the impact that the experience will have on your user	Specify the Outcomes/ Deliverables to be created for each user	Write User Stories or Hypotheses that break down the Deliverables into small chunks
	Customer	Receives order in less than 20 minutes	Easy-to-use customer ordering application on tablet device at their table	Enter order into tablet application
Increase restaurant average review from 4 to 5 stars within 6 months	Kitchen Staff	Less time using computer & more time cooking	Printed, easy-to-read order ticket vs. reading/deciphering a hand-written note	Receive printed order ticket
	Server	100% correct orders - focus on serving customer and not writing down orders correctly	Pop-up notification at the POS (Point of Sale) system that order is ready to pickup from kitchen	Receive order ready notification

Fig. 3: Impact Mapping Template

How to Build an Impact Map (Step by Step)

Download our free template from structured-conversations.com to follow along:

Start with your goal (Why). Write it as VERB + NOUN to keep it concrete. "Increase order volume by 15%" beats "improve the customer experience" every time. Be specific about what success looks like.

Identify your actors (Who). List the people who can make or break your goal. Think customers, staff, partners—anyone whose behavior matters. "Busy parents ordering dinner" and "restaurant kitchen staff" are way more useful than generic "customers."

Map the impacts (How). What would each actor need to do differently to help you hit your goal? Pull from your empathy maps here. "Order more frequently during weeknight dinner rush" and "process orders 25% faster" give you something concrete to work toward.

List deliverables (What). Now you can brainstorm features that might drive those behavior changes. "Add one-tap reorder button for family favorites" and "automate order status notifications to kitchen" are specific enough to actually build.

Review and ruthlessly prioritize. Get the team together and ask: Do these deliverables actually align with customer needs and business goals? If not, eliminate them. Yes, even that cool feature everyone's excited about.

Real Example: Restaurant App Impact Map

Why? Increase weeknight order volume by 25%

Who? Busy families, restaurant kitchen staff

How? Families reorder their usual meals quickly; kitchen staff process orders without confusion

What? One-tap reorder button for previous family orders, automated kitchen notifications with special instructions

This map led the team to prioritize the reorder button first. Smart move—it boosted weeknight orders by double digits in the first month, way faster than expected. The kitchen notifications came next and reduced order errors by 80%.

Notice how specific this is compared to "boost customer engagement." Everyone knew exactly what behavior they were trying to change and how they'd measure success.

Making Impact Mapping Work in Real Life

Impact maps aren't just a one-time exercise. Here's how to weave them into your actual workflow:

Strategy planning. Get stakeholders aligned around goals like "increase customer retention by 20%" and figure out which deliverables will actually move the needle.

Sprint planning. Turn your deliverables into proper user stories. "As a busy parent, I want one-tap reorder, so that I can get dinner sorted in under a minute."

Backlog refinement. Use your impact map as a filter. If a feature doesn't connect back to an impact on your map, maybe it doesn't belong in your backlog. (Sorry, fancy animations that don't drive behavior change.)

Stakeholder reviews. Show how features like delivery tracking directly tie to business goals. Makes for a much better conversation than "trust us, this is important."

One retail team mapped their goal of "reduce customer service burden" and realized their return process was causing most support tickets. They streamlined it and saw both customer satisfaction and support efficiency improve dramatically.

Try This Right Now

Next time you're looking at your backlog, sketch a quick impact map:

1. Pick a goal like "improve customer retention"

2. Write it in the center as: "Increase retention by 20%"

3. Add 2-3 key actors: "New customers," "Support team"

4. List 2-3 impacts per actor: "New customers come back within 30 days," "Support resolves issues in first contact"

5. Brainstorm 3-5 deliverables: "Onboarding email sequence," "Live chat support," "Proactive check-in calls"

Then ask your team: Which of these deliverables are most likely to actually drive the behavior changes we want?

Pay attention to what surprises come up during this exercise—they're usually the most valuable insights.

Alternative Mapping Techniques

Impact Mapping is great for alignment, but sometimes you need different approaches for different situations:

Opportunity Solution Trees (OST). Perfect when you're exploring new territory and need to visualize paths from outcomes to opportunities, solutions, and experiments (Fig. 4). Teresa Torres (2021) developed this for teams doing continuous discovery and rapid iteration.

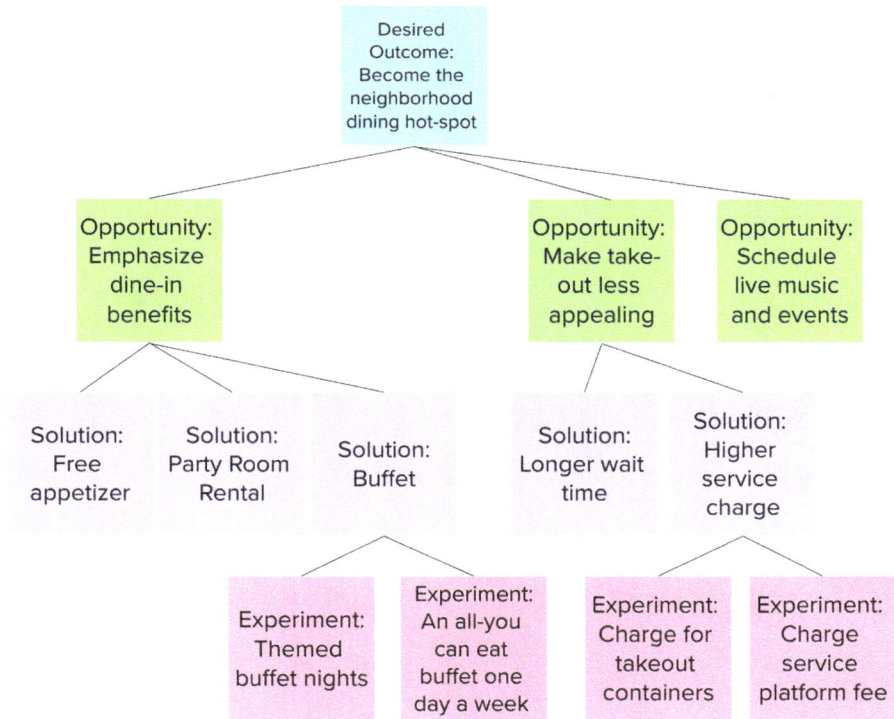

Fig. 4: Opportunity Solution Tree Template

GIST (Goals-Ideas-Steps-Tasks). Breaks goals down into ideas, steps, and tasks. Itamar Gilad (2023) developed this for lean planning and execution when you need to get tactical fast (Fig. 5).

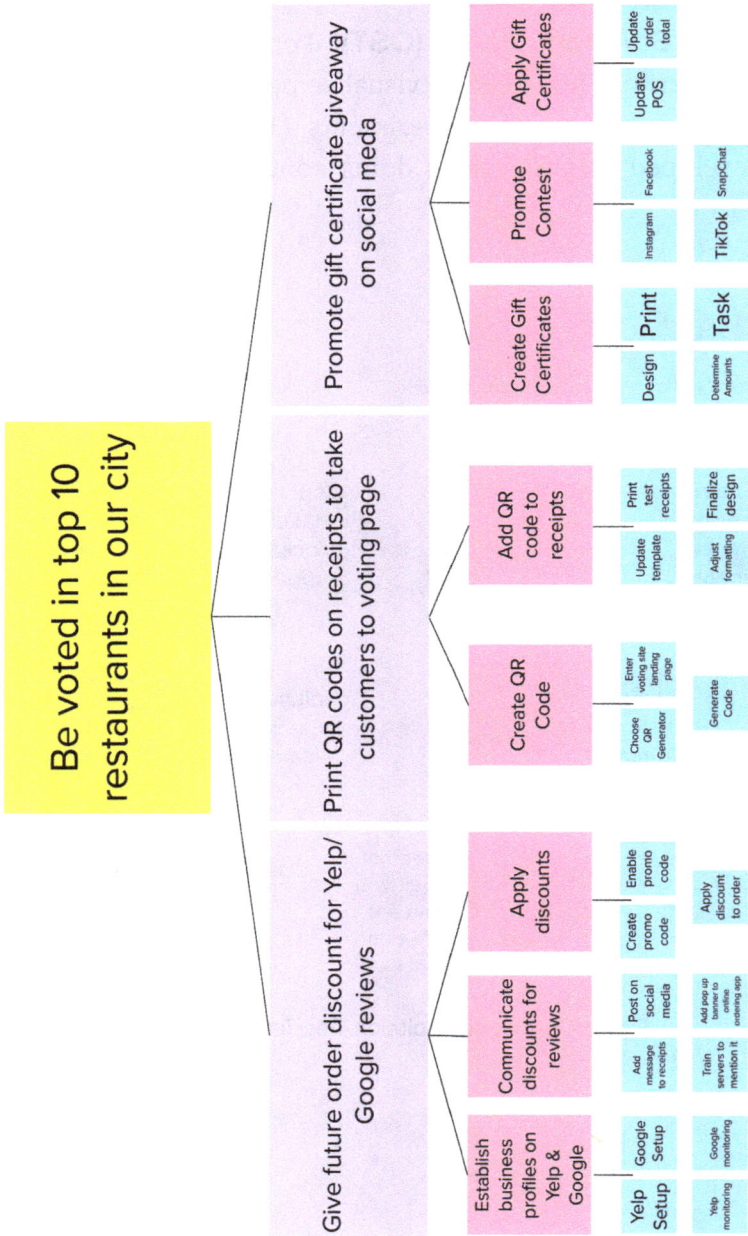

Fig. 5: GIST Template

Technique	Best For	Flow	Example
Impact Mapping	Getting aligned, clarifying assumptions	Goal → Actors → Impacts → Deliverables	Simplify app menu for faster orders
OST	Innovation, opportunity discovery	Outcome → Opportunities → Solutions → Experiments	Test voice ordering for speed
GIST	Lean planning, execution	Goals → Ideas → Steps → Tasks	Redesign menu as one task toward better reviews

Use Impact Mapping when you need alignment, OST when you're exploring new territory, or GIST when you need to get stuff done quickly.

Making Impact Mapping Stick

To make this a habit instead of a one-off exercise:

Always start with goals. Use that VERB + NOUN format. It forces clarity about what you're actually trying to achieve.

Make it a team sport. Co-create these maps with product, design, and engineering. The magic happens when everyone contributes their perspective and challenges assumptions together.

Keep them fresh. Revisit your maps when priorities shift or you learn something new about your customers. Maps should evolve as your understanding deepens.

Combine with empathy maps. Use those customer insights to make your "how" section more specific and actionable. The behavior changes should feel natural given what you know about customer motivations.

Connect to daily work. Reference your impact map during sprint planning. Every user story should trace back to a deliverable on your map, which creates an impact (behavior change) for a specific actor, which serves your overall goal.

During sprint planning, try mapping something like "reduce checkout abandonment" to help you prioritize a streamlined payment flow. Every feature should earn its place by contributing to real behavior change that drives real value.

What's Next

In Chapter 7, we'll dive into **Customer Journey Mapping**. You'll learn how to build on your impact maps to chart the entire customer experience across touchpoints, spot pain points before they become problems, and design interactions that actually feel seamless.

We'll keep building on this foundation of understanding what customers truly need, but we'll zoom in on the complete experience they have with your product from start to finish.

CHAPTER 7

Customer Journey Mapping

Designing the Customer Experience

What You'll Learn

- How customer journey maps reveal what's really happening across every touchpoint
- A straightforward process to create customer journey maps that actually improve satisfaction
- Ways to use customer journey maps to get teams aligned and design products people love

When Polish Isn't Enough

The restaurant app team was riding high after launching their sleek new checkout feature. They'd spent weeks perfecting every detail— smooth animations, gorgeous color transitions, pixel-perfect typography. The design team was proud. The developers were satisfied with the clean code. The product manager was excited about the customer experience improvements.

This was going to be their moment.

Then the complaints started rolling in. "Where's the confirm button?" "Why did my payment fail?" "I ordered twice by accident!" Instead of celebrating their beautiful design, they were firefighting customer frustration.

Here's what happened: they'd gotten so focused on making individual screens look perfect, they forgot to think about what it actually felt like to move through the entire experience. The fancy new interface buried important buttons behind animations. The payment flow had confusing steps that seemed logical in isolation but felt frustrating in sequence. And customers were bailing out left and right.

They'd optimized for screenshots, not for real people trying to get dinner ordered while juggling three other things.

The team had been designing features. Their customers were experiencing journeys. And those are very different things.

This is exactly why our Structured Conversations Manifesto says *"Visual maps show the path."* Customer Journey Mapping helps teams see the entire experience from the customer's perspective, not just individual features in isolation.

Where This Fits

You've already dug deep into what customers think and feel (Empathy Mapping in Chapter 5) and connected those insights to business goals (Impact Mapping in Chapter 6). Now Customer Journey Mapping helps you see their entire experience from start to finish—every click, every wait, every moment of confusion or delight.

This technique builds naturally on your empathy insights while setting you up perfectly for Chapter 8 on Value Stream Mapping, where you'll optimize the internal processes that make those customer experiences possible.

Why Customer Journey Mapping Matters

Many teams design features in isolation—"Let's make checkout better" or "Let's improve search." But customers don't experience your product as isolated features. They experience it as a continuous story, and right now, that story probably has some pretty frustrating plot holes.

Here's the problem: when you optimize individual touchpoints without understanding the full journey, you often create new problems while solving old ones.

Customer journey maps help you:

See the full experience, not just the parts you're currently working on. That amazing new feature doesn't matter if customers never make it that far in their journey.

Spot the real friction points that cause people to give up or get frustrated. Often these happen between features, not within them.

Prioritize improvements based on where they'll actually make a difference in someone's day, not just where they're technically easiest to implement.

Understand emotional context for every interaction. The same interface element feels completely different when someone's stressed versus when they're relaxed.

Here's a real example: A travel booking team thought their biggest problem was the final payment page because that's where their analytics showed the highest drop-off rates. But when they mapped the full customer journey, they discovered the real issue was way earlier—customers couldn't easily compare flight options, so they were getting frustrated and leaving before they ever reached payment.

They'd been optimizing the wrong part of the experience entirely.

As UX researcher Kate Kaplan (2016) puts it, journey maps help organizations stop letting internal processes drive customer experience decisions and start focusing on what customers actually think, feel, and do. This connects directly to your Empathy Mapping work from Chapter 5—you're taking those insights about what customers think and feel and seeing how those emotions play out over time.

What Is a Customer Journey Map?

A customer journey map (Fig. 6) is basically a timeline that shows what customers experience as they interact with your product or service over time. It captures six key elements:

Actor. The specific customer persona you're mapping (like "Restaurant Customer—Middle-Aged Man").

Stages. The major phases they go through (like "Before Ordering," "While Ordering," "After Ordering").

Activities & Touchpoints. What they're actually doing and every place they interact with you at each step (sitting at table, opening your menu, tapping buttons in your app, receiving confirmations).

Needs. What they're trying to accomplish or what's important to them at each stage (finding desired menu sections, easy ordering process, receiving information).

Experience. How they're feeling and what they're experiencing throughout the journey (ease of menu navigation, frustration with app buttons, satisfaction with service).

Notes, Ideas. Where things go wrong and where you can make them significantly better (training hosts, server improvements, payment process optimization).

The key difference from Empathy Mapping? Empathy maps are like a detailed snapshot of someone's mindset in a specific moment. Customer journey maps are like a movie of their entire experience unfolding over time.

Both techniques work together—your empathy insights inform the emotional layers of your customer journey maps.

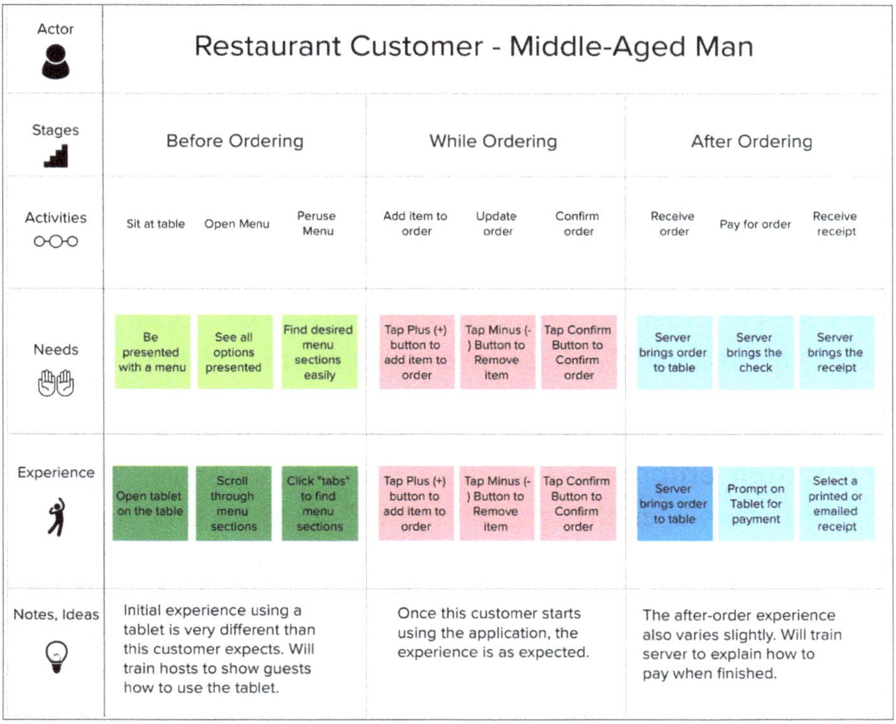

Fig. 6: Customer Journey Mapping Template

How to Build a Customer Journey Map (Step by Step)

Download our free template from structured-conversations.com to follow along:

Pick your actor. Get specific about who you're mapping. "John, 40, busy professional trying to order lunch between meetings" gives you way more to work with than generic "mobile customers."

Define the stages. Break their experience into major phases. For a restaurant app, that might be "Deciding what to eat," "Placing the order," "Waiting for delivery," and "Receiving and eating the food."

Map what they do. At each stage, what actions are they taking? "Opens the app, scrolls through restaurant options, reads reviews, and adds items to cart." Get granular here—the details matter.

Capture what they need. What are they hoping will happen at each step? "Quick menu loading," "Clear delivery time estimates," "Easy way to modify order before payment." This is where your empathy mapping insights become crucial.

Document what actually happens. Now for the reality check. What's their actual experience? "Menu loads slowly," "Can't find delivery time estimate," "Modification options are buried in confusing sub-menus."

Track their emotions. How do they feel at each stage? "Optimistic" when they open the app, "frustrated" when it's slow, "anxious" when they can't find delivery info, "relieved" when order finally goes through.

Spot the pain points and opportunities. Where are the biggest gaps between what they need and what they get? These become your prioritized improvement areas.

Real Example: Restaurant App Customer Journey Map

Let's review what this looks like in practice:

Stage 1: Deciding What to Eat (Before Opening App)

- *Actions:* Feeling hungry during work meeting break, remembering our app exists
- *Needs:* Quick decision-making, reliable option that won't disappoint
- *Reality:* Opens app hoping for fast solution to immediate hunger
- *Emotions:* Optimistic but pressed for time, slightly stressed about limited break time
- *Pain Points:* None yet—this is the honeymoon phase

Stage 2: Browsing Restaurant Options

- *Actions:* Scrolling through restaurant list, checking ratings and delivery times
- *Needs:* Clear options, quick loading, helpful filters for dietary preferences
- *Reality:* Slow loading, overwhelming choices, unclear delivery time estimates
- *Emotions:* Getting frustrated and impatient, starting to second-guess app choice
- *Pain Points:* Too many options without good filtering, no easy way to sort by actual delivery speed

Stage 3: Selecting and Customizing Food

- *Actions:* Choosing restaurant, browsing menu, selecting items, customizing orders
- *Needs:* Clear food descriptions, easy customization, visible running total
- *Reality:* Confusing customization interface, surprise add-on costs, hidden delivery fees
- *Emotions:* Annoyed by unexpected complexity, worried about time running out
- *Pain Points:* Surprise fees appearing late in process, unclear customization options

Stage 4: Checkout and Payment

- *Actions:* Reviewing order, entering payment info, confirming purchase
- *Needs:* Clear order summary, quick payment, confidence order went through
- *Reality:* Confusing final summary, payment form errors, unclear confirmation
- *Emotions:* Anxious about whether order worked, frustrated by payment friction
- *Pain Points:* Multiple payment attempts needed, unclear success confirmation

Stage 5: Waiting for Delivery

- *Actions:* Returning to work, occasionally checking order status
- *Needs:* Accurate timing updates, ability to track progress, easy contact if issues

- *Reality:* Vague "30-45 minutes" estimate with no real tracking updates
- *Emotions:* Anxious about timing, can't plan rest of workday, feeling powerless
- *Pain Points:* No real-time updates, can't contact driver or restaurant directly

When the team mapped this complete journey, they realized their biggest opportunity wasn't adding more restaurant partners (what they'd been planning) but fixing the communication and tracking experience during delivery. That single focus area had a huge impact on overall customer satisfaction because it addressed the longest and most anxiety-inducing part of the journey.

Making Customer Journey Mapping Work in Your Workflow

Customer journey maps work best when they're integrated with your other mapping techniques and daily processes:

User research. Use your empathy maps to inform the emotions and pain points in your journey maps. They complement each other beautifully—empathy maps give you the psychological insights, customer journey maps give you the temporal context.

Design sprints. Start design work with the customer journey map to make sure you're solving problems that actually matter to the full experience, not just optimizing isolated touchpoints.

Sprint planning. Prioritize features based on where they'll have the biggest impact on the overall journey, not just where they're easiest to build or most technically interesting.

Stakeholder reviews. Show the full customer experience to help stakeholders understand why certain improvements matter more than others, even if they seem less impressive in isolation.

Feature prioritization. Use customer journey maps to identify which features will have the biggest impact on customer emotions and outcomes across the entire experience.

One e-commerce team mapped their return process and discovered that customers weren't just frustrated with the return form itself—they were anxious about potential returns from the moment they made their original purchase. So instead of just improving the return flow, they added clear return policy information right on product pages. Result: fewer actual returns and more confident purchases.

Try This Right Now

In your next team meeting, pick a key customer scenario (like "ordering lunch" or "booking a service appointment") and spend 30 minutes sketching a customer journey map:

1. List 4-5 major stages of the experience

2. Add 2-3 key actions per stage

3. Capture the emotional highs and lows throughout

4. Identify the 2-3 biggest pain points

5. Ask the team: What surprised you? Which pain point should we tackle first?

The surprises are where the real insights live. Often you'll discover that the problem you thought you had isn't actually the problem customers are experiencing, or that the solution you were planning would only address part of a larger journey issue.

Making Customer Journey Mapping a Team Habit

To make this more than a one-off exercise:

Start new features with journey context. Before diving into detailed requirements, map out where this feature fits in the customer's overall experience and what they'll be thinking/feeling when they encounter it.

Include different perspectives. Get product, design, engineering, and especially customer support in the room. Support sees the pain points and emotional reactions that may not make it into your analytics dashboards.

Keep them current. Update your customer journey maps when you get new customer feedback, support ticket patterns, or usage analytics that reveal how people actually behave.

Connect to action. Turn journey pain points into clear goals using the VERB + NOUN syntax from Chapter 2. "Reduce checkout confusion" or "Improve delivery communication" give you something concrete to work toward.

Test journey improvements, not just feature functionality. When you ship changes, measure their impact on the overall journey experience, not just the specific feature metrics.

During one design review, a team's Customer Journey Mapping exercise revealed that their planned visual updates would actually make the checkout flow more confusing by changing familiar patterns customers had learned. Instead, they prioritized adding Apple Pay integration—a change that removed three steps from the payment process. Way better impact on the actual journey experience.

Common Customer Journey Mapping Mistakes (And How to Avoid Them)

Mistake 1: Making the journey too generic. "Customers browse, select, and purchase" doesn't give you actionable insights. Get specific about your actor and their context.

Mistake 2: Focusing only on your product touchpoints. Customers' journeys include what happens before they find you and after they stop using your product. Map the complete experience.

Mistake 3: Ignoring emotional context. The same interaction feels completely different when someone's stressed versus relaxed, new versus experienced, mobile versus desktop.

Mistake 4: Creating beautiful maps that gather dust. If your customer journey map doesn't influence what you build and when you build it, it's just expensive wallpaper.

Mistake 5: Mapping what you think happens instead of what actually happens. Base your maps on real customer behavior data, support tickets, and customer research, not assumptions.

What's Next

In Chapter 8, we're flipping the perspective from customer-facing to internal with **Value Stream Mapping**. You'll learn how to optimize your team's workflows and processes so you can deliver those great customer experiences faster and more reliably.

Because the best customer journey in the world doesn't matter if your team can't actually build and maintain it efficiently. It's time to map how value flows through your organization.

CHAPTER 8

Value Stream Mapping

Optimizing the Flow of Value

What You'll Learn

- How value stream maps expose the hidden inefficiencies impacting your delivery speed
- A step-by-step process to create value stream maps that actually accelerate delivery
- Ways to use value stream maps to get teams aligned and working more efficiently

When "Fast" Isn't Actually Fast

The restaurant app team was pretty proud of themselves. They'd spent weeks optimizing their order processing system—orders were now flying from the app to the kitchen in record time. Their dashboards were all green, their performance metrics looked fantastic, and everyone was patting themselves on the back for a job well done.

But customers were still complaining about slow deliveries. The team was baffled. "We're processing orders faster than ever!" they insisted at their weekly review. "What's the problem?"

Here's what they missed: Sure, the order got to the kitchen in lightning-fast 15 seconds. But then it sat there for five minutes while a busy staff member noticed it and manually typed the details into their separate kitchen display system. Then the completed food sat on the counter for another four minutes until someone remembered to call the delivery driver. Then the driver spent three minutes trying to figure out the correct address because the GPS coordinates in their system were wrong.

The team had optimized one tiny piece of a much bigger, messier process. They could see the trees, but they were completely missing the forest.

This is exactly why our Structured Conversations Manifesto says "*Visual maps show the path*." Value Stream Mapping helps you see the entire flow of work from start to finish, so you can spot the bottlenecks and waste that are actually slowing things down.

Where This Fits

You've mapped what customers experience (Customer Journey Mapping in Chapter 7) and now you need to optimize the internal processes that create those experiences. Value Stream Mapping helps you see where work gets stuck, where effort gets wasted, and where small changes can have big impacts on what customers actually feel.

This technique builds naturally on your customer journey insights while setting you up perfectly for Chapter 9 on User Story Mapping, where you'll organize all this optimized work into deliverable chunks that make sense.

Why Value Stream Mapping Matters

Many teams think they know where their processes are slow or wasteful. "Oh, it's definitely the approval process" or "QA is always the bottleneck." But when you actually map out the full flow of work, the real culprits are usually surprising.

Here's the thing about waste in product development: it's mostly invisible. Teams focus on optimizing the work they can see (writing code, designing interfaces, testing features) while ignoring the hidden delays that eat up most of their time.

Value stream maps help you:

See the whole picture, not just the parts that feel slow. Often the biggest delays happen in the handoffs between steps, not within the steps themselves.

Distinguish between work that adds value and work that's just administrative overhead. You'd be shocked how much time gets spent on stuff that doesn't actually improve the customer experience.

Find the real bottlenecks, which are usually not where you think they are. That approval process everyone complains about? It might only add 30 minutes. But the time work sits in someone's inbox waiting to be noticed? That's where days disappear.

Align teams around what actually matters. When everyone can see the full flow, it's easier to make decisions that optimize for the whole process, not just a piece of it.

Quantify the cost of your current process. It's one thing to say "handoffs are slow." It's another thing to say "handoffs add an average of 3.2 days to every feature delivery."

Here's a real example: A software team was frustrated that features took forever to ship. They assumed it was because development was slow, so they started pushing developers to work faster. But when they mapped their value stream, they discovered the real problem: completed features sat in a "ready for review" queue for an average of four days before anyone looked at them. One simple process change—daily review check-ins—cut their delivery time in half without anyone working harder.

What Is a Value Stream Map?

A value stream map is basically a detailed timeline that shows how work actually flows through your process (not how you think it flows or how it's supposed to flow according to your documentation). It captures several key elements:

Every step in the process, from the moment work starts until it's completely done and delivered to customers.

How long each step takes and, crucially, how long work waits between steps.

Who's responsible for each step and where handoffs happen between people or teams.

Which steps actually add value for customers versus which steps are just internal overhead.

Where work gets stuck, gets redone, or takes unexpected detours.

The flow of information alongside the flow of work—what communication happens when.

The key insight that surprises many teams: in typical product development processes, the actual work time is tiny compared to the waiting time. You might spend 30 minutes writing code, but that code sits in a review queue for three days. You might spend an hour creating a design mockup, but it waits two weeks for stakeholder feedback.

Most of your "delivery time" is actually "waiting time."

How to Build a Value Stream Map (Step by Step)

This is going to take some dedicated time and honest conversation with your team, but it's worth every minute. Download our free template from structured-conversations.com to follow along:

1. Define your boundaries. Pick one specific process to map. "From customer submits support ticket to customer gets resolution" or "From feature idea to feature in production." Be specific about the start and end points. Don't try to map everything at once (Fig. 7)

2. List every step (and we mean every step). Walk through the process chronologically and capture everything that happens. Don't just list the big obvious steps like "Development" or "Testing." Include the small stuff like "Developer updates ticket status," "Product Owner sends notification email," or "Designer exports assets." The details matter because that's where the waste hides. (Fig. 8)

3. Figure out who does what. Map each step to specific roles or teams. This helps you see where work is moving between different people or departments, which is often where delays occur. (Fig. 9)

4. Measure the time (this is the eye-opening part). For each step, capture three key metrics:

- **Work time:** How long does the actual work take when someone is actively doing it?
- **Wait time:** How long does work sit idle before the next step begins?
- **Lead time:** Total time from when this step starts until it's completely finished

The ratio between work time and wait time is usually pretty shocking. (Fig. 10)

5. Spot the bottlenecks and handoffs. Look for places where work consistently gets stuck or where it has to move between different people, teams, or systems. These are your highest-impact problem areas. (Fig. 11)

6. Identify rework loops. Map out what happens when something goes wrong—defects that need fixing, approvals that get rejected, requirements that change midstream. How often does this happen? What percentage of work goes through these loops? (Fig. 12)

7. Connect to customer impact. Use your customer journey maps from Chapter 7 to understand how these internal delays affect what customers experience. Long internal delays often translate directly to customer frustration.

8. Calculate your totals. Add up your total lead time and compare how much of that is actual value-adding work versus waiting and waste. The results are usually eye-opening.

9. Design your future state. Now that you can see the problems clearly, brainstorm improvements. What if you automated certain handoffs? What if you reduced approval layers? What if you caught errors earlier in the process? (Fig. 13)

Value Stream Mapping

Fig. 7: Start and End Boundaries

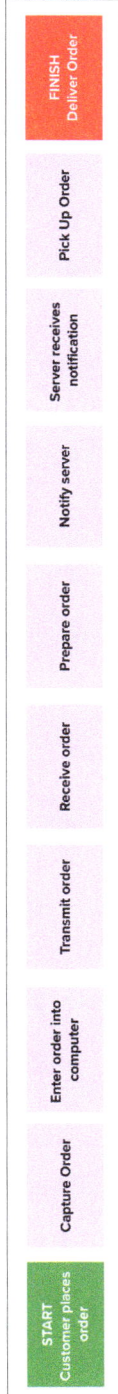

Fig. 8: High-Level Steps in a Product Value Stream

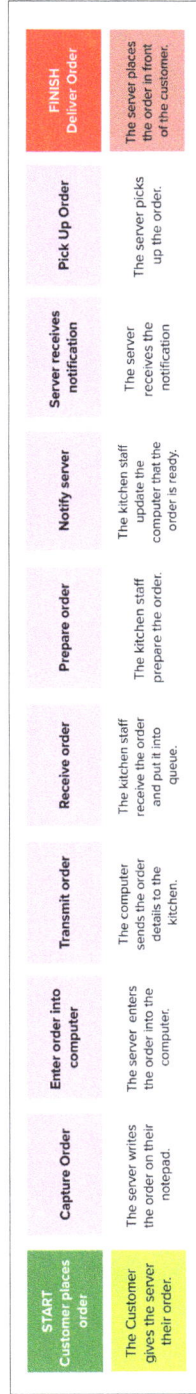

Fig. 9: Swimlanes by Role

93

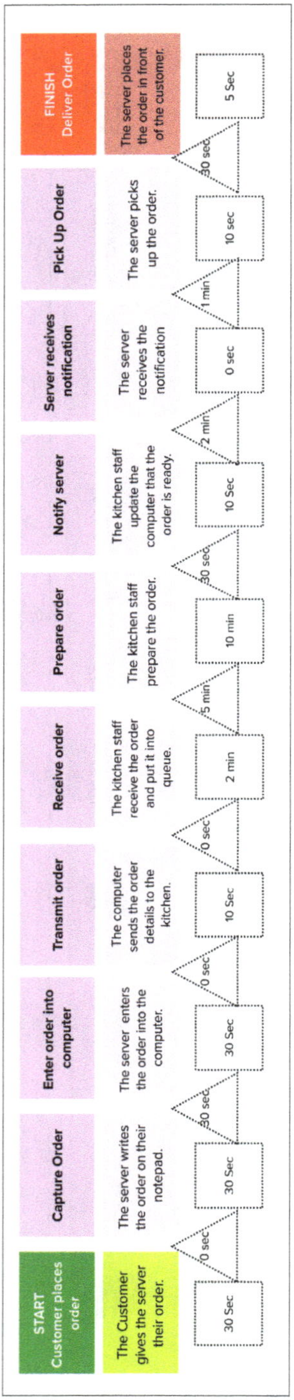

Fig. 10: Annotated Time Metrics

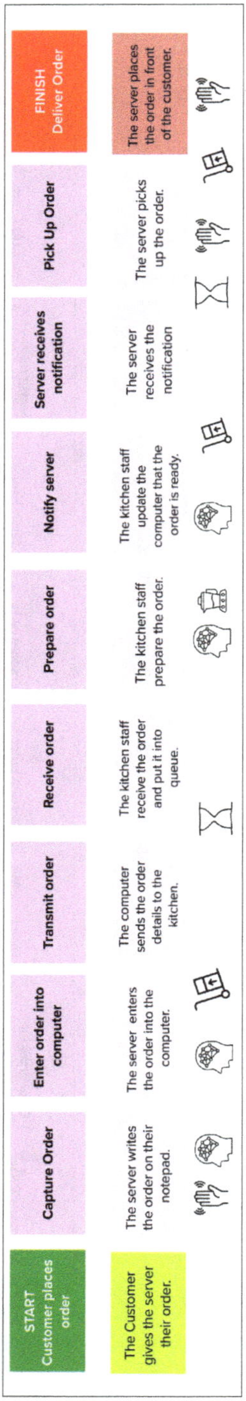

Fig. 11: Handoff and Bottleneck Callouts

Value Stream Mapping

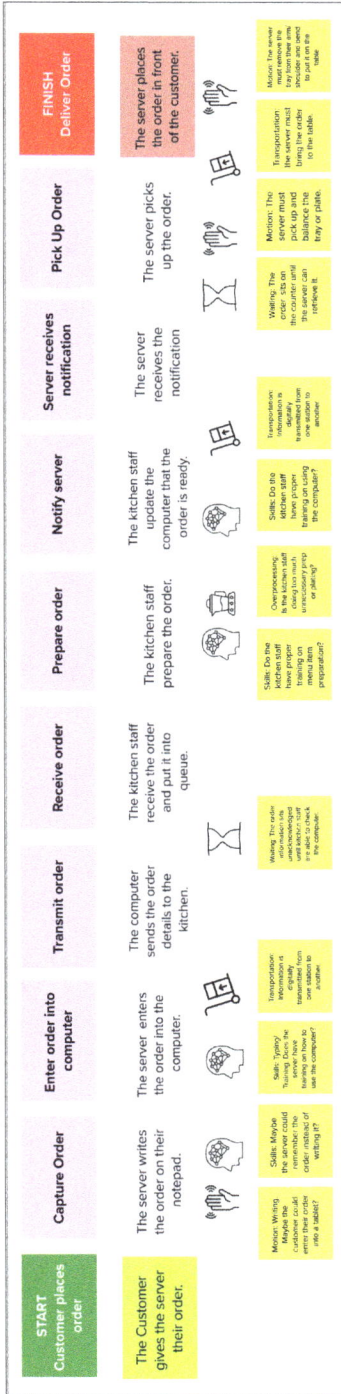

Fig. 12: Rework Loops

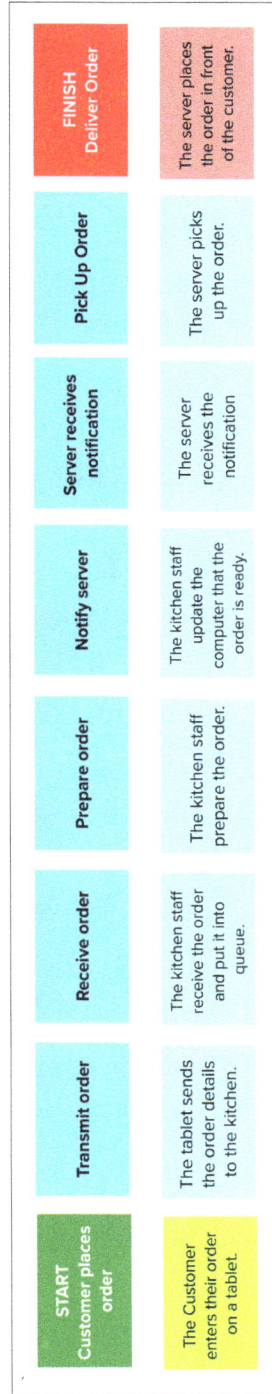

Fig. 13: Future State Value Stream Sketch

Real Example: Restaurant App Value Stream Map

Let's review what this looks like with our restaurant app team's order processing:

1. Customer places order (App interaction, 2 minutes)—**Value-added**

2. Order sits in processing queue (Wait, 30 seconds)—**Waste**

3. System processes payment (Automated, 15 seconds)—**Value-added**

4. Order waits for restaurant notification (System delay, 1 minute)—**Waste**

5. Staff member notices order, manually enters into kitchen system (Manual entry, 3 minutes)—**Waste**

6. Order waits in kitchen preparation queue (Wait, 2 minutes)—**Waste**

7. Kitchen prepares food (Cooking, 12 minutes)—**Value-added**

8. Food waits for driver notification (Wait, 4 minutes)—**Waste**

9. Staff manually calls/texts driver (Manual coordination, 2 minutes)—**Waste**

10. Driver picks up and delivers (Delivery, 15 minutes)—**Value-added**

Results:

- **Total lead time:** 42 minutes
- **Value-added time:** 29 minutes (69%)
- **Waste time:** 13 minutes (31%)

When the team saw this mapped out, they realized their biggest opportunity wasn't making the kitchen faster (it was already efficient)—it was eliminating those manual handoffs and wait times. They automated the kitchen notifications and driver alerts, cutting the waste time in half and improving customer satisfaction significantly.

The insight that changed everything: they'd been optimizing the wrong things.

Making Value Stream Mapping Work in Your Daily Flow

Value Stream Mapping isn't an exercise that you do once and then forget. Here's how to weave it into your regular work:

Process reviews. When something feels slow or broken, map the current state before jumping to solutions. Often the obvious fix isn't the right fix.

Retrospectives. Instead of just talking about what went wrong, map out how work actually flowed through your process and where it got stuck. This turns complaints into actionable improvements.

Planning sessions. Use value stream insights to prioritize improvements that will actually speed up delivery, not just the improvements that feel important.

Stakeholder conversations. Show the full cost of process changes, not just the obvious parts. Help executives understand that "adding one approval step" might add days to delivery time.

Continuous improvement. Update your maps as you make changes so you can see what actually worked versus what just moved the bottleneck somewhere else.

For teams ready to dive deeper into systematic flow improvement, Steve Pereira and Andrew Davis's *Flow Engineering: From Value Stream Mapping to Effective Action* (2024) provides five key flow engineering maps for turning value stream insights into sustainable process improvements and building organizational capabilities around flow optimization.

A healthcare team mapped their patient intake process and discovered that patients were filling out the same information on three different forms across two different systems. They streamlined it to one digital form that populated all their systems automatically. Result: happier patients, less frustrated staff, and hours of time saved every week.

Try This Right Now

In your next retrospective, pick a workflow that's been frustrating your team:

1. List out 6-8 steps from start to finish

2. Estimate how long each step takes (work time vs. wait time)

3. Mark which steps actually add value for customers

4. Identify 1-2 biggest improvement opportunities

5. Ask the team: What surprised you about this process? Where did we think the problem was versus where it actually is?

The surprises are where the real improvements hide. Often you'll discover that the thing everyone complains about isn't actually the biggest time sink, or that problems you thought were technical are actually communication or handoff issues.

Making Value Stream Mapping a Team Habit

To make this more than a one-off exercise:

Start with customer pain points. Use insights from your customer journey maps to pick internal processes that directly impact customer experience. Fix the internal problems that cause external frustration.

Include everyone who touches the process. Developers, testers, support staff, operations, product managers—they all see different pieces of the flow. The full picture only emerges when everyone contributes.

Measure before and after. When you make improvements, update your value stream map to see if they actually worked or just moved the problem somewhere else.

Connect to clear goals. Turn waste reduction into specific objectives using the VERB + NOUN syntax from Chapter 2: "Eliminate manual handoffs" or "Reduce approval delays," or "Automate status updates."

Focus on system problems, not people problems. Value stream mapping usually reveals that delays are caused by process design, not individual performance. Keep the focus on improving the system.

During one retrospective, a team mapped their defect-fixing workflow and realized that defects were spending more time in various "pending" statuses than they were being actively worked on. They simplified their status tracking from eight states to three and saw immediate improvements in resolution time.

Common Value Stream Mapping Pitfalls (And How to Avoid Them)

Pitfall 1: Mapping the idealized process instead of reality. Map what actually happens, not what's supposed to happen according to your documentation. Shadow real work for a few days if necessary.

Pitfall 2: Focusing only on obvious work steps. The biggest waste often happens in the spaces between work—waiting for approvals, sitting in queues, or during handoffs between people.

Pitfall 3: Optimizing locally instead of globally. Making one step faster might just create a bigger bottleneck somewhere else. Always optimize for the whole process.

Pitfall 4: Ignoring rework and error correction. Map what happens when things go wrong, not just the happy path. Failed deployments, rejected designs, and changed requirements are part of your real process.

Pitfall 5: Creating beautiful maps that never drive action. If your value stream map doesn't lead to specific process improvements, it's just an expensive consulting exercise.

What's Next

In Chapter 9, we'll dive into **User Story Mapping**, which builds on all this process optimization to help you organize features into customer-centric backlogs. You'll learn how to break down big ideas into deliverable chunks while keeping everyone focused on customer value.

Because all the process optimization in the world doesn't matter if you're building the wrong things in the wrong order. It's time to map your product development from the customer's perspective.

CHAPTER 9

User Story Mapping

Building the Right Features, Step by Step

What You'll Learn

- How user story maps turn chaotic backlogs into a clear, customer-focused plan
- A practical process to create user story maps that actually align teams around what matters
- Ways to use user story maps to guide development and deliver features customers will actually use

When Everything Is a Priority, Nothing Is

The restaurant app team was feeling pretty good about their latest release. They'd packed it full of features customers had asked for: loyalty points, advanced menu filters, delivery tracking, restaurant reviews, dietary restriction tags, social sharing, group ordering—the works. This was going to be their big moment.

Instead, the reviews were brutal. "Too confusing now," "Can't find anything," "Just want to order food quickly," "App used to be simple, now it's a mess."

Customers were actually less happy than before.

What went wrong? The team had built everything customers said they wanted, but they'd never thought about the order or the overall experience. The simple "quick reorder" button that busy parents desperately needed? Buried under three menu layers behind the loyalty program. The delivery tracking that would reduce anxiety? Hidden in a separate section that most people never found.

They'd prioritized everything, which meant they'd prioritized nothing. Without a clear map of how customers actually move through their app, they'd created a feature museum instead of a useful tool.

This is exactly why our Structured Conversations Manifesto says "*Visual maps show the path.*" User Story Mapping helps teams see the customer's journey from start to finish and organize features in a way that actually makes sense for how people operate.

Where This Fits

You've uncovered customer needs (Empathy Mapping in Chapter 5), connected them to business goals (Impact Mapping in Chapter 6), mapped their experience (Customer Journey Mapping in Chapter 7), and optimized your internal processes (Value Stream Mapping in Chapter 8). Now User Story Mapping gives you the visual backbone for your entire product—a way to organize all that insight into something your team can actually ship that drives the customer outcomes and business impact you mapped out.

This technique synthesizes everything you've learned about customers and translates it into a practical development plan. It sets you up perfectly for Chapter 10, where you'll learn to communicate your product vision in a way that gets everyone excited and aligned.

Why User Story Mapping Matters

Most backlogs are just lists—a random collection of features, defects, and technical tasks that somebody thought were important at some point. They don't tell a story, and they definitely don't help teams understand how everything fits together.

Here's the problem with traditional backlogs: they're organized around what's easy for teams to track, not around what makes sense for customers to use.

User Story Mapping, pioneered by Jeff Patton (2014), changes that by organizing your backlog around the customer's actual journey. It helps teams:

Keep customers at the center instead of getting lost in feature lists and technical requirements. Every story connects to a real customer need.

Make smart trade-offs by seeing how features relate to each other and what customers actually need first. You can see the forest and the trees.

Align everyone around a single story instead of having product, design, and engineering working from different assumptions about what you're building.

Plan releases that make sense by grouping features that work together to solve complete customer problems, not just random collections of functionality.

Spot gaps and overlaps before you waste time building the wrong things or building the same thing twice in different places.

Communicate progress to stakeholders in terms they actually care about—customer value delivered, not just features shipped.

Here's a real example: An e-commerce team had a backlog with 17 different checkout improvements scattered across multiple categories. They used User Story Mapping to realize that most of those improvements wouldn't matter if customers couldn't easily find products in the first place. So they prioritized search and navigation first, then tackled checkout systematically. The result was much better conversion rates because they'd improved the whole experience, not just one piece of it.

What Is a User Story Map?

A user story map (Fig. 14) is basically your product backlog reorganized as a story instead of a list. Instead of features scattered all over the place, you organize them around how customers actually use your product.

It has four main parts:

The backbone. High-level activities that customers go through (like "Find restaurant," "Place order," "Get food delivered"). These form the horizontal backbone of the map.

User tasks. Specific tasks needed to complete each activity, organized horizontally under their parent activities.

User stories. Specific functionality under each user task, written from the customer's perspective and organized vertically by priority beneath their parent tasks.

Release slices. Horizontal cuts that group user stories into deliverable chunks that provide complete customer value.

The magic happens when you can see the whole customer journey laid out horizontally at the activity level, with tasks organized under each activity, and all the supporting user stories organized vertically underneath each task. Suddenly it's obvious what needs to be built first, what can wait, and what might not be needed at all.

Think of it like planning a road trip: the backbone (activities) is your route from city to city, the user tasks are the specific stops and actions needed in each city, the user stories are all the different ways you might accomplish each task, and the release slices are how you decide what to include in each leg of the journey to make it valuable and manageable.

User

Goal

Type your paragraph...

Understand your User and their Goal(s).

Mapping your user stories depends on understanding your users and their goals. In our restaurant example, one of the users is the Customer, who has complained of waiting 30 minutes or longer to receive their order. We will set a goal for orders to arrive in fewer than 20 minutes. Each goal will ultimately become a theme.

Describe User Activities.

You can use the future state process map steps that you created to describe each activity that your selected user will take. In this case, we will show the Restaurant Customer activities.

Describe the User Tasks within each Activity.

Each activity is made up of smaller steps, called tasks. Think through the specific actions that the user must take in order to complete each activity. Organize your tasks below the activity to which they correspond. You will notice that in our example, the activity "Customer Places order" is very detailed, while the second activity, "Customer Receives Order" requires no action from the customer at all - they must simply receive their order (our confirmation that the process is complete).

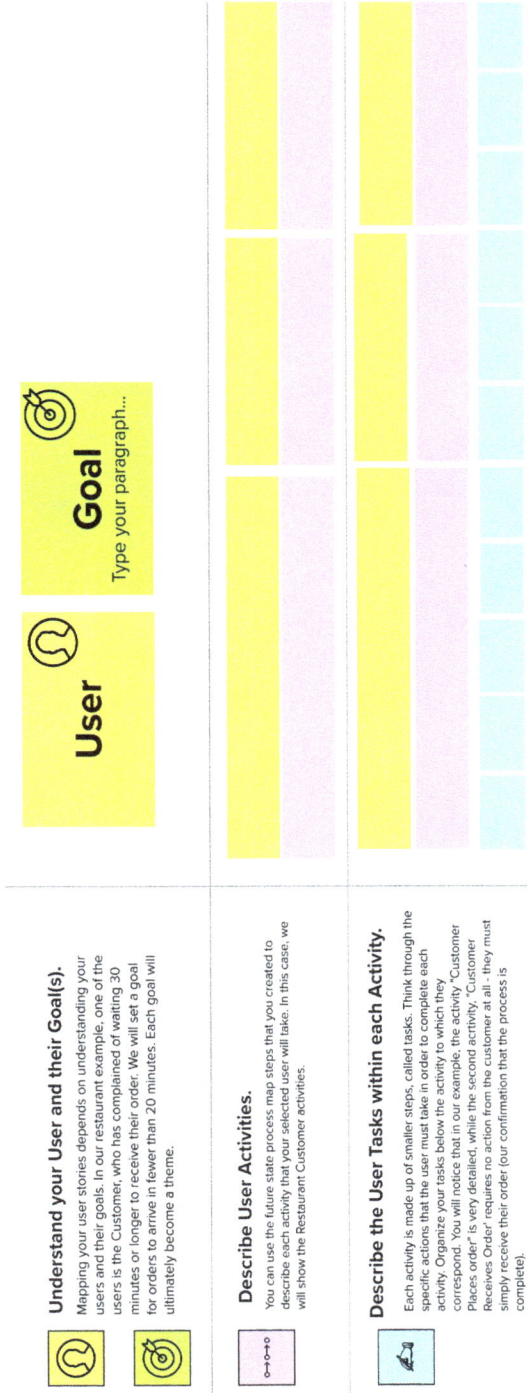

Fig. 14: User Story Mapping Template

(continued on next page)

107

(continued from previous page)

Create your user stories.

Your user stories will capture the user, their desire, and ultimate outcome of each step.

Title: <Task name or breakdown of task name>

If you need multiple user stories to satisfy each step, stack them vertically below the task.

Create horizontal slices to define your releases.

It is possible that not all user stories will be completed in a typical release period. Understanding your teams' typical velocity will enable you to estimate what may be feasible in each release. Draw horizontal lines across the map to indicate which stories should be completed in Release 1, Release 2, Release 3, etcetera.

Release 1

Release 2

Fig. 14: User Story Mapping Template

108

How to Build a User Story Map (Step by Step)

This works best as a collaborative workshop with your whole team. Set aside a few hours and download our free template from structured-conversations.com to follow along:

1. Start with your user and their goal. Pull from your empathy and impact maps from previous chapters. "Sarah, busy parent, wants to order dinner in under 5 minutes" gives you way more direction than generic "improve customer experience." (Fig. 15)

2. Map out the major activities. What are the big things customers do to accomplish their goal? For the restaurant app: "Decide what to eat," "Place order," "Wait for delivery," "Receive food." Keep these high-level—you're telling the story of their journey. (Fig. 16)

3. Break activities into specific tasks. Under each activity, what smaller things do customers need to do? Under "Place order" you might have "Browse menu," "Customize items," "Choose delivery time," "Enter payment info." (Fig. 17)

4. Turn tasks into user stories. Use the VERB + NOUN syntax from Chapter 2 to write clear user stories. Instead of vague "Payment processing," write specific "Process payment quickly" or "Save payment methods for future use."

5. Stack related user stories vertically. Group user stories that serve the same basic customer need. All the different ways to browse the menu stack under "Browse menu," with the most essential at the top and nice-to-haves below. (Fig. 18)

6. Slice horizontally for releases. Now comes the crucial part. Draw horizontal lines to create releases. Your first release should include the absolute minimum features customers need to accomplish their core goal. Each subsequent release adds more value. (Fig. 19)

7. Involve everyone. The real power comes from getting product, design, engineering, customer support, and business stakeholders in the same room, looking at the same map, having the same conversations about trade-offs and priorities.

Understand your User and their Goal(s).

Mapping your user stories depends on understanding your users and their goals. In our restaurant example, one of the users is the Customer, who has complained of waiting 30 minutes or longer to receive their order. We will set a goal for orders to arrive in fewer than 20 minutes. Each goal will ultimately become a theme.

User

Goal
Receive order in <20 Minutes

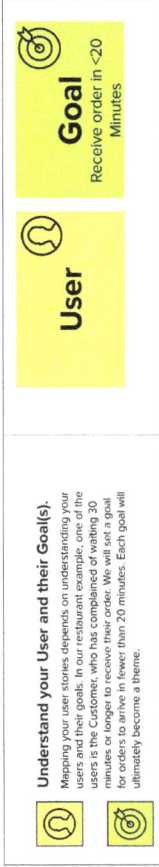

Fig. 15: User and Goal

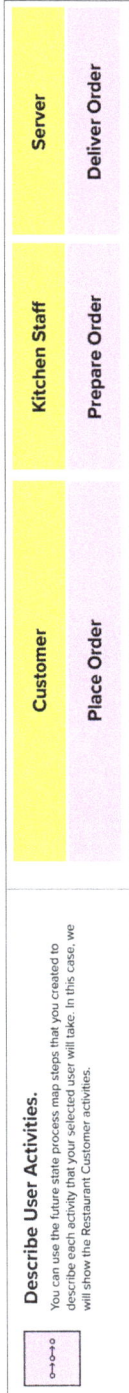

Describe User Activities.

You can use the future state process map steps that you created to describe each activity that your selected user will take. In this case, we will show the Restaurant Customer activities.

Customer	Kitchen Staff	Server
Place Order	Prepare Order	Deliver Order

Fig. 16: User Activities

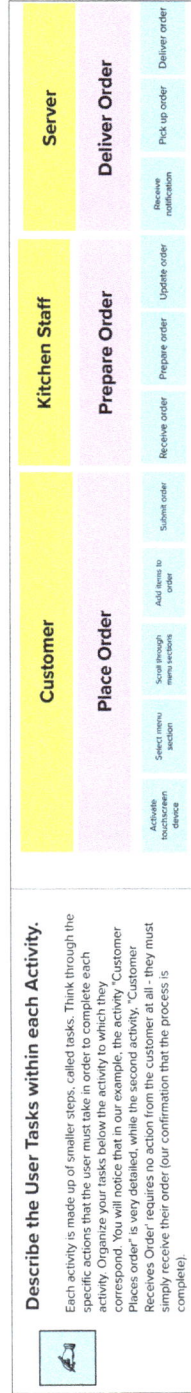

Describe the User Tasks within each Activity.

Each activity is made up of smaller steps, called tasks. Think through the specific actions that the user must take in order to complete each activity. Organize your tasks below the activity to which they correspond. You will notice that in our example, the activity "Customer Places order" is very detailed, while the second activity, "Customer Receives Order" requires no action from the customer at all - they must simply receive their order (our confirmation that the process is complete).

Customer					Kitchen Staff			Server		
Place Order					**Prepare Order**			**Deliver Order**		
Activate touchscreen device	Select menu section	Scroll through menu sections	Add items to order	Submit order	Receive order	Prepare order	Update order	Receive notification	Pick up order	Deliver order

Fig. 17: User Tasks

Create your User Stories.

Your user stories will capture the user, their desire, and ultimate outcome of each step.

Title: <Task name or breakdown of task name>

If you need multiple user stories to satisfy each step, stack them vertically below the task.

Customer		Kitchen Staff		Server	
Place Order		**Prepare Order**		**Deliver Order**	

Customer — Place Order	Kitchen Staff — Prepare Order	Server — Deliver Order
Activate touchscreen device · Select menu section · Scroll through menu sections · Add items to order · Submit order	Receive order · Prepare order · Update order	Receive notification · Pick up order · Deliver order
Activate touchscreen device · Select menu section · Scroll through menu section · Add items to order · Review all items in order	Acknowledge receipt of order · Prepare order · Update that order is ready	Acknowledge that order is ready · Pick up order from kitchen · Deliver order to customer
Change menu section · Remove item from order · Submit order	Place order into work queue · Send notification that order is ready	
Update number of order items · Transmit order to kitchen	Order cannot be completed	
Add note to item in order		

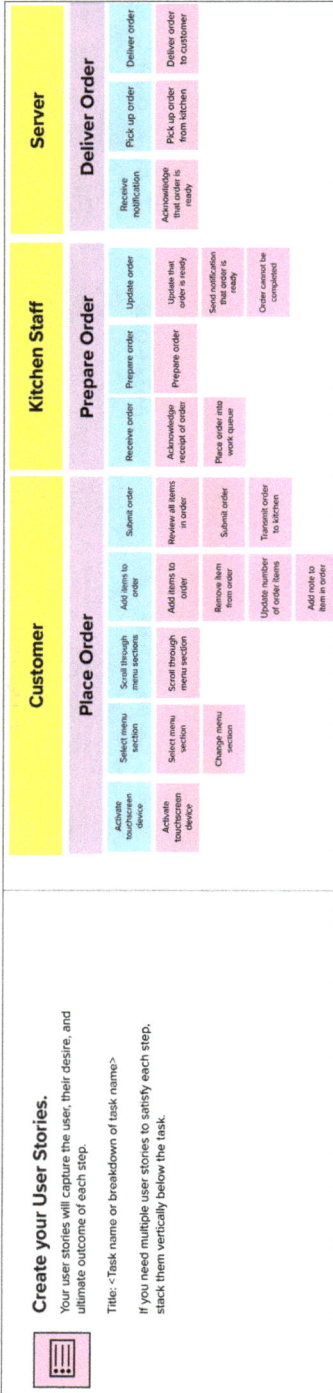

Fig. 18: Vertical Story Stack

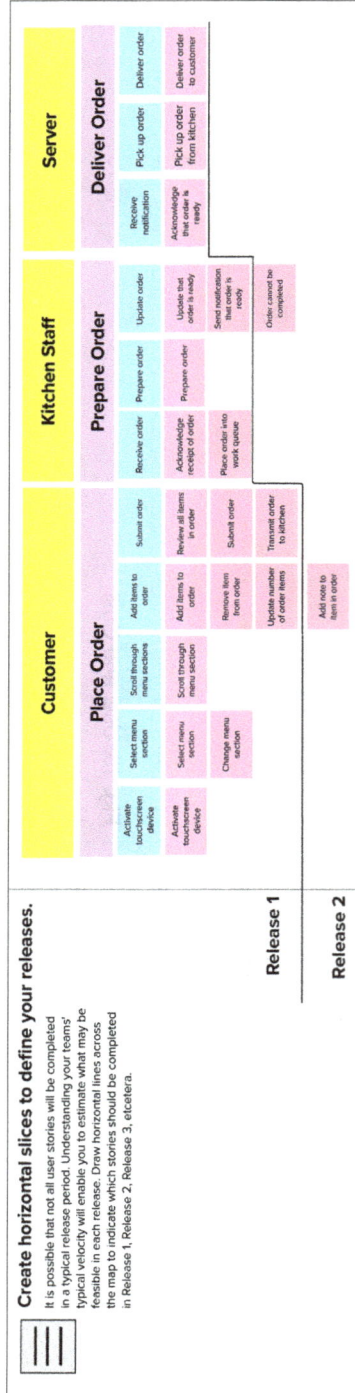

Create horizontal slices to define your releases.

It is possible that not all user stories will be completed in a typical release period. Understanding your teams' typical velocity will enable you to estimate what may be feasible in each release. Draw horizontal lines across the map to indicate which stories should be completed in Release 1, Release 2, Release 3, etcetera.

Customer		Kitchen Staff		Server	
Place Order		**Prepare Order**		**Deliver Order**	

Release 1

Release 2

Fig. 19: Release Slice

Real Example: Restaurant App User Story Map

Let's walk through what this looks like for our restaurant app team:

Activities (the backbone): Decide What to Eat → Place Order → Track Delivery → Receive Food

User Tasks by Activity

Activity 1: Decide What to Eat

- Browse restaurants
- View restaurant details
- Search and filter

Activity 2: Place Order

- Build cart
- Provide delivery details
- Complete payment
- Confirm order

Activity 3: Track Delivery

- Monitor order status
- View delivery progress
- Receive updates

Activity 4: Receive Food

- Complete delivery
- Provide feedback
- Access support

User Stories by Task & Priority

Activity 1: Decide What to Eat

Task: Browse restaurants (Essential, Release 1):
- Browse restaurant list
- View menu items with prices

Important (Release 2):
- See restaurant ratings and reviews

Nice to Have (Release 3):
- Get personalized recommendations
- See trending/popular items

Task: View restaurant details (Important, Release 2):
- View dietary information (vegetarian, gluten-free, etc.)

Nice to Have (Release 3):
- Filter by dietary restrictions

Task: Search and filter (Essential, Release 1):
- Search for restaurants

Important (Release 2):
- Filter by cuisine type

Activity 2: Place Order

Task: Build cart (Essential, Release 1):
- Add items to cart

Important (Release 2):
- Customize order (add/remove ingredients)

Nice to Have (Release 3):
- Save favorite orders for reordering

Task: Provide delivery details (Essential, Release 1):
- Enter delivery address

Nice to Have (Release 3):
- Schedule orders for later delivery
- Add special delivery instructions

Task: Complete payment (Essential, Release 1):
- Process payment

Important (Release 2):
- Save payment methods

Nice to Have (Release 3):
- Split payment between multiple methods

Task: Confirm order (Essential, Release 1):
- Submit order

Important (Release 2):
- View order confirmation details

Activity 3: Track Delivery

Task: Monitor order status (Essential, Release 1):
- View order status (received, preparing, out for delivery)
- See estimated delivery time

Important (Release 2):
- View order history

Nice to Have (Release 3):
- See detailed preparation timeline

Task: View delivery progress (Important, Release 2):
- Track driver location on map

Nice to Have (Release 3):
- Share live tracking link with others

Task: Receive updates (Important, Release 2):
- Receive push notifications for status updates

Nice to Have (Release 3):
- Chat with driver

Activity 4: Receive Food

Task: Complete delivery (Essential, Release 1):
- Mark order as received
- View receipt

Nice to Have (Release 3):
- Tip driver after delivery

Task: Provide feedback (Important, Release 2):
- Rate order and delivery

Nice to Have (Release 3):
- Upload photos in reviews
- Earn and redeem loyalty points

Task: Access support (Important, Release 2):
- Report issues with order
- Contact customer support

Release Slices (Horizontal Cuts)

Release 1—Minimum Viable Product (Essential)

Goal: Customers can complete a basic order from start to finish
- Browse restaurant list
- View menu items with prices

- Search for restaurants
- Add items to cart
- Enter delivery address
- Process payment
- Submit order
- View order status (received, preparing, out for delivery)
- See estimated delivery time
- Mark order as received
- View receipt

Release 2—Enhanced Experience (Important)

Goal: Improve usability and provide key conveniences
- Filter by cuisine type
- See restaurant ratings and reviews
- View dietary information
- Customize order (add/remove ingredients)
- Save payment methods
- View order confirmation details
- View order history
- Track driver location on map
- Receive push notifications for status updates
- Rate order and delivery
- Report issues with order
- Contact customer support

Release 3—Advanced Features (Nice to Have)

Goal: Delight customers and encourage loyalty
- Get personalized recommendations
- See trending/popular items
- Filter by dietary restrictions
- Save favorite orders for reordering
- Schedule orders for later delivery
- Split payment between multiple methods

- Add special delivery instructions
- Chat with driver
- See detailed preparation timeline
- Share live tracking link with others
- Earn and redeem loyalty points
- Tip driver after delivery
- Upload photos in reviews

When the team laid this out visually, the user story map revealed that customers needed to trust the basic ordering experience before they'd engage with features like a rewards program.

Making User Story Mapping Work in Your Daily Flow

User story maps aren't something you create once and forget. Here's how to weave them into your regular workflow:

Backlog refinement. Use your customer journey insights from Chapter 7 to make sure user stories actually address customer pain points, not just technical requirements or competitive features.

Sprint planning. Pull from your impact maps from Chapter 6 to prioritize user stories that drive business outcomes, not just features that sound cool or are easy to build.

Design reviews. Check whether new features fit into the customer's story and support the overall experience rather than creating confusion.

Stakeholder conversations. Use release slices to show what's coming when and why certain features are grouped together. This helps with resource planning and expectation setting.

Customer feedback sessions. Use the story map to understand where customer suggestions fit and how they might affect the overall experience.

One team used their user story map during quarterly planning and realized they'd been building features for three different types of customers but never completing the experience for any of them. They refocused on nailing the experience for their primary customer type first, then expanding to others.

Try This Right Now

In your next backlog refinement, pick one key user workflow and spend 30 minutes story mapping:

1. List 3-5 major activities your customer goes through

2. Write 2-3 user stories under each activity (use VERB + NOUN syntax from Chapter 2)

3. Draw a line for Release 1: What's the absolute minimum needed?

4. Draw a line for Release 2: What would make it noticeably better?

5. Ask the team: Are we building the right things in the right order?

The "right order" question is where the real insights happen. Often teams discover they're building advanced features before they've nailed the basics, or that they're optimizing parts of the experience that customers barely use.

Making User Story Mapping a Team Habit

To make this more than a one-off workshop:

Ground everything in customer research. Start every user story mapping session by reviewing your empathy maps and customer journey insights. Keep real customer needs front and center.

Make it collaborative. The magic happens when different perspectives collide in the same room looking at the same map. Product sees business priorities, design sees user experience, engineering sees technical dependencies.

Keep it current. Update your user story map based on what you learn from customers, analytics, support feedback, and market changes. It should be a living document.

Write clear user stories. Use the VERB + NOUN syntax from Chapter 2 to keep user stories actionable and focused on specific outcomes.

Review releases regularly. As you complete features and learn more about customers, adjust your release slices. What seemed important six months ago might not be what customers actually need.

Connect to business goals. Reference your impact maps from Chapter 6 to ensure your user story map supports measurable business outcomes, not just feature completeness.

During one backlog refinement, a team's user story map revealed that they'd been treating "customer onboarding" as one user story when it actually needed to be broken into five different user stories across three releases. That insight helped them ship a basic onboarding flow quickly and iterate based on customer feedback, rather than spending months building a comprehensive system that might not work.

Common User Story Mapping Mistakes (And How to Avoid Them)

Mistake 1: Making the backbone too detailed. The backbone should be high-level customer activities, not specific features. "Place Order" is good; "Click Add to Cart Button" is too specific.

Mistake 2: Organizing by teams instead of customer value. Don't create sections for "Frontend Stories" and "Backend Stories." Organize everything around what customers are trying to accomplish.

Mistake 3: Making release 1 too big. Your first release should be uncomfortably small. If it feels complete, it's probably too big. You want to learn from customers as quickly as possible.

Mistake 4: Forgetting about the whole experience. Don't just map the happy path. Include error handling, edge cases, and support scenarios that customers will actually encounter.

Mistake 5: Treating the map as permanent. User story maps should evolve as you learn more about customers and market needs. Keep them current and relevant.

What's Next

In Chapter 10, we'll dive into the **Product Elevator Pitch**, which builds on everything you've mapped to help you communicate your product vision clearly and compellingly. You'll learn how to distill all your customer insights and feature planning into a pitch that gets stakeholders excited and keeps teams aligned on what you're building and why.

You've got the foundation—now it's time to tell the story.

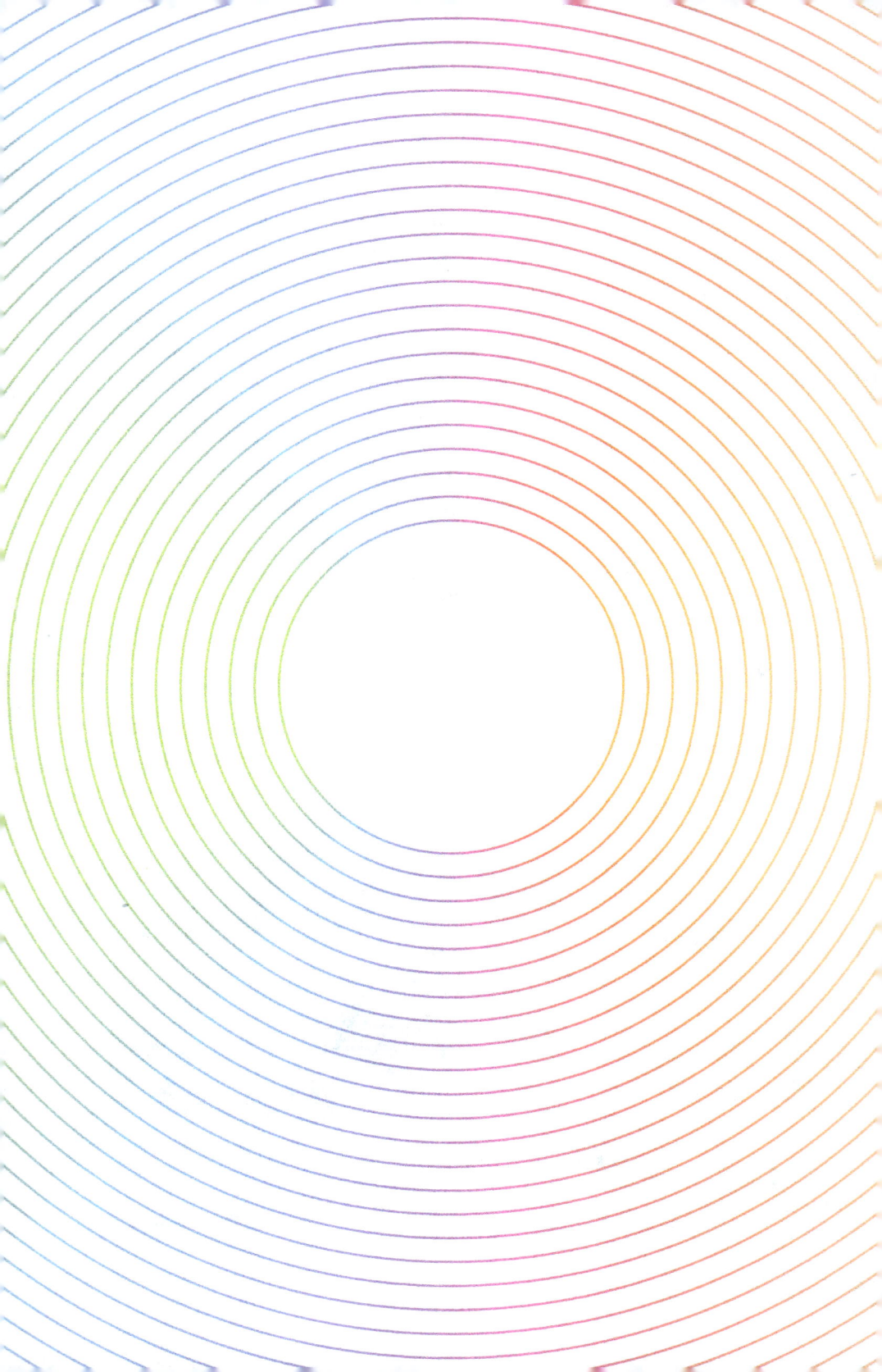

PART 3

CRAFTING DELIVERABLES

CHAPTER 10

Product Elevator Pitch

Telling Your Product's Story

What You'll Learn

- How to craft a pitch that actually gets people excited about your product
- Ways to align teams and stakeholders around a vision everyone can remember
- Practical steps to create a pitch that inspires action (not yawns)

When Buzzwords Attack Your Product Vision

The restaurant app team was pumped to present their latest progress to the executive team. They'd prepared beautiful slides, gathered impressive metrics, and crafted what they thought was the perfect pitch: "We're building an enhanced customer platform with robust functionality and seamless integration capabilities that leverage cutting-edge technology to optimize customer engagement through innovative solutions."

The room went quiet. Not the good kind of quiet where people are absorbed and thinking—the "what did they just say?" kind of quiet where everyone's trying to decode corporate speak.

One executive asked about the loyalty program they'd mentioned (they hadn't). Another wanted to know about the new interface design (also not mentioned). A third person asked if this was the same project they'd discussed last month (it was, but nobody could tell from the description).

The meeting ended with the dreaded "let's schedule a follow-up to clarify the vision." Translation: "We have no idea what you're actually building or why anyone would want it."

Here's what went wrong: they'd used so much jargon and corporate speak that their actual product got completely lost. Instead of painting a clear picture of what they were building and why it mattered to real people, they'd created a buzzword cloud that could mean anything to anyone.

This is exactly why our Structured Conversations Manifesto says *"Clear language sparks action."* A product elevator pitch cuts through the noise and gets everyone on the same page about what you're building and why it matters.

Where This Fits

You've done the deep work of understanding customers (Empathy Mapping), connecting to business goals (Impact Mapping), mapping their journeys (Customer Journey Mapping), optimizing your processes (Value Stream Mapping), and organizing features into a coherent plan (User Story Mapping). Now you need to communicate all of that insight in a way that gets people excited and aligned.

This technique pulls together everything from your previous mapping work into one clear, compelling statement that anyone can understand and remember. It prepares you perfectly for Chapter 11's Future Press Release, where you'll expand this pitch into a full vision of success.

Why Product Elevator Pitches Frequently Fail (And Why It Matters)

Too often, product descriptions are either too vague ("We're disrupting the food space with innovative solutions") or too detailed (a 20-minute explanation of every feature and technical specification). Neither approach helps people understand what you're actually building or why they should care.

Here's the problem: when people can't quickly understand what you're building, they can't help you build it. They can't make good decisions about resources, priorities, or partnerships. They can't give you useful feedback. And they certainly can't get excited about the vision.

A good product elevator pitch helps you:

Get everyone on the same page instead of having five different interpretations of what you're building floating around the organization.

Focus your team on what really matters instead of getting distracted by every shiny new idea or competition that comes up.

Make decisions faster because everyone knows what fits the vision and what doesn't, what supports the core mission and what's just feature bloat.

Get buy-in from stakeholders who don't have time to dive into the details but need to understand the big picture well enough to support your work.

Test your own understanding—if you can't explain it simply, you probably don't understand it clearly enough yet.

Here's a real example: A team was struggling to get approval for their mobile banking app redesign. Their original pitch was full of technical jargon about "API integrations," "omnichannel experiences," and "customer experience optimization." When they simplified it to "For busy professionals frustrated by our current app's complexity, our new version lets you handle banking tasks in under 30 seconds, unlike traditional banking apps that require multiple screens and confirmations, our product enables instant one-tap transactions, completes tasks with 90% fewer steps, and processes requests without any confirmation delays", suddenly everyone got it. Approval came quickly because the value was crystal clear.

The 7-Line Syntax That Actually Works

Geoffrey Moore gave us this template (Fig. 20) in "Crossing the Chasm" (originally from 1991, still works today), and it's stuck around because it forces you to be specific about the important stuff:

For. Who exactly is this for? (Not "customers"—be specific about the actual people)

Who. What problem are they struggling with? (Real pain, not theoretical issues)

The. What are you calling this thing? (Names matter—they shape how people think about it)

Is a. What category does it fit into? (Helps people understand context quickly)

That. What's the main benefit? (Why would someone want this in their life?)

Unlike. What's the obvious alternative? (What are people using now that's not working?)

Our product. What makes yours different/better? (This is your big differentiating moment)

Product Elevator Pitch

Everybody is a salesperson first

Purpose: To "sell" your product by succinctly describing the benefits of your product to your customer, highlighting the salient characteristics in a small amount of time.

Audience: While your customers will ultimately be the ones who hear the pitch, this should be crafted by Product Owners and/or Product Managers. You can involve the development team, or a focus group as needed to refine your pitch.

Process Steps:

1. **Outline your customer personas or user types**. Your elevator pitch may vary depending on your target audience.
2. **Complete the syntax** for each user type, working vertically across the canvas. Add as many columns as needed to ensure all target users are represented.
3. **Read** each completed elevator pitch aloud or test it with actual users. **Refine** it until it is as succinct as possible while effectively conveying the benefits of your product.

	User: Working Parents
For [Explains who the product is for or who would benefit from its usage]	**Working Parents**
Who [Expands on the problem or need the customer has to solve]	**Need a quick weeknight family meal**
The [Gives life to the product by giving it a name. Names are important because they communicate intent]	**4 for $20 Special**
Is/Are [Explains what this service or product actually is or does]	**a pre-cooked meal**
That [Explains why our customer would want to buy this product in the first place]	**is prepared fresh daily**
Unlike [Covers why we wouldn't already use what's out there]	**Meal Kits that require chopping, frying and baking**
Our product [Differentiates and explains how our product differs from the competing alternatives.]	**Goes from our Kitchen to your table in as little as 10 minutes**
Product Elevator Pitch Write out the full pitch, read it aloud, and refine it as needed.	For working parents who need a quick weeknight family meal, our 4 for $20 Special is a pre-cooked meal that is prepared fresh daily, unlike meal kits that require chopping, baking and frying, our meals go from our kitchen to your table without the hassle!

Fig. 20: Product Elevator Pitch Template

Product Elevator Pitch

User: Business Executives	User: Young Couples	User: Groups of Girlfriends
Business Executives	Young Couples	You and your girlfriends
want to treat their clients to a delicious meal	desire an evening of romance	are seeking a restaurant that offers brunch all day
Daily Specials	Lover's Special	Weekend Brunch Special
rotating dinner favorites	a candlelight dinner for two	a full menu of brunch favorites
will satisfy any craving	includes a shared appetizer and dessert	are available from 8 am to 8pm
fast casual restaurants	fast casual restaurants	other restaurants who only offer brunch for a few hours
uses fresh, local ingredients that will delight the senses	meals are enjoyed in an intimate, romantic setting making the perfect date night	is available all day long
For business executives who want to treat their clients to a delicious meal, our daily dinner specials are rotating favorites that will satisfy any craving, unlike fast casual restaurants our kitchen uses fresh, local ingredients that will delight the senses	For young couples who desire an evening of romance, our Lover's Special is a candlelight dinner for two that includes a shared appetizer and dessert, unlike fast casual restaurants, our meals are enjoyed in an intimate setting making the perfect date night.	For when you and your girlfriends are seeking a restaurant that offers brunch all day, our Weekend Brunch special is a full menu of brunch favorites that are available from 8am to 8pm, unlike other restaurants who only offer brunch for a few hours, our Brunch Special is available all day long!

Here's how we'd pitch this book using the template:

For product teams building customer-focused software

Who struggle with misaligned goals and wasted effort

The book *Connecting Goals to Impacts and Outcomes*

Is a practical toolkit of clear syntax and visual mapping techniques

That helps teams align around customer value from discovery to launch

Unlike books that focus primarily on process frameworks

Our book provides hands-on techniques you can use immediately to cut miscommunication before it kills your product

A Simpler Version When You Need It

Sometimes you don't need the full 7-line treatment. For quick conversations, early-stage discussions, or when you're still figuring things out, try this shorter format (Sandy, 2020):

Product: QuickBite restaurant app

Solves: Slow, confusing food ordering during busy lunch hours

For: Busy professionals with limited time

By providing: One-tap reordering of your usual favorites

Unlike alternatives: Actually remembers what you ordered last time and makes it effortless to get again

This works great for hallway conversations, elevator encounters (hence the name), or when you're still refining your full vision.

Real Example: Building a Pitch That Works

Let's watch how our restaurant app team developed their pitch through iteration:

First attempt (too vague). For restaurant customers who want better experiences, our app provides enhanced ordering capabilities with improved functionality and streamlined processes.

Second attempt (getting clearer). For busy professionals who don't have time for complicated food ordering, our restaurant app provides fast, simple ordering unlike other apps that have too many confusing steps.

Final version (specific and compelling). For busy professionals who have 30 minutes or less for lunch, QuickBite is a restaurant ordering app that lets you reorder your favorites in under 10 seconds, unlike other food apps that make you browse through endless menus every single time, our product saves your top 5 orders on the home screen, uses one-tap reorder with saved payment methods, and remembers your preferences and locations for instant ordering.

Notice how the final version paints a specific picture? You can immediately imagine the professional standing in an office break room, trying to order lunch quickly while checking their phone between meetings. You understand exactly how this app would make their day better.

The magic is in the specificity—"30 minutes or less," "under 10 seconds," "endless menus every single time." These details make the value concrete and believable.

Making Product Elevator Pitches Work in Your Daily Flow

Your product elevator pitch isn't just for external presentations or funding conversations. Here's how to use it throughout your regular workflow:

Team kickoffs. Start sprints by reading the pitch to remind everyone what you're building and why it matters to real people.

Stakeholder meetings. Lead with the pitch instead of diving immediately into features, timelines, and technical details.

Backlog refinement. Use the pitch to evaluate whether proposed features actually support your core vision or just add complexity.

Hiring conversations. Help candidates understand what they'd be working on and why it matters, not just what technologies they'd use.

Customer conversations. Test your pitch with actual customers to see if it resonates with their experience and language.

Decision-making. When facing tough trade-offs, ask "Which option better supports the vision in our pitch?"

One team printed their pitch on a poster and stuck it on their meeting room wall. Whenever someone suggested a new feature or questioned a prioritization decision, they'd point to the poster and ask, "Does this support our vision?" It became their north star for staying focused instead of chasing every interesting idea.

Try This Right Now

Pick something your team is currently working on and spend 20 minutes crafting an elevator pitch:

1. **Start with your customer:** Who specifically are you building for? (Use insights from your empathy maps from Chapter 5)

2. **Identify their struggle:** What problem keeps them frustrated or stuck?

3. **Name your solution:** What are you calling this thing? (Keep it simple and memorable)

4. **Categorize it:** What type of product/feature is this? (Helps people understand context)

5. **Highlight the benefit:** What's the main value they'll get from using this?

6. **Acknowledge alternatives:** What do they use now that's not working well?

7. **Differentiate clearly:** Why is yours better/different/ worth switching to?

Read it out loud to someone who doesn't know your product. If they can't immediately understand what you're building and why someone would want it, keep refining. The goal is clarity, not cleverness.

Common Product Elevator Pitch Mistakes (And How to Fix Them)

Mistake 1: Using internal jargon instead of customer language.

- **Bad**: We're building a comprehensive customer engagement platform
- **Good**: We're building an app that reminds busy parents when their kids need to schedule a doctor's appointment

Mistake 2: Focusing on features instead of benefits.

- **Bad**: Our app has advanced filtering, real-time notifications, and integrated payment processing
- **Good**: Our app lets you find and book the perfect restaurant in under 30 seconds

Mistake 3: Being too broad or generic.

- **Bad**: For anyone who wants better food delivery
- **Good**: For working parents who need to feed their family on weeknight evenings

Mistake 4: Not identifying a clear alternative. Without a clear "unlike" comparison, people don't understand why your solution is needed or different.

Mistake 5: Making claims you can't support. Don't promise "revolutionary" or "game-changing" unless you can back it up with specific, believable benefits.

Making Product Elevator Pitches a Team Habit

To make this more than a one-time exercise:

Ground it in customer research. Pull from your empathy maps and customer journey insights to make sure your pitch reflects real customer language and real problems, not just what you think they should care about.

Make it collaborative. Get product, design, engineering, and marketing voices involved. Different perspectives help you spot assumptions and improve clarity.

Test it regularly. Share your pitch with customers, stakeholders, and new team members. Their reactions and questions will tell you if it's working or if it needs refinement.

Keep it current. As you learn more about your customers while refining the product, update your pitch to reflect new insights and priorities.

Use it consistently. Don't have one pitch for executives and a different one for customers. Consistency builds shared understanding across your organization.

Here's a pitch that evolved through real customer feedback:

Original. For small business owners who need better financial management, our app provides comprehensive expense tracking unlike complicated accounting software.

After customer feedback. For freelancers who lose money because they forget to track expenses, TaxSaver is a receipt-scanning app that automatically categorizes business expenses in real-time, unlike manual spreadsheets that require you to remember and enter everything later, our product uses AI to instantly read and sort receipts by tax category, integrates with your bank to match transactions automatically, and learns your spending patterns to predict categories before you even scan.

The second version came from learning that their customers weren't "small business owners" managing comprehensive finances—they were freelancers who specifically struggled with expense tracking for tax purposes. They refined the pitch that speaks directly to that specific pain point.

Testing Your Pitch in the Wild

The real test of your product elevator pitch isn't whether your team likes it—it's whether it resonates with the people you're building for. Here are ways to test it:

Customer interviews. Start conversations by sharing your pitch and asking "Does this sound like something that would help you? Why or why not?"

Stakeholder meetings. Watch faces and body language when you deliver the pitch. Confusion, excitement, or boredom will be obvious.

New team member onboarding. See how quickly new hires understand what they're working on based on your pitch.

Casual conversations. Try explaining your product to friends or family using your pitch. If they get it, you're probably on the right track.

The best pitches generate immediate follow-up questions that show understanding: "Oh, so it's like Uber but for . . ." or "That sounds really useful for when I . . ."

What's Next

In Chapter 11, we'll expand your product elevator pitch into a **Future Press Release**—a compelling narrative that envisions your product's success and keeps your team motivated about the impact you're trying to create. You'll learn how to paint a detailed picture of the future that gets everyone excited about the work ahead and helps guide tough decisions along the way.

Future Press Release

Painting a Vision of Customer Success

What You'll Learn

- How a future press release creates a shared vision that everyone can actually get excited about
- A step-by-step guide to crafting a press release that aligns teams around real customer value
- Practical ways to use future press releases to get stakeholder buy-in and guide tough decisions

Why Everyone Has a Different Movie in Their Head

The restaurant app team was absolutely buzzing about their new loyalty program. Product was excited about the engagement metrics. Design had created beautiful point-tracking animations. Engineering was proud of the sophisticated rewards algorithm. Marketing was already planning the launch campaign.

Six months later, the feature launched to crickets. Customers found the point system confusing ("How many points for a free drink again?"). The rewards weren't compelling enough to change behavior. Orders actually decreased because the loyalty flow interrupted the checkout process.

In the post-mortem, something became painfully clear: everyone had been building toward a different definition of success. Product thought success meant higher engagement scores. Design thought it meant customers would love the interface. Engineering thought it meant the system would scale. Marketing thought it meant increased orders.

Nobody had ever sat down and said, "What does success actually look like for our customers? What story will we tell when this works?"

This is exactly why our Structured Conversations Manifesto says "*Clear language sparks action.*" A future press release forces your team to agree on what success looks like **before** you start building—and crucially, it defines success from the customer's perspective, not just your internal metrics.

We're building on your product elevator pitch from Chapter 10 and all the mapping work you've done. Now you're going to paint a vivid picture of the future that gets everyone rowing in the same direction.

Where This Fits

You've crafted a product elevator pitch that explains what you're building and why it matters. Now you need to expand that into a compelling vision of what success looks like when customers are actually using your product and loving it.

This prepares you perfectly for Chapter 12 on Feature Mapping, where you'll break this vision down into specific features and acceptance criteria.

Why Future Press Releases Matter

Too often, teams have vague ideas about success: "Customers will be happy" or "We'll increase engagement." But when you force yourself to write about success as if it's already happened, you quickly discover all the assumptions hiding in those vague statements.

A future press release helps you:

Get everyone aligned on the same definition of success instead of having five different success stories in five different heads.

Think from the customer's perspective rather than getting caught up in internal metrics that don't actually matter to customers.

Make better decisions because you have a clear vision to evaluate features against.

Create excitement by painting a picture of the impact you're trying to make.

Surface hidden assumptions about what customers will actually do with your product.

Amazon pioneered this with their "Working Backwards" process. As Colin Bryar and Bill Carr (2021) explain in their book, Amazon teams write a future press release **before** they write code because it forces clarity about what customer problem they're solving and what success looks like.

Here's what Jeff Bezos reportedly said about this: "*We don't do PowerPoint presentations at Amazon. Instead, we write narrative memos with full sentences, topic sentences, verbs, and nouns.*" The future press release is that narrative memo for your product vision (Gallo, 2018).

What Is a Future Press Release?

A future press release is exactly what it sounds like: a press release written as if your product has already launched successfully and customers are raving about it. But it's not a marketing document—it's an internal alignment tool.

The key insight is writing in present tense, as if the success has already happened. This forces you to be specific about:

- **What problem you actually solved** (not just what features you built)
- **How customers' lives are different** (not just what your product does)
- **What success metrics look like** (not just what you hope will happen)
- **Who's excited about this** (and what they're saying)

It typically includes:

Headline. A bold statement about customer success.

Problem. What was broken before.

Solution. How your product fixed it.

Customer impact. What's different in customers' lives.

Quotes. What customers and team members are saying.

Metrics. Specific improvements you've achieved.

Unlike a real press release, this one is meant to surface assumptions and guide decisions, not impress journalists.

Three Ways to Structure Your Future Press Release

There's no single 'right' way to write a future press release—the best structure depends on your product, audience, and organizational culture. Amazon popularized this approach with their PR/FAQ format, which Walker (2024) calls "one of the most powerful tools" for clarifying thinking and aligning organizations.

Download our free template from structured-conversations.com (Fig. 21) showing you three different approaches, depending on your context:

Option 1: The Structured Announcement

Good for formal environments or when you need to hit specific talking points:

Title: [Company] launches [Product] to help [Customer] achieve [Benefit]

Subtitle: Additional context or specific improvement

Launch Info: Date and location (imagine it's 6-12 months from now)

Introduction: 3-4 sentences summarizing what launched and why it matters

Problem: The customer pain points you solved

Solution: How your product addresses those problems

Leadership Quote: What your product leader would say about the vision

How It Works: Simple customer experience walkthrough

Customer Quote: What a happy customer would say

Call to Action: How people can get started

Option 2: The Story-Driven Version

Good for consumer products or when you want to emphasize customer experience:

Heading: Product name in customer-friendly language

Subheading: One sentence about the value

Summary: A compelling paragraph that tells the whole story

Problem: The frustration you eliminated

Solution: What you built and how it works

Team Quote: Why you built this

Customer Quote: How it changed someone's day

Getting Started: First steps for new customers

Option 3: The Comprehensive Launch Story

Good for complex products or when you need to address multiple audiences:

Heading + Subheading: Product vision from customer perspective

Summary: Executive overview of the impact

Problem Statement: What was broken and why it mattered

Solution: Your approach to fixing it

Customer Experience: Day-in-the-life story

FAQ: Questions from customers and internal teams

Internal Notes: Design, technical, and go-to-market considerations

Connecting Goals to Impacts and Outcomes

	Option 1		Option 2
Title	[Company] announces [Service/Technology/Tool] to enable [Customer Segment] to [Benefit Statement]	**Heading**	Name the product in a way the reader (i.e. the target customers) will understand
Subtitle	Frame the main announcement in a different way or provides another element of detail	**Subheading**	Describe who the market for the product is and what benefit they get. One sentence only underneath the title
Introductory Paragraph	3-4 sentences that reiterate and expand on the title with a little more detail on the customers served and what is being launched	**Summary**	Give a summary of the product and the benefit. Assume the reader will not read anything else so make this paragraph good
Problem Paragraph	Lay out the top 3-4 (max) problems for the customers your product or service is intended to serve. Describe each problem briefly and talk about the negative impact of it	**Problem**	Describe the problem the product solves
Solution Paragraph	Describe how the product/service elegantly solves the problem. Give a brief overview of how it works, and then go through and talk about how it solves each problem listed above	**Solution**	Describe how the product elegantly solves the problem
Quote from a Leader	Pick a leader in the company and make up a quote that talks about why the company decided to tackle this problem and (at a high level) how the solution solves it	**Quote from you**	A quote from you or a spokesperson in the company
How the Product/Service Works	Describe what a customer has to do to start using the product/service and how it works. Go into enough detail to give them the confidence it actually solves the problem	**How to get started**	Describe how easy it is to get started
Quote from a Customer	Create a fake quote by a fake customer, but one that sounds like it could be real. The customer should describe her pain point or the goal she needs to accomplish, and then how the product you launched enables her to do so	**Customer Quote**	Provide quote from a hypothetical customer that describes how they experienced the benefit
Learn More	How to get started/To learn more, go to [URL]: provide a URL or other information on the first place a customer should go to get access to the product/service [provide our 1-page Website URL for ordering the book via amazon]	**Closing & Call to Action**	Wrap it up and give pointers where the reader should go next

Fig. 21: Future Press Release Template (Syntax Comparison)

Future Press Release

	Option 3
Heading	Short, catchy name for the product that a given target audience can relate to
Subheading	One-liner explaining who the target market is, what the product does, and what it hopes to achieve
Summary	A brief paragraph, explaining what the product is and its benefits
Problem Statement	A brief paragraph explaining what problem the company is trying to solve with this product and why they are trying to solve this problem. This paragraph may also include pain points on existing products or processes that can be alleviated using the product
Solution	A brief explanation on how the company hopes to resolve the problem mentioned in the problem statement section. Usually, it would be helpful to provide research or numbers to back the assumptions made for the resolution
User Experience	A paragraph explaining how a user would interact with the product itself. In this section one could add an internal quote; something regarding the product for example, why the company feels it's essential for the given customer base to purchase this product. One could also add hypothetical customer quotes. This kind of information gives more insight to the product or the features
FAQ	This section would include all plausible questions target customers may want to ask. This includes the typical what, why, when, how and who questions from the customer's perspective. This could also serve as a justification for the company to launch given product
Internal Section	This part of the document involves questions that the internal teams would ask. These questions could be regarding technical, sales, marketing or design inquiries. The section would also delve into the solutions for any said questions and would make it transparent for teams to see where this product/feature is heading and what the ask is, especially from the stakeholders. It could also act as an aid to stakeholders for decision making purposes. Typically, visuals could be added to avoid having to write out large chunks for words and would help keep it brief

Real Example: Restaurant App Future Press Release

Let's review what this looks like in practice:

QuickBite's New One-Tap Ordering Saves Busy Parents 10 Minutes Every Dinner

Streamlined checkout eliminates menu browsing frustration, increases family satisfaction

January 1, 2027—New York, NY

QuickBite today announced that its redesigned ordering experience has transformed weeknight dinners for thousands of busy families. The new one-tap reordering feature eliminates the daily stress of menu browsing, letting parents order family favorites in seconds instead of minutes.

The Problem We Solved

Before this update, parents like Sarah spent 5-7 minutes every night navigating cluttered menus, trying to remember what her kids actually liked, and wrestling with a slow checkout process. "By the time I finally placed an order, the kids were melting down and I was stressed," Sarah said. "It felt like a chore instead of solving a problem."

How We Fixed It

QuickBite's new smart reordering system learns from previous orders and surfaces family favorites with a single tap. No more scrolling through endless restaurants or remembering customizations. The app remembers that Sarah's family always orders chicken tenders with no pickles and her husband's favorite Thai curry order.

What's Different Now

"Now dinner ordering takes 30 seconds," Sarah explained. "I tap 'Order Again,' confirm the delivery time, and I'm done. The kids stay calm, and I actually feel like I accomplished something instead of fighting technology."

Since the beta launch, families are reordering 3x more frequently, and customer satisfaction scores have jumped from 6.2 to 8.7 out of 10.

"This isn't about building more features," said Alex, Product Manager. "It's about understanding that parents at 6 PM on a Tuesday don't want to browse—they want dinner handled so they can focus on their family."

Getting Started

Current QuickBite users will see the new reordering option automatically. New families can download the app and start building their favorites list with their first order.

Notice how this future press release tells a specific story about a specific customer's improved experience? It's not about the app's features—it's about how Sarah's evenings got better.

Making Future Press Releases Work in Your Team

A future press release isn't just a writing exercise. Here's how to use it throughout your workflow:

Vision alignment meetings. Start major initiatives by writing the future press release together as a team. The disagreements that surface are where the real alignment work happens.

Feature prioritization. When debating what to build next, ask "Which features get us closer to the story in our future press release?"

Design reviews. Test whether proposed designs support the customer experience described in your future press release.

Stakeholder updates. Share the future press release to help executives understand the customer impact you're working toward.

Team motivation. When the work gets tough, remind everyone of the customer story you're trying to make real.

One team we worked with printed their future press release and stuck it on the wall. During every sprint planning meeting, they'd ask, "Are we building toward this vision or getting distracted by other stuff?"

Try This Right Now

Pick something your team is currently working on and spend 20 minutes drafting a mini future press release:

1. **Pick your customer and their current frustration** (pull from your empathy maps)

2. **Write a headline** about their success, not your product features

3. **Describe the problem** in their words, not your technical language

4. **Explain your solution** in terms of how their life gets better

5. **Add a customer quote** that captures the emotional improvement

6. **Include one specific improvement** they'll experience

Share it with your team and ask: "Does this story excite us? Are we building toward this vision?"

The magic happens when people realize they've been thinking about different success stories.

Making Future Press Releases a Team Habit

To make this more than a one-off exercise:

Start with customer research. Ground your future press release in real customer language from your Empathy Mapping and Customer Journey Mapping work.

Write it collaboratively. The disagreements that come up when writing together are where alignment happens.

Test your assumptions. The future press release will make claims about customer behavior—find ways to validate those assumptions early.

Keep it visible. Put it somewhere the team sees regularly, not buried in a document folder.

Update it as you learn. As you get customer feedback and see how people actually use your product, refine the story.

Use it for decisions. When facing tough choices, ask whether options A or B gets you closer to the future press release vision.

What's Next

In Chapter 12, we'll dive into **Feature Mapping**, where you'll take this compelling vision from your future press release and break it down into specific features and acceptance criteria. You'll learn how to translate customer success stories into buildable, testable pieces while keeping that customer vision front and center.

Feature Mapping

The Fast Track to Actionable Acceptance Criteria

What You'll Learn

- How feature maps transform product vision into clear, testable user stories that actually work
- A simple visual technique to explore rules, examples, steps, consequences, and all those pesky edge cases everyone forgets about
- Practical ways to get your team aligned and turn fuzzy feature ideas into rock-solid acceptance criteria

When Good Intentions Meet Real Life

The restaurant app team was absolutely buzzing after writing their future press release about "one-tap ordering" for busy parents. They had their empathy maps (Chapter 5), their impact maps (Chapter 6), their customer journey maps (Chapter 7), and now this compelling vision. The vision was crystal clear, everyone was pumped, and they dove straight into development thinking they had it all figured out.

Three weeks later, Sarah (remember her from Chapter 11?) finally got to try the new feature. She tapped "Order Again" expecting magic and got charged twice for the same meal. Her kids' dietary restrictions were completely ignored. The restaurant had changed their menu two weeks ago, but the app was still showing old items that weren't even available anymore.

"Seriously? I thought this was supposed to make my life easier," Sarah muttered, canceling both orders and opening a different app instead.

Back at the office, the post-mortem was painful but predictable. The team had this gorgeous vision but hadn't worked through all the nitty-gritty details that make features actually work in the real world. What happens when someone gets tap-happy and hits the button twice? How do we handle it when restaurants change their menus? What if payment processing goes sideways?

This is exactly why our Structured Conversations Manifesto says "*Visual maps show the path*." Having a standout future press release is awesome, but you need to map out all the specific steps to get there without face-planting on the details everyone forgot to think about.

Where This Fits

You've painted this amazing picture of success with your future press release from Chapter 11. You've got a solid product elevator pitch from Chapter 10. Now you need to bridge the gap between that inspiring vision and the actual user stories your team is going to build.

Feature Mapping takes all your mapping work from Chapters 5-9 and turns it into specific, testable user stories. This sets you up perfectly for Example Mapping in Chapter 13 and detailed User Stories in Chapter 15.

Why Feature Mapping Matters

Look, we get it. Another mapping technique might feel like process overload. But here's the thing: Feature Mapping was invented by John Ferguson Smart (2017) precisely because teams kept shipping features with defects and unintended consequences because they hadn't fully explored the rules, examples, steps, and edge cases. Smart saw that traditional approaches weren't solving this problem, so he created a technique that would.

A retail team thought they were totally aligned on building "faster checkout." Six weeks later, they launched this beautiful one-click purchase button that completely bypassed their fraud detection system. Customers loved how fast it was—until fraudsters discovered they could breeze through purchases without any checks. The chargeback requests piled up so fast they had to yank the feature within 48 hours.

If they'd spent just one hour Feature Mapping beforehand—talking through the business rules, walking through examples, asking "what could possibly go wrong?"—they would have caught that missing fraud check before anyone wrote a single line of code.

Feature Mapping helps you:

Stop shipping features with critical gaps by forcing everyone to agree on what "done" actually looks like.

Catch expensive screw-ups early instead of discovering them when customers are screaming.

Turn vague ideas like "make it faster" into testable pieces your team can actually build.

Have better conversations about edge cases instead of stumbling into them at 2 AM during a production incident.

Actually deliver what customers need instead of what sounded cool in the meeting.

Combine it with Impact Mapping from Chapter 6, and you'll build features that actually drive the outcomes you mapped—not just check boxes.

What Is Feature Mapping?

Think of Feature Mapping as the detailed blueprint that turns your architectural vision into something a contractor can actually build without calling you every five minutes with questions. Your future press release is the artist's rendering of the finished house. Feature Mapping is the plan that shows where every pipe goes and what happens when someone flushes the toilet.

Download our free template (Fig. 22) from structured-conversations. com to follow along for a collaborative exercise where you take any feature and break it down into six parts that everyone can understand:

Actor. Who's actually going to use this thing? (And "customers" doesn't count—be specific).

Rules. What are the business rules that absolutely have to work? (The stuff that keeps lawyers and compliance people happy).

Examples. Real scenarios that show how those rules play out when humans get their hands on your product.

Steps. What does the person actually have to do to use this feature?

Consequences. What happens when they do that? (Both when everything goes right and when it all goes sideways).

Questions. What don't we know yet? What assumptions are we making that could cause problems later?

While User Story Mapping from Chapter 9 gives you a high-level view of user activities and workflow for your product, Feature Mapping zooms way in on one specific feature and maps out every single detail that needs to work.

Connecting Goals to Impacts and Outcomes

Features	Actors	Business Rules	Examples
Customize an order	Customers	Menu items have a fixed price	The one where a customer makes no modifications
			The one where added ingredients have an
			The one where removed ingredients do not impact price
			The one where a custom note is added
Cancel an order	Customers	Orders can be canceled if not yet confirmed by kitchen	The one where the order is not yet confirmed
			The one where the order is confirmed but not in progress
			The one where the order is confirmed and in progress

Fig. 22: Feature Mapping Template

Feature Mapping

Steps					Consequences/ Outcomes	Questions
Scroll through menu	Add items to order	See prompt: Would you like to make any modifications?	Select "no"	Submit Order	Customer pays price shown on menu	
			Add extra tofu	Submit Order	Price is increased by $1.00 for each extra item	
			Remove egg	Submit Order	Customer pays price shown on menu	What if the request is really an extra item, and the customer should be charged more?
			Request to make extra spicy	Submit Order	Customer pays price shown on menu	
Open recent orders	Select order to cancel	Order status shows not confirmed	Confirm cancelation		Order is canceled	
		Order status shows confirmed but not in progress	Wait for kitchen to acknowledge request to cancel		Order is canceled	What if the kitchen staff doesn't see the request to cancel before they start making it?
		Order status shows confirmed and in progress			Order is not canceled	What if only part of the order is in progress, and some items could still technically be canceled?

How to Build a Feature Map (Step by Step)

Let's see this thing in action: The restaurant app's "One-Tap Reordering". Instead of rushing into development like last time, let's walk through how the restaurant app team could have used Feature Mapping to actually build the right thing:

Actor: Busy parents like Sarah who've ordered from the same restaurant before and just want dinner handled without drama

Rules:

- Only show "Order Again" if they've ordered from this restaurant in the past 30 days (nobody wants to reorder from that place they tried once and hated)
- Make sure the restaurant is actually open and taking orders right now
- Double-check that everything from their previous order is still on the menu
- Apply any current promotions automatically (customers shouldn't miss out on deals)
- For the love of all that's holy, don't charge them twice if they get impatient and tap multiple times

Examples:

- Sarah ordered pizza last Tuesday, opens the app Thursday at 6 PM, restaurant's open, everything's available → Show that beautiful "Order Again" button
- Mike ordered sushi 45 days ago → Don't show the reorder option because that's ancient history
- Lisa tries to reorder at 10 PM when the restaurant is closed → Show her the hours and let her schedule it for tomorrow

Steps:

1. Sarah opens the restaurant's page in the app

2. She sees and taps the "Order Again" button

3. App shows her order summary with current prices (in case anything changed)

4. She confirms her delivery details haven't changed

5. She completes payment and gets on with her evening

Consequences:

- When everything works: Order's confirmed, she sees the delivery time, gets a confirmation email, and can stop thinking about dinner
- Restaurant's closed: Clear message about when they're open again, maybe an option to schedule the order for later
- Some items aren't available anymore: Show her what's changed, suggest substitutions, or just remove stuff with a clear explanation
- Payment goes wrong: Give her a clear error message and an easy way to try again

Questions:

- What if prices have gone up since her last order? Do we warn her or just show the new total?
- How do we handle it if her kids' dietary restrictions don't match the current menu items?
- Should we remember how much she tipped last time or make her choose again?
- What happens if she gets distracted and leaves the confirmation screen open for 20 minutes?

See how this maps out all the stuff Sarah might actually run into? Instead of assuming everything will work perfectly in some fantasy world, the team thinks through the realistic complications that happen when real people use your product in their messy, chaotic lives.

Making Feature Mapping Work in Your Team

Feature Mapping isn't something you do by yourself in a corner—it works best when you get different perspectives in the room and hash things out together. Here's how to make it actually useful:

Start with real customer problems. Pull from your Empathy Maps (Chapter 5) and Customer Journey Maps (Chapter 7) to ground your feature in stuff customers actually care about. Don't map features that sound cool in theory but don't solve problems real people actually have.

Get the right people in the room. You need someone who understands the business rules (product person), someone who knows what's technically possible without breaking everything (engineer), someone who's thinking about whether customers will actually figure out how to use this thing (designer), and ideally someone who talks to customers when they're upset (customer support).

Focus on one feature at a time. Don't try to map your entire product roadmap in one marathon session. Pick one specific feature and go deep on it. You can always do another mapping session for the next feature—your brain will thank you.

Make those hidden assumptions visible. The magic happens when someone says, "Wait, I totally assumed we were handling that differently." Those moments of "oh wait, we're not aligned" are exactly why you're mapping instead of just building and hoping for the best.

Test your logic with real scenarios. Walk through your examples as a team. If Sarah does this, then what happens? If the system responds that way, then what does Sarah do next? Keep going until you've covered the realistic paths customers will actually take, not just the happy path you drew on the whiteboard.

Try This Right Now

Pick a feature your team is planning to work on in the next couple of weeks. Grab a whiteboard or shared template and spend 30 minutes working through these questions with whoever's around:

1. Who exactly is going to use this feature? (Get way more specific than just "customer")

2. What are three business rules this thing absolutely has to follow?

3. Give me two concrete examples of how someone would actually use this in real life

4. What are all the steps they have to go through?

5. What happens when it works perfectly? What happens when it doesn't?

6. What's one thing we're assuming that we probably should double-check?

If you start disagreeing about stuff or realize you don't actually know the answer to something important, congratulations! You just saved your team from shipping something incomplete or having to rebuild it later when customers start complaining.

Making Feature Mapping a Team Habit

To turn Feature Mapping from a one-off exercise into something your team actually does:

Map before you code, every single time. Make Feature Mapping part of your backlog refinement process. Before any user story gets the "Ready for Development" stamp, make sure the team has mapped out the key scenarios and thought through what could go wrong.

Keep your maps where people can see them. Don't let your feature maps disappear into some document folder that nobody ever opens. Print them out, stick them on the wall, or keep them in a shared space where developers can look at them when they're actually building the thing.

Update them when you learn something new. Customer feedback, customer testing, and real usage data are going to teach you stuff you had no idea about when you first mapped the feature. Update your maps so they stay useful instead of becoming outdated fiction.

Connect them to your other stuff. Use your feature maps to write better acceptance criteria for your user stories. Reference them during design reviews to make sure the designs you're proposing actually handle all the scenarios you mapped out.

Celebrate when it actually works. When a feature launches smoothly because you caught edge cases early in mapping, make sure the team knows that spending time thinking upfront prevented a bunch of pain later. It'll make everyone way more willing to invest the effort next time.

What's Next

In Chapter 13, we're diving into **Example Mapping**, which takes your feature maps and gets even more specific about rules and acceptance criteria. You'll learn how to use concrete examples to drive out all the ambiguity and create user stories that are actually testable instead of just wishful thinking.

Example Mapping

Bringing User Stories to Life with Concrete Examples

What You'll Learn

- How example maps turn vague user stories into crystal-clear requirements that everyone actually understands
- A simple visual technique that gets your whole team on the same map about what you're really building
- Practical ways to catch all those sneaky edge cases before they blow up in production

When "It's Obvious" Clearly Isn't

The restaurant app team was feeling pretty good about themselves. They'd mapped out their "one-tap checkout" feature in Chapter 12, everyone seemed aligned, and they jumped into development with confidence.

Launch day arrived, and Sarah was excited to finally try the new feature. She tapped "Order Again," expecting the smooth experience they'd promised. Instead, her loyalty discount didn't apply (wait, was she even supposed to get one?), and the payment failed with a vague error. Only after digging into her account settings did she realize her card had expired—why hadn't the app warned her upfront?"

"Seriously? This was supposed to be the easy button," Sarah said, giving up and ordering pizza from a competitor instead.

Back at the office, the team was scratching their heads. "But we thought it was obvious that loyalty discounts would apply automatically," said the product manager. "And obviously we'd validate payment methods," added the developer. "I designed the flow assuming all that stuff just worked," the designer chimed in.

Turns out, when everyone assumes something is "obvious," that's usually when the most important details fall through the cracks.

This is exactly why our Structured Conversations Manifesto says *"Every story is a conversation."* Example Mapping makes sure those conversations happen before you write code, not after customers start complaining.

Where This Fits

You've got your inspiring future press release from Chapter 11 and your detailed feature map from Chapter 12. Now you need to take those features and get really specific about what they actually do in the real world.

Example Mapping bridges the gap between your feature maps and the detailed user stories you'll write in Chapter 15. It's where you turn "apply loyalty discounts" into "when Sarah has a 10% loyalty discount and orders $50 worth of food, she pays $45 and sees the savings clearly on her receipt."

Why Example Mapping Matters (And Saves You from "Obvious" Disasters)

Look, every team thinks their requirements are clear until development starts. Then suddenly everyone discovers they had completely different ideas about how things should work.

A grocery delivery team spent weeks building "same-day delivery" only to realize on launch day that nobody had defined what "same-day" actually meant. Did it mean orders placed by noon? By 6 PM? What about orders placed at 11:59 PM? And in whose time zone—the customer's or the warehouse's? They had to scramble to add zip code validation, time cutoff rules, and timezone handling, delaying launch by two weeks.

Twenty minutes of Example Mapping would have caught all of that.

Example Mapping helps you:

Turn fuzzy ideas like "make checkout faster" into specific, testable scenarios everyone can understand.

Catch all those edge cases that seem "obvious" until they're not.

Get your whole team—product, design, engineering, QA—aligned on exactly what you're building.

Prevent those brutal "wait, I thought we were doing it differently" conversations in the middle of development.

Actually deliver features that work the way customers expect them to.

Matt Wynne (2015) pioneered the technique after discovering that "we all understood the requirements" was a myth.

What Is Example Mapping?

Example Mapping is like having a really focused conversation about one user story, except you write everything down on sticky notes so nobody can pretend they didn't hear something later.

You break down a user story as follows (Fig. 23):

The Story (Yellow sticky). The main thing you're trying to build, written so a human can understand it.

Rules (Blue stickies). The business logic that absolutely has to work—stuff like "loyalty discounts apply automatically" or "payment must be validated before confirming."

Examples (Green stickies). Real scenarios that show exactly how those rules play out—like "Sarah with a 10% discount ordering $50 of food pays $45."

Questions (Red stickies). All the stuff you realize you don't actually know yet—like "what happens if the discount expired yesterday?"

It's basically a way to have all the important conversations about a feature in one focused session, instead of discovering missing pieces when you're trying to demo to stakeholders. As John Ferguson Smart (2023) writes: *Example Mapping is a simple, fast, and effective way to drill into a requirement and get high test coverage to boot*.

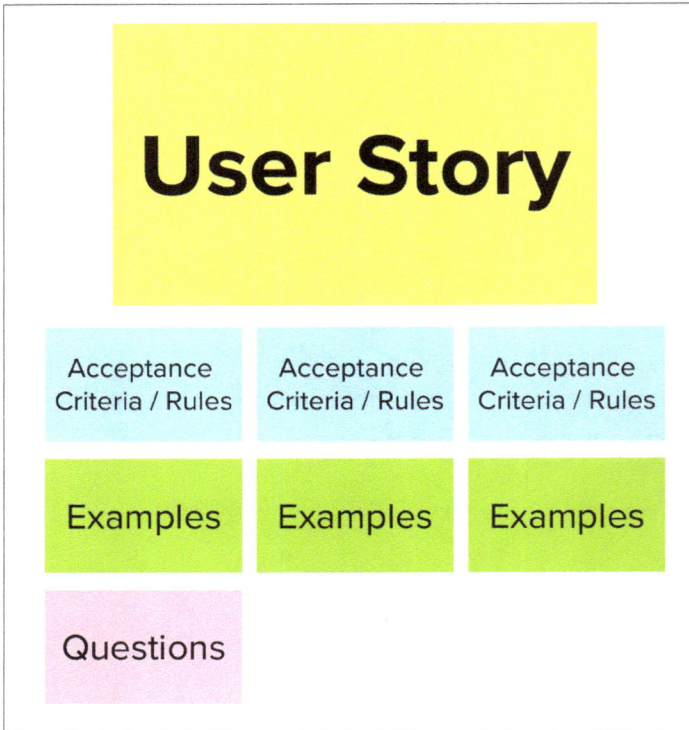

Fig. 23: Example Mapping Template

Real Example: The Restaurant App's Loyalty Discount Nightmare

Instead of assuming everyone was on the same map about loyalty discounts, let's see how the restaurant app team could have used Example Mapping to figure out what they were really building:

The Story (Yellow):

As a returning customer, I want my loyalty discount to apply automatically during checkout, so I don't have to remember coupon codes or worry about missing my savings.

Rules (Blue stickies):

- Loyalty discounts apply automatically if the customer is logged in and has an active discount
- Discount amount shows clearly in the order summary before payment
- Expired discounts don't apply (obviously, but let's be explicit)
- Discounts can't stack with other promotional offers
- Minimum order amounts must be met for percentage discounts

Examples (Green stickies):

- Sarah logs in, has a 10% loyalty discount, orders $50 of food → Pays $45, sees "$5.00 loyalty savings" on receipt
- Mike has a 15% discount but only orders $8 worth of food with $10 minimum → Discount doesn't apply, sees message explaining why
- Lisa has an expired discount from last month → No discount applied, doesn't see any mention of expired offers
- James has both a 10% loyalty discount and a "FREE DELIVERY" promo code → Gets free delivery, loyalty discount doesn't apply, sees explanation

Questions (Red stickies):

- What if someone logs in after adding items to their cart? Does the discount apply retroactively?
- How do we handle it if the discount would make the order total negative? (Like a $5 discount on a $3 order)
- Do discounts apply to tax and delivery fees, or just food?
- Should we show expired discounts in the customer's account or pretend they never existed?

See how this maps out all the stuff that seemed "obvious" until you actually think about it? Instead of everyone making different assumptions, the team talks through exactly how this feature should behave in all the messy real-world scenarios customers will encounter.

How to Build an Example Map (Step by Step)

Example Mapping works best when you get the right people in a room and actually hash things out together. Download our free template (Fig. 24) from structured-conversations.com to follow along:

Keep it short and focused. Don't try to map every user story in your backlog in one marathon session. Pick one user story, set a timer for 25-30 minutes, and go deep on just that one thing. Your brain will thank you, and you'll actually finish instead of getting overwhelmed.

Get the right mix of people. You need someone who knows the business rules (product person), someone who understands what's technically possible (developer), someone thinking about the user experience (designer), and someone who knows what goes wrong in the real world (QA or customer support).

Start with what you think you know. Write down the user story and the rules everyone thinks are "obvious." You'll be amazed how quickly you discover that your "obvious" isn't the same as everyone else's "obvious."

Get specific with examples. Avoid vague phrases like "customer gets a discount." They don't provide enough detail to be useful. Write "Sarah with a 10% loyalty discount ordering $50 worth of Thai food pays $45 and sees 'You saved $5.00 with loyalty rewards' on her receipt." The more specific you get, the more edge cases you'll discover.

Embrace the questions. When someone says "Wait, what happens if . . ."—celebrate! Those questions are exactly why you're doing this exercise. Write them down on red stickies and figure out who needs to find the answers.

Make decisions or park them. For each question, either decide on the spot (if it's simple) or assign it to someone to figure out later (if it needs research). Don't let questions sit in limbo forever.

Using Example Mapping

Example maps shine in multiple contexts:

Backlog refinement. Sharpen user stories from feature maps (Chapter 12) for the backlog (Chapter 15).

Sprint planning. Align developers and testers on acceptance criteria.

Design reviews. Validate that designs cover all rules and examples.

Stakeholder alignment. Share maps to justify priorities, supported by Chapter 6's Impact Mapping.

As a restaurant Customer, I want to customize my order via an app so that the kitchen makes it to my liking

- I can add or remove ingredients
- I can add a text note
- I can choose the spice level

- The one where I don't want hard boiled egg
- The one where I only want rice noodles and no egg noodles
- The one where I like it as spicy as possible

- The one where I want extra tofu
- The one where I ask for a special sauce
- The one where I forget to choose a spice level

- The one where I want fried tofu, not steamed tofu
- What happens if the customer forgets to choose a spice level?

- Is there an extra charge for these modifications?

As a member of the Kitchen Staff, I want to see each modification on a separate line, so that I prepare the order correctly

- Menu Item name and number appear as a new line entry
- Added ingredients have the word "Add" before them on an indented new line
- Removed ingredients have the word "no" before them on an indented new line

- 52. Vegetarian Pho
- -Add Fried Tofu -Add Special Sauce
- -No egg noodles -No hard-boiled egg

- What does an order look like with more than one item?

As a restaurant owner, I want to ensure that customers pay the correct price for their order

- Each menu item has a set price
- Added ingredients increase the price
- Removed ingredients do not affect the price
- Text notes do not impact the price

- 52. Vegetarian Pho $10.99
- Customer adds fried tofu
- Customer removes egg noodles
- Customer does not enter a note

- Customer asks for extra sauce

- What if the note asks to add another ingredient?

As a restaurant Customer, I want to pay for my order on the app

- I can add a tip
- I can use a credit card
- I can choose how to receive my receipt

- The one where I choose a pre-set tip amount
- The one where I tap my credit card
- The one where I ask for an email

- The one where I enter a custom tip amount
- The one where I insert my credit card
- The one where I ask for a printed receipt

- The one where I do not leave a tip
- The one where I swipe my credit card
- The one where I ask for a text receipt

- What should custom tip amounts be?
- What happens if credit card is declined?
- The one where I ask for no receipt

- What happens if customer wants to pay by cash?
- What happens if customer wants to pay using another app?

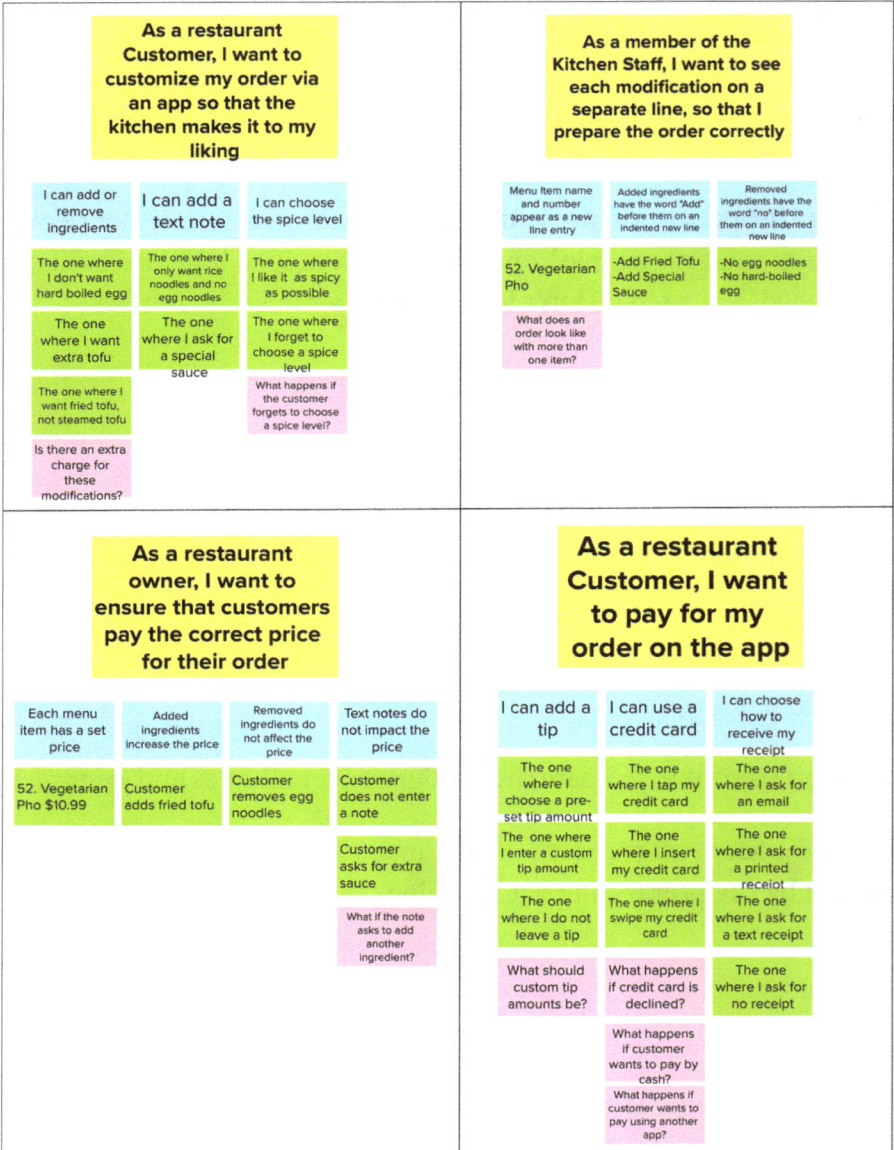

Fig. 24: Example Mapping Template

Try This Right Now

Pick a user story from your backlog—something you're planning to work on in the next week or two. Grab some sticky notes (or a digital equivalent) and spend 20 minutes working through this:

1. **Write the user story on a yellow sticky** (make sure it's something a human would actually want to do)

2. **List 3-4 rules on blue stickies** (the business logic that absolutely has to work)

3. **Create 2-3 examples per rule on green stickies** (get really specific—use names, dollar amounts, actual scenarios)

4. **Write down every question that comes up on red stickies** (there will be more than you expect)

If you end up with a bunch of red stickies, congratulations! You just prevented a bunch of "wait, how should this work?" conversations during development.

Making Example Mapping a Team Habit

To make Example Mapping a regular part of how your team works:

Map before you commit to building. Make Example Mapping part of your backlog refinement process. Before a user story gets marked "ready for development," make sure the team has mapped out the key rules and examples.

Keep the maps visible. Don't let your example maps disappear into a digital folder somewhere. Take photos of the sticky note walls, or recreate them in whatever tool your team actually looks at. Developers should be able to reference them while they're coding.

Update when you learn new stuff. Customer feedback, testing, and real usage will teach you things you didn't know when you first mapped the user story. Update your maps so they stay useful instead of becoming historical artifacts.

Use them for more than just requirements. Reference your example maps during design reviews to make sure proposed designs handle all the mapped scenarios. Use them during testing to make sure you're covering all the examples. Use them in stakeholder demos to show exactly what behavior you built.

Celebrate when it prevents problems. When Example Mapping catches a missing rule or edge case before it becomes a production defect, make sure the team knows that taking the time upfront saved everyone pain later. It builds commitment to the practice.

What's Next

In Chapter 14, we'll dive into **Writing Epics**—those bigger chunks of work that connect multiple user stories to your overall strategy. You'll learn how to frame larger initiatives in a way that keeps teams focused on customer outcomes instead of just shipping features.

Writing Epics

Framing Strategic Initiatives for Impact

What You'll Learn

- How to write epics that actually align everyone instead of creating more confusion
- How to craft an epic pitch for turning initiatives into clear, outcome-focused plans
- How to connect your epics to measurable outcomes using product OKRs

When Big Ideas Meet Messy Reality

The restaurant app team was pumped. They'd just pitched their biggest initiative yet to the executive team: "Revolutionize the customer experience with AI-powered personalization." The room was nodding, people were excited, and they got the green light for a six-month project.

Three months later, things were not going well.

The engineering team was building a recommendation engine. The design team was working on a new interface for showing suggestions. The product team was focused on improving search functionality. Marketing was planning campaigns around "smart ordering." Everyone was busy, everyone was working hard, but nobody could really explain how all these pieces fit together or why they mattered to customers.

During the quarterly review, the CEO asked the dreaded question: "So how do we know if this is working?"

Awkward silence.

"Well, customers seem to like the new interface," offered the designer. "The recommendation algorithm is getting more accurate," said the engineer. "We're seeing some engagement with the new features," added the product manager.

More awkward silence.

"But are people actually ordering more food?" asked the CEO.

Nobody had a good answer. They had activity metrics, feature adoption rates, and algorithm accuracy scores—everything except evidence that customers' lives had actually improved.

That's when they realized: they'd been measuring their work instead of measuring the outcome.

This is what happens when you have a big vision but no clear way to measure whether you're actually making progress toward something that matters. As our Structured Conversations Manifesto says, "*Intentional syntax surpasses accidental semantics.*" Well-structured epics turn exciting but vague initiatives into focused plans that everyone can understand and measure.

Where This Fits

You've been mapping features (Chapter 12) and drilling into specific requirements (Chapter 13). Now you need to step back and frame those features as part of bigger, strategic initiatives that stakeholders actually care about.

Epics take all your mapping work from Chapters 5-9 and package it into high-level initiatives that connect daily work to measurable business outcomes. This sets you up perfectly for writing detailed user stories in Chapter 15.

Why Many Epics Miss the Mark (And How to Fix Them)

Here's the uncomfortable truth: many epics are just big user stories dressed up with fancy language. They sound important in planning meetings, but they don't actually help teams make decisions or measure progress.

A retail team wrote an epic called "Enhance the customer journey experience." Six months and half a million dollars later, they had a bunch of new features that customers barely used. When they finally asked customers what they actually wanted, it turned out the biggest pain point was not being able to easily reach a human when they had questions about their order.

The epic sounded strategic, but it wasn't connected to any real customer problem or measurable outcome.

Good epics are different. They:

Actually explain why you're building something instead of just describing what you're building.

Give teams a clear way to know if they're succeeding instead of just hoping for the best.

Help everyone make better decisions about what to prioritize and what to cut.

Connect daily work to business results so people understand why their work matters.

Prevent scope creep by giving you something concrete to evaluate new ideas against.

The secret is treating epics like hypotheses that you're trying to prove, not just to-do lists that you're trying to complete.

What Makes an Epic Actually Epic

Think of an epic as a focused bet you're making about how to improve your product. You're saying "If we build this stuff, then these specific good things will happen, and here's how we'll know if we're right."

A good epic has all the pieces you need to make that bet intelligently:

A clear, actionable name. Use VERB + NOUN so people actually know what you're trying to accomplish. "Simplify checkout process" tells you way more than "Checkout improvements."

A compelling pitch. Explain who this helps, what problem it solves, and why it's different from what exists today. Think of it like the product elevator pitch from Chapter 10, but focused on one specific initiative.

Measurable outcomes. Specific results you expect to see, not vague hopes like "improve customer satisfaction." More like "reduce checkout abandonment from 35% to 25% within 90 days."

Early warning signs. Leading indicators that tell you if you're on the right track before waiting for the final results. Like "50% of returning customers try the new checkout flow in the first month."

Clear constraints. The non-negotiable requirements like performance, scale, or compliance that could harm the product if you ignore them.

Let's fix the restaurant app's epic disaster: Instead of that vague "revolutionize customer experience" epic that went nowhere, let's see how the restaurant app team could have written something actually useful:

Epic Name: Personalize reordering experience

Epic Pitch:

For busy parents like Sarah

Who want to reorder family favorites without thinking about it

The QuickBite app

Is a food delivery platform

That learns your preferences and surfaces the right options at the right time

Unlike generic apps that make you search through endless menus every time

Our epic remembers what your family actually eats and makes it effortless to order again

Business Outcomes:

- Increase repeat orders from current customers by 25% within 4 months
- Reduce average time from app open to order completion by 80% for returning customers

Product OKRs:

- 60% of returning customers use personalized reorder suggestions within 60 days
- Personalized recommendations achieve 35% click-through rate
- Customer satisfaction score for ordering experience increases from 7.2 to 8.5

Leading Indicators:

- 40% of eligible customers see personalized suggestions in first month
- Average time spent browsing menus decreases by 30% for customers who engage with recommendations
- Support tickets related to "finding previous orders" decrease by 90%

Non-Functional Requirements:

- Recommendation engine responds within 200ms
- System handles 10,000 concurrent customers during peak dinner hours
- All customer data handling complies with industry-leading privacy standards

See how this epic tells a specific story about a specific outcome? Instead of "revolutionizing everything," it focuses on making reordering easier for people who already love the app. Instead of hoping for vague "engagement," it measures specific behaviors that matter to the business.

The Magic of Product OKRs (Beyond the Corporate Version)

Here's the challenge with many OKRs: they're often too high-level to guide product decisions. A goal like "increase revenue by 20%" doesn't tell a product team what to prioritize or build.

Product OKRs work differently. They focus on measurable product behaviors that drive business outcomes. Instead of "increase revenue," you'll see objectives like "increase repeat purchase rate," "reduce onboarding drop-off," or "improve feature adoption."

For the restaurant app's personalization epic, the product OKRs tell you exactly what success looks like:

- **60% adoption** means people actually find the feature and try it
- **35% click-through** means the recommendations are relevant, not just visible
- **8.5 satisfaction score** means the experience feels better, not just different

These aren't arbitrary numbers—they're based on what you learned from your customer research in Chapters 5-7. Sarah told you she wants ordering to be "effortless," so you're measuring how much effort you're actually removing.

How to Write Epics That Don't Disappoint

Writing good epics is like writing good user stories—you need to know who the hero is, what problem they're facing, and what success looks like.

Start with real customer problems. Pull from your empathy maps (Chapter 5) and customer journey maps (Chapter 7). What's actually frustrating customers? Don't make up problems because they sound strategic.

Be specific about outcomes. "Improve the experience" is not an outcome. "Reduce the time Sarah spends placing her weekly family dinner order from 8 minutes to 2 minutes" is an outcome.

Connect to business results. Your product metrics should roll up to business metrics. If Sarah orders faster and more often, that means more revenue per customer and better retention.

Make it measurable from day one. Don't wait until the end to figure out if it worked. Define leading indicators that tell you if you're on track before you've spent months building the wrong thing.

Get everyone aligned before you start. Write the epic collaboratively. The disagreements that come up during writing are way easier to resolve than the ones that come up during development.

Try This Right Now

Pick a big initiative your team is working on (or about to work on). Spend 30 minutes writing it up as a proper epic:

1. **Give it a VERB + NOUN name** that actually tells people what you're trying to accomplish

2. **Write a one-paragraph pitch** explaining who this helps and why they should care

3. **Define 2-3 specific, measurable outcomes** you expect to see (with numbers and timeframes)

4. **List 1-2 early indicators** that would tell you if you're on the right track

5. **Identify any constraints** that could harm the product if you ignore them

Then ask yourself: If I showed this to a customer, would they understand why we're building it? If I showed it to an executive, would they understand how we'll know if it worked?

If the answer to either question is "not really," you've got more work to do.

Making Epics Actually Useful (Instead of Just Required)

To make epic-writing a valuable part of your process instead of just bureaucracy:

Write them collaboratively. Don't let one person go off and write epics in isolation. Get product, design, engineering, and business stakeholders in a room and hash it out together.

Keep them visible. Your epics should live somewhere the whole team can see them, not buried in a planning document. When people are debating what feature to build next, they should be able to look at the epic and see how it connects.

Update them when you learn stuff. Customer feedback, usage data, and market changes will teach you things that change your epic. Don't treat them like contracts carved in stone.

Use them to make decisions. When someone suggests a cool new feature, ask how it connects to the current epic. If it doesn't, either it's not a priority right now or you need to write a different epic.

Measure what you said you'd measure. Track your product OKRs and leading indicators consistently—they're meant to drive learning and course correction, not just scorekeeping. Falling short reveals important insights about what's working and where you need to adjust.

Download our free template from structured-conversations.com to co-create epics with your team.

What's Next

In Chapter 15, we'll dive into **Writing User Stories**—breaking these big epics down into specific, testable pieces your team can actually build. You'll learn different ways to structure user stories so they connect back to the epic outcomes you just defined.

Writing User Stories

The Atomic Unit of Getting Stuff Done

What You'll Learn

- How to write user stories that actually help your team build the right thing instead of just keeping everyone busy
- Multiple ways to structure user stories so you can pick the right format for the job
- How to make sure your user stories are ready for development (and won't come back to haunt you later)

When Everyone's Building Different Things

The restaurant app team got their epic approved (remember the personalization one from Chapter 14?) and immediately dove into development. The designer started mockups for a beautiful recommendation interface. The backend developer began building a machine learning system to analyze order patterns. The product manager started writing requirements for a loyalty point system.

Three weeks later, they demoed their progress to Sarah, their favorite customer tester.

"This is . . . interesting," Sarah said, trying to be polite. "But I was hoping you'd just remember that I always order the chicken Pad Thai with no peanuts for my daughter. Instead, I'm getting recommendations for sushi, which none of us eat, and something about earning points that I don't really understand."

Back in the team meeting, everyone was confused. "But we're personalizing the experience!" said the designer. "The algorithm is learning from customer data!" said the developer. "We're increasing engagement with gamification!" said the product manager.

Meanwhile, Sarah just wanted to reorder last Tuesday's dinner without having to remember whether her daughter's Pad Thai was medium or mild spice.

This is what happens when you have a great epic but don't break it down into specific, actionable pieces that everyone can understand. As our Structured Conversations Manifesto says, "*Intentional syntax surpasses accidental semantics.*" User stories are where the rubber meets the road—they're the specific, testable pieces that teams actually build.

Where This Fits

You've defined your big strategic initiative with an epic in Chapter 14. Now you need to break that epic down into bite-sized pieces your team can actually deliver in a sprint.

User stories take all your mapping work from Chapters 5-13 and turn it into specific, actionable tasks. Each user story should connect back to real customer needs you discovered in your Empathy Mapping and solve specific problems you identified in your customer journey work.

Why User Stories Are Often Terrible
(And How to Fix Them)

Here is a common problem: User stories often focus more on technical features than on real customer needs. They sound official and cover all the bases, but they don't help teams understand what customers actually want to accomplish.

A retail team wrote this user story: As a customer, I want to have an enhanced shopping experience so that I can purchase products more efficiently.

What does that even mean? What's "enhanced"? What counts as "efficient"? How would you know if you built it right?

Three months later, they shipped a bunch of features that nobody used because the user story didn't actually describe a real person with a real problem.

Well-written user stories are different. They:

Describe specific people doing specific things instead of vague "customers" having vague "experiences."

Focus on outcomes customers actually care about instead of features that sound cool.

Give the team enough context to make good decisions without micromanaging every detail.

Create space for conversation and iteration instead of trying to lock everything down upfront.

Connect to measurable results so you know if you're actually solving the problem.

The secret is remembering that user stories aren't requirements documents—they're conversation starters about what to build and why it matters.

Crafting Effective User Stories

User stories thrive on simplicity and focus. Structured syntax ensures clarity and reinforces the Manifesto's principle: *"Clear language sparks action."* Six syntax patterns—each suited to different contexts—help teams craft user stories that resonate.

User Story Syntax Options

Syntax Type	Format Template	Best Used For	Example
Traditional	As a <user>, I want to <goal> so that <benefit>	General user-facing functionality	As a customer, I want to reorder a meal so that I can save time
Hypothesis-Driven Development (HDD)	We believe that <capability> will result in <outcome>	Testing risky ideas	We believe that adding reminders will increase return visits
Feature-Driven Development (FDD)	<Action> the <result> <by/for/to> an <object>	System-level functionality	Log the error to a dashboard for admin visibility

Syntax Type	Format Template	Best Used For	Example
Job Story	When <situation>, I want to <motivation> so that <outcome>	Contextual behaviors	When I close the register, I want a report so I can check totals
Jobs to Be Done (JTBD) / Outcome-Driven Development (ODD)	Even when <constraint>, I want to <job> so that <result>	Outcome-driven product thinking	Even when I'm busy, I want to schedule posts so my feed stays active
Event-Based	When <event happens>, <actor> should <respond> to <achieve>	Event-driven systems or reactive flows	When a login is detected, prompt for MFA to ensure secure access

Traditional User Story Syntax

Choose one syntax format that resonates with your team and use it consistently. The specific wording matters far less than ensuring every story clearly expresses who needs what and why. Don't let syntax debates delay the more important work of understanding your customers' needs.

- As a <user>, I want to <goal> so that <benefit>
- As a <type of user>, I want to <action> so that <value>
- As a <role>, I would like to <action> to achieve <business value>
- As a <user>, I can <do something> so that <value>
- As a <person>, I can <do something> so that <value>

- In order to <value>, as a <user>, I want to <goal>
- In order to <achieve a goal>, as a <type of user>, I want to <do something>

Hypothesis-Driven Development (HDD) Syntax

- We believe that <capability> will result in <outcome>, we will know we have succeeded when <we see a measurable signal>

This syntax is useful when exploring uncertainty or assumptions and pairs well with hypothesis-based planning (Chapter 23).

Feature-Driven Development (FDD) Syntax

For system-level, backend, or non-user-facing stories (Cohn, 2015):
- <Action> the <result> <by/for/of/to/on/from/in> an <object>

Example: "Log the error to a central dashboard for administrator visibility."

Job Stories

- When <situation>, I want to <motivation> so that <outcome> (Cohn, 2019)

Example: "When I'm closing the register at night, I want to view the daily sales summary so that I can confirm totals and flag discrepancies."

Jobs To Be Done (JTBD) / Outcome-Driven Development (ODD)

- Even when <constraint>, I want to <job> so that <desired outcome>

Example: "Even when I'm too busy to post manually, I want to schedule content so that my restaurant's social presence remains consistent."

Event-Based

For user stories derived from domain events:

- When <event happens>, <actor> should <respond this way> to <achieve outcome>

Example: "When a customer logs in from a new device, the system should prompt for MFA to ensure secure access."

Choosing the Right Syntax

Traditional. Ideal for most customer-facing features, emphasizing who, what, and why.

HDD. Best for experimental features with uncertain outcomes.

FDD. Suited for technical or system-level tasks with less customer focus.

Job Stories. Captures situational needs for nuanced customer contexts.

JTBD/ODD. Focuses on overcoming specific barriers to achieve customer goals.

Event-Based. Perfect for systems reacting to triggers or security needs.

For example, a restaurant app team might use traditional for "As a customer, I want to track my delivery, so that I know when it arrives," and FDD for "Send order confirmation to the kitchen for faster processing."

Making Sure Your User Stories Are Actually Ready to Build

Before your team starts working on a user story, it should pass what we call the INVEST criteria. They help you avoid those painful mid-sprint conversations where everyone realizes the user story wasn't really ready:

Independent. Can you build this user story without depending on other user stories being done first? If not, you might need to split it differently.

Negotiable. Is there room for the team to make decisions about how to implement this, or have you locked down every detail? User stories should guide decisions, not eliminate them.

Valuable. Does this user story deliver something that actually matters to customers or the business? If you can't explain why it's valuable, maybe it shouldn't be a priority.

Estimable. Can your team look at this user story and have a reasonable conversation about how much work it is? If not, you probably need to break it down more or do some research first.

Small. Can you build and test this user story within a sprint? If it's going to take months, it's probably an epic, not a user story.

Testable. How will you know when this user story is done? If you can't define "done," you can't test it successfully.

For example, "As a customer, I want a better ordering experience, so that I can be happier" fails most of these criteria. It's not specific enough to estimate, you can't test whether it's done, and "better" doesn't tell you what's valuable.

But "As a returning customer, I want to see my last three orders when I open the app, so I can reorder quickly" passes all the readiness criteria.

When to Use Spikes Instead

If a user story is too uncertain to estimate—say, "Integrate a new payment gateway"—frame it as a spike (Chapter 17). Spikes are time-boxed research efforts that resolve uncertainty before delivery.

Try This Right Now

Pick a user story from your backlog and run it through this quick test:

1. **Can you picture a specific person who would want this?** (Not just "customer")

2. **Is the thing they want to do concrete and specific?** (Not vague like "have a better experience")

3. **Do you understand why they want it?** (The outcome should make sense)

4. **Could your team build and test this in a week or two?** (If not, it needs to be split)

5. **Would you know how to demo this to a customer?** (If not, it's probably too vague)

If you answered "no" to any of these questions, your user story probably needs more work before it's ready for development.

How to Write User Stories That Work

Writing good user stories is like writing good emails—you need to know your audience and get to the point quickly.

Start with real people. Use the personas and insights from your Empathy Mapping (Chapter 5). Don't write for generic "customers"—write for Sarah who's trying to feed her family on a Tuesday night.

Focus on outcomes, not features. Instead of "I want a recommendation engine," write "I want to discover meals my family will actually eat." The team can figure out the best way to make that happen.

Keep it conversational. Write like you're talking to a colleague. "As a busy parent" is better than "As a user persona representing the demographic of working parents aged 25-45."

Include just enough context. Give the team enough information to understand the situation, but not so much that you're micromanaging the implementation.

Make the value clear. The "so that" part should describe an outcome that actually matters to the person, not just what the system does.

Test it with real scenarios. Can you walk through how Sarah would actually use this? If the user story feels artificial, it probably is.

Making User Stories Work for Your Team

To make user story writing actually helpful instead of just another process:

Write them together. Don't let one person go off and write all the user stories alone. The conversation that happens while writing user stories is often more valuable than the user stories themselves.

Keep them visible. Your user stories should live somewhere the whole team can see them and reference them during development.

Update them when you learn. Customer feedback and testing will teach you things that change your user stories. Don't treat them like sacred contracts.

Connect back to your epic. Each user story should clearly connect to the bigger initiative you defined in Chapter 14. If you can't explain the connection, maybe the user story isn't a priority.

Focus on conversations, not documentation. The user story is just the starting point. The real work happens in the conversations about how to implement it.

As our Manifesto states: *"Every story is a conversation."*

What's Next

In Chapter 16, we'll dive into **Splitting User Stories**—because inevitably, some of your user stories are going to be too big to fit in a sprint, and you'll need to break them down further without losing the customer focus that makes them valuable.

Splitting User Stories

Cakes, Hamburgers, and Spiders

What You'll Learn

- Why big user stories slow momentum and how to slice them into manageable pieces
- Simple techniques to break down big user stories without losing the customer value
- How to deliver working software faster by thinking like you're serving cake (trust us on this one)

When "Simple" Updates Become Six-Month Death Marches

The restaurant app team was feeling confident after writing some solid user stories in Chapter 15. Then they looked at their backlog and found this beast: "As a restaurant owner, I want to completely redesign the menu management system so that I can update items, prices, photos, descriptions, categories, dietary tags, and availability across web and mobile platforms while automatically notifying customers about changes."

"This should be pretty straightforward," said the product manager during sprint planning.

Three months later, they were still building it. The backend team was knee-deep in database migrations. The frontend team was waiting for APIs that kept changing. The mobile team was blocked by design decisions that weren't finalized yet. The restaurant owners who'd requested this feature had stopped asking for updates because they assumed it was never going to ship.

"Maybe we should have broken this down a bit more," the product manager finally admitted during a particularly painful retrospective.

This is what happens when user stories grow into these massive, multi-headed monsters that nobody can actually finish. As our Structured Conversations Manifesto says, *Visual maps show the path.* Sometimes that path needs to be broken into smaller steps that humans can actually walk.

Where This Fits

You've written some solid user stories using the techniques from Chapter 15. Now you need to look at those user stories and figure out which ones are actually too big to build in a reasonable amount of time.

Story splitting takes your user stories and breaks them into smaller, more manageable pieces that still deliver real value to customers. It's the difference between trying to eat an entire pizza in one bite and cutting it into slices you can actually handle.

Why Big User Stories Are Actually Evil

Here's the thing about big user stories: they seem efficient until you actually try to build them. Then they turn into these soul-crushing monsters that drag on forever and make everyone miserable.

A retail team wrote this user story: As a customer, I want a personalized shopping experience that remembers my preferences, suggests relevant products, tracks my browsing history, integrates with my social media, and provides customized promotions based on my purchase patterns.

Ten months later, they'd built a recommendation engine that nobody used, a social media integration that creeped people out, and a promotion system that mostly suggested dog food to people who'd never owned pets.

The problem wasn't that the idea was bad—it was that they tried to build everything at once instead of starting with one small piece that actually solved a real problem.

Big user stories are problematic because they:

Take forever to finish, which means you don't get feedback until it's too late to change course.

Hide a bunch of different problems that should probably be solved separately.

Make it impossible to prioritize what's actually important vs. what's just nice-to-have.

Create dependencies between teams that turn simple changes into coordination nightmares.

Make demos really awkward because nothing actually works end-to-end until everything's done.

The secret is learning how to slice big user stories into smaller pieces that each deliver something useful on their own.

How to Split User Stories Effectively

Splitting user stories is both art and science. Below are four engaging techniques, supported by our free template at structured-conversations.com. Use it during backlog refinement to spark collaboration.

Slicing User Stories Like You're Serving Cake (The Vertical Slice Approach)

The best way to think about story splitting is like cutting a cake.

You could cut the cake horizontally—first *all* the fluffy whipped cream, then *all* the sweet cherry filling, then *all* the chocolate layers soaked in cherry syrup. But eating each component separately misses the magic—you want that perfect bite with *tangy* cherry, *rich* chocolate, and *light, fluffy* cream all together.

Instead, you cut the cake vertically, so each slice has some of every layer. That way, every piece is a complete, delicious experience— *cherry on top and all* (Fig. 25).

The same thing applies to user stories. You could split them horizontally by technical layers—build the database stuff first, then the backend, then the frontend. But that means nobody gets any real value until everything's done.

Vertical slicing means each piece includes a little bit of every technical layer, so each piece delivers something a customer can actually use and provide feedback on.

Fig. 25: Cake Slicing Analogy

The Hamburger Technique: Build Bite-Sized Value

This playful metaphor, developed by Gojko Adzic (2012, 2014), helps teams break down user stories into flavorful, digestible pieces (Fig. 26) while retaining business value. It's particularly useful when teams are stuck thinking in technical terms and struggle to find smaller user stories that still deliver end-to-end functionality.

Steps:

1. **Identify a user story that resists splitting.** Pick a user story where the team can only see horizontal technical splits ("let's do the backend first, then the frontend") rather than smaller end-to-end deliverables.

2. **List the technical workflow tasks.** Work with the team in their comfort zone—break down the user story into the technical steps needed to implement it. These become the layers of your hamburger like lettuce (UI), tomato (interactions), onions (validation), cheese (business logic), and patty (data storage).

3. **Brainstorm quality options for each task.** For each technical task, identify what would make it "good" and write down multiple options at different quality levels. Consider factors like speed, accuracy, volume, personalization, and automation.

4. **Combine and trim.** Arrange all options from lowest to highest quality for each task. Remove options that take similar effort to higher-quality alternatives, and identify the maximum quality needed (anything beyond brings diminishing returns).

5. **Take the first bite.** Decide the minimum acceptable quality level for each task to create your first vertical slice. Some tasks might even be skipped initially if "doing nothing" is acceptable.

6. **Take another bite.** Each subsequent increment adds more quality to one or more tasks, progressively enhancing the feature.

Example user story: As a restaurant owner, I want to add new dishes to my website menu so customers can see what's available.

The team identifies technical workflow tasks:

- **Lettuce (UI):** Collect dish information
- **Tomato (Interactions):** Validate input data
- **Onions (Validation):** Organize dishes by category
- **Cheese (Business Logic):** Store dish data
- **Patty (Data):** Display on website

Now the team brainstorms quality options for each task:

Lettuce — Collect dish information:

- Option A: Paper form, manually entered by developer (slow, but works)
- Option B: Simple web form with name and price only
- Option C: Web form with name, price, and description
- Option D: Rich form with image upload, description, dietary tags
- Option E: Bulk import from spreadsheet

Tomato — Validate input data:

- Option A: Do nothing, trust the input (risky but fast)
- Option B: Basic required field checking
- Option C: Format validation (price must be number, reasonable length limits)
- Option D: Business rule validation (duplicate detection, category exists)
- Option E: Real-time validation with helpful error messages

Onions—Organize dishes by category:

- Option A: No categorization, flat list (simple but chaotic)
- Option B: Manual category assignment via dropdown
- Option C: Auto-suggest categories based on dish name
- Option D: Drag-and-drop ordering within categories

Cheese—Store dish data:

- Option A: Single flat table, no relationships
- Option B: Normalized tables with foreign keys
- Option C: Include audit trail (who added, when modified)
- Option D: Version history for changes

Patty—Display on website:

- Option A: Plain text list, no styling
- Option B: Basic formatted list with categories
- Option C: Card layout with images
- Option D: Searchable, filterable menu display

After trimming (removing options that don't make sense), the team takes their first bite:

Bite 1—Bare minimum:

- **Lettuce:** Simple web form with name and price (Option B)
- **Tomato:** Basic required field checking (Option B)
- **Onions:** No categorization (Option A)
- **Cheese:** Single flat table (Option A)
- **Patty:** Plain text list (Option A)

Bite 2—Better validation and organization:

- **Lettuce:** Same (Option B)
- **Tomato:** Format validation with error messages (Option E—similar effort to C/D but better UX)
- **Onions:** Manual category dropdown (Option B)
- **Cheese:** Normalized tables (Option B)
- **Patty:** Basic formatted list with categories (Option B)

Bite 3—Rich content:

- **Lettuce:** Rich form with images and descriptions (Option D)
- **Tomato:** Same (Option E)
- **Onions:** Same (Option B)
- **Cheese:** Same (Option B)
- **Patty:** Card layout with images (Option C)

Bite 4—Enhanced user experience:

- **Lettuce:** Bulk import capability added (Option E)
- **Tomato:** Same (Option E)
- **Onions:** Drag-and-drop ordering (Option D)
- **Cheese:** Audit trail (Option C)
- **Patty:** Searchable, filterable display (Option D)

Each bite is a complete mini-hamburger—it includes all necessary tasks at varying quality levels (Onuta, 2019). Restaurant owners can start adding dishes to their menu after the first increment, then progressively improve the feature's sophistication and usability.

When to use this technique: The Hamburger technique works best when your team is stuck thinking in horizontal technical slices ("let's build the API first, then the UI") and needs help visualizing how to deliver working features incrementally. If your team can already identify different capabilities and split user stories effectively, you may not need this technique. This technique works particularly well as a collaborative workshop activity with the whole team.

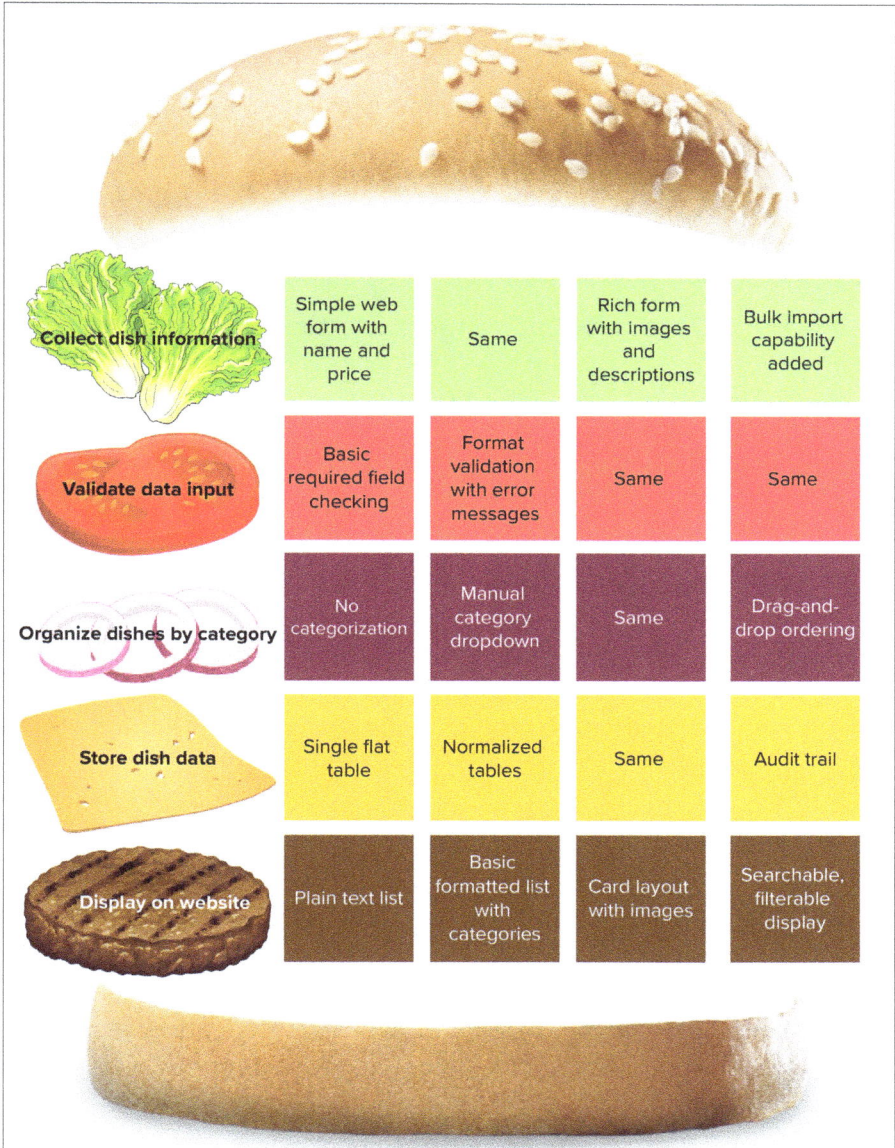

Collect dish information	Simple web form with name and price	Same	Rich form with images and descriptions	Bulk import capability added
Validate data input	Basic required field checking	Format validation with error messages	Same	Same
Organize dishes by category	No categorization	Manual category dropdown	Same	Drag-and-drop ordering
Store dish data	Single flat table	Normalized tables	Same	Audit trail
Display on website	Plain text list	Basic formatted list with categories	Card layout with images	Searchable, filterable display

Fig.26: Hamburger Story Breakdown

The SPIDR Technique: Slice by Dimensions

Sometimes you need a more systematic way to think about splitting user stories. SPIDR (Cohn, 2017) is a handy framework that gives you five different ways to slice:

S—Spike. If part of your user story is really uncertain, split out the research.

- "Investigate whether the payment API can handle international cards"

P—Paths. Split by different user journeys through your feature.

- "Order pickup" vs. "Order delivery" vs. "Order for later"

I—Interfaces. Split by different ways people interact with your system.

- "Web interface" vs. "Mobile app" vs. "Voice ordering"

D—Data. Split by different types of information.

- "Handle credit cards" vs. "Handle PayPal" vs. "Handle gift cards"

R—Rules. Split by different business logic.

- "Apply regular pricing" vs. "Apply loyalty discounts" vs. "Apply promotional codes"

SPIDR is especially useful when you have a complex user story that could be split in multiple ways and you need to think through all the options.

Rule
Mark email addresses as contacted

Spike
Research 3rd party integration tool

Rule
Remove bounced email addresses

Path
Notify via email manually

Data
Email addresses

As a < restaurant owner >
I want to < notify my followers about our new tasty dishes via email >
So that < they can order them and help us generate more revenue >

Path
Notify via email automated

Interface
Restaurant mobile app Android

Interface
Restaurant mobile app iOS

Interface
Restaurant website

Interface
Download report

Interface
Export report to file format of choice

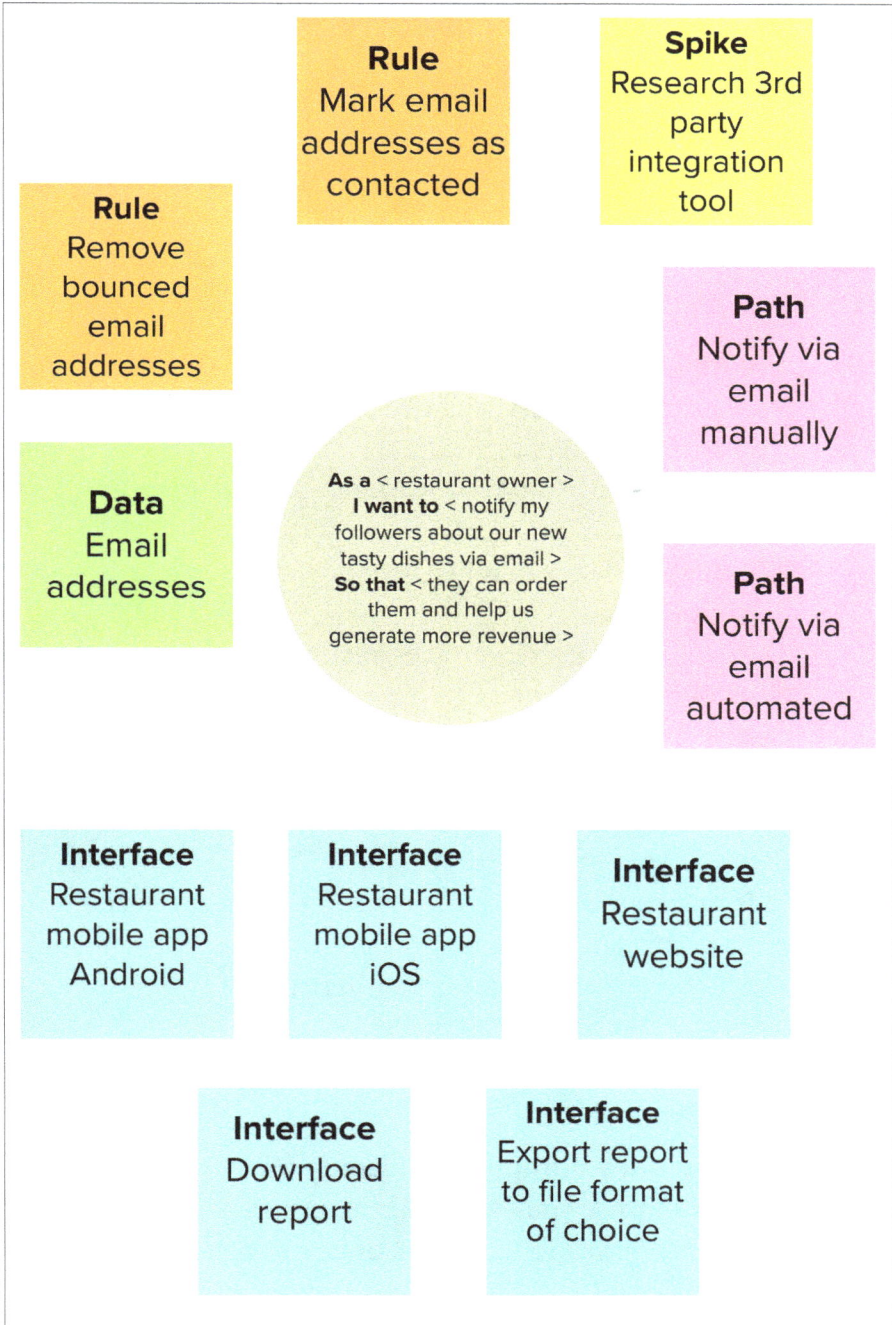

Fig.27: SPIDR Template

The Q&A Decision Tree: Ask the Right Questions

The Q&A Decision Tree, developed by Lawrence and Green (2023), uses targeted questions to uncover splitting opportunities, especially for ambiguous or risky user stories.

Steps:

1. **Ask key questions.** Use prompts to identify splits:
    - Does the user story include multiple operations (e.g., create, read, update, delete)?
    - Does it involve multiple workflow steps or approval processes?
    - Can we deliver a minimal version first, then add complexity?
    - Are multiple user interfaces, platforms, or actors involved?
    - Does the user story combine several business rules or data variations?
    - Are there different data entry methods we could implement separately?
    - Is there a major effort component that could be split from smaller additions?
    - Are there performance or non-functional requirements we could defer?
    - Is part of the user story uncertain enough to warrant a research spike?

2. **Find the core complexity.** Identify what's most likely to surprise you—often the part involving human behavior, external integrations, or new dependencies. Then reduce all variations to focus on one complete slice through that complexity first.

3. **Map answers to slices.** Turn answers into smaller user stories.

4. **Validate and choose the best split.** Ensure each slice meets the INVEST criteria, then:
    *   Choose splits that let you deprioritize or eliminate low-value user stories
    *   Prefer splits that create more equally-sized user stories for better prioritization flexibility

Example user story: As a customer, I want to manage my account settings, so that I can personalize my experience.

Q&A Decision Tree Process:

*   Multiple operations? → Yes: view, create, update, delete settings
*   Minimal version first? → Yes: start with updating just email address
*   Multiple interfaces? → Yes: web vs mobile have different constraints
*   Workflow steps? → No: direct updates, no approvals needed
*   Multiple business rules or data variations? → Yes: email/ password/phone have different validation; privacy rules vary by region
*   Different data entry methods? → Yes: text input, file upload
*   Major effort component to split? → Yes: 2FA setup is much more complex than basic updates
*   Non-functional requirements to defer? → Yes: real-time sync, audit logs, data export
*   Research spike needed? → Possibly: OAuth integration, account deletion compliance

Resulting Slices (in priority order):

The original user story splits into 7 smaller user stories (listed below in priority order). During sprint planning, developers can then sub-task each user story into implementation tasks (Chapter 18).

Foundation (View & Basic Updates)

User Story: As a customer, I want to view and update my basic account credentials on the web, so that I can keep my contact information and password current.

Implementation sub-tasks (examples):

- View current account settings on web interface
- Update email address on web interface
- Update password on web interface
- Handle validation errors for email/password updates on web

Mobile Parity

User Story: As a mobile customer, I want to view and update my basic account credentials on my mobile device, so that I can manage my account on the go.

Implementation sub-tasks (examples):

- View current account settings on mobile app
- Update email address on mobile app
- Update password on mobile app
- Handle validation errors for email/password updates on mobile

Profile Management

User Story: As a customer, I want to update my profile information and picture across all platforms, so that others can identify me and I can share accurate contact details.

Implementation sub-tasks (examples):

- Update basic profile information (name, phone) on web interface
- Update basic profile information on mobile app
- Upload/change profile picture on web interface
- Upload/change profile picture on mobile app

Communication Preferences

User Story: As a customer, I want to control how and when the platform communicates with me, so that I only receive relevant notifications through my preferred channels.

Implementation sub-tasks (examples):

- Update email notification preferences on web interface
- Update push notification preferences on mobile app
- Update SMS notification preferences on web interface
- Manage marketing communication preferences on web interface

Privacy & Security

User Story: As a customer, I want to control my privacy settings and monitor my account security, so that I can protect my personal information and detect unauthorized access.

Implementation sub-tasks (examples):

- Update privacy settings (profile visibility, data sharing) on web interface
- Update privacy settings on mobile app
- View login history/account activity on web interface
- Enable two-factor authentication on web interface
- Manage connected devices/active sessions on web interface

Advanced Features

User Story: As a customer, I want to have full control over my account lifecycle including data portability and account deletion, so that I can exercise my data rights and account ownership.

Implementation sub-tasks (examples):

- Export account data on web interface
- Temporarily deactivate account on web interface
- Permanently delete account on web interface
- Recover recently deleted account on web interface

Integration & Sync

User Story: As a customer, I want my settings synchronized across platforms and integrated with third-party services, so that I have a seamless experience and can leverage external tools.

Implementation sub-tasks (examples):

- Sync settings across web and mobile platforms
- Connect/disconnect third-party accounts (Google, Facebook, etc.)
- Manage API keys/developer settings (if applicable)

This order prioritizes core functionality first, then adds mobile parity, followed by increasingly sophisticated features. Each user story is independently deployable and delivers incremental value.

The Q&A Decision Tree is especially helpful for ambiguous or risky work. This technique clarifies scope, reducing ambiguity and ensuring actionable slices through systematic questioning that reveals hidden complexity and variation points.

Choosing the Right Technique

Cake. Best for ensuring technical layers align for end-to-end value.

Hamburger. Best when teams can only see horizontal technical splits and need help finding vertical slices with incremental quality.

SPIDR. Suited for complex user stories with multiple platforms or rules.

Q&A Decision Tree. Perfect for ambiguous user stories needing structured exploration.

Try This Right Now: The User Story Surgery Session

Pick the biggest, scariest user story from your backlog. Grab your team and spend 30 minutes doing surgery on it:

1. **Write the user story on a whiteboard** and read it out loud.

2. **Ask the uncomfortable questions**: How many different things is this user story trying to accomplish? How many different types of customers are involved? How many platforms or systems does it touch?

3. **List all the different pieces** you can identify—don't worry about making them perfect yet.

4. **Pick the smallest piece that would still be valuable** to a real customer.

5. **Write that as a new user story** and check if it passes the INVEST criteria from Chapter 15.

6. **Repeat until you have 3-5 smaller user stories** that could each be built in a week or less.

If you end up with a bunch of smaller user stories that each make sense on their own, congratulations! You just prevented a multi-month death march.

Making User Story Splitting Part of Your Regular Process

To make user story splitting a natural part of how your team works:

Make it a backlog refinement habit. Every time you look at a user story and think "this feels big," spend 10 minutes trying to split it. It's way easier to split user stories during refinement than in the middle of a sprint.

Involve the whole team. Developers often have good insights about technical ways to split user stories. Designers can suggest splitting by user experience flows. Product people can split by business value. Get everyone's perspective.

Start with the most valuable slice. When you split a user story, ask which piece would deliver the most value to customers with the least work. Build that first, get feedback, then decide what to tackle next.

Don't split everything. Not every user story needs to be split. If your team can comfortably build and test a user story in a week or two, it's probably fine as is. Only split user stories that feel too big or risky.

Keep the customer focus. Every split should still be something a real person would find valuable. If your split is "build the database tables," you've gone too technical. Keep each piece focused on delivering something customers can actually experience.

What's Next

In Chapter 17, we'll talk about **Spikes**—those time-boxed research tasks you use when part of a user story is too uncertain to estimate. Sometimes the right answer isn't to split a user story, but to do some investigation first to reduce the uncertainty.

Writing Spikes

Tackling Uncertainty with Focused Research

What You'll Learn

- How spikes turn uncertainty into focused research that actually moves your team forward
- A simple process for writing spikes that answer the right questions in the right amount of time
- Practical ways to transform spike findings into user stories your team can actually build

When Everyone's Building Toward Different Unknowns

The restaurant app team was three weeks into their biggest feature yet: integrating a new payment system that promised faster checkouts and lower fees. Everyone was excited—until they hit the first real technical question.

"So the API documentation says it supports real-time updates," said Maya, the lead developer. "But what does that actually mean for our order tracking?"

"I assume it means customers see payment confirmation instantly," replied Jake from product.

"But what about our delivery status updates?" asked Sarah from design. "Do we need to build a separate system for that?"

"Wait," said Tom, the tech lead, "I just realized we don't even know if this API can handle our peak dinner rush. What if it crashes when we get 500 orders in ten minutes?"

The room went quiet. They'd been building toward this integration for weeks, but suddenly everyone realized they were making different assumptions about how it would actually work. Maya thought it was about payment speed. Jake thought it was about customer experience. Sarah thought it was about order tracking. Tom thought it was about system reliability.

Three weeks of development, and they didn't actually know if their solution would work.

When uncertainty is hiding in your backlog, it doesn't just slow you down—it makes everyone build toward different versions of success. Spikes help you tackle those unknowns head-on, so your team can move forward with confidence instead of crossed fingers.

We're building on all your Empathy Mapping and user story work. You've identified what customers need and written user stories about how to deliver it. Now you need a way to handle the inevitable unknowns that pop up when you start building real solutions.

Where This Fits

You've written user stories that capture what customers need (Chapter 15) and split them into manageable pieces (Chapter 16). But sometimes you hit a user story that makes everyone pause: "How exactly would we build this?" or "Will this approach actually work?"

This prepares you perfectly for Chapter 18 on sub-tasking, where you'll break down clear, de-risked user stories into specific development tasks.

Why Spikes Can Save Your Sprint

Some teams struggle with uncertainty. They either dive in and hope for the best (leading to mid-sprint surprises and missed commitments), or they endlessly debate without actually learning anything (leading to analysis paralysis and frustrated stakeholders).

Spikes give you a third option: focused research that turns unknowns into knowns.

Here's what happened when our restaurant app team finally wrote a proper spike for their payment integration: Instead of continuing to argue about assumptions, they wrote a two-day spike: "Test payment API with realistic order volume to confirm real-time capabilities and identify performance limits."

Maya spent half a day setting up a test environment. By the end of day one, she'd discovered the API had a 100-requests-per-minute rate limit—way below their dinner rush needs. Day two revealed a premium tier that could handle their volume, but it required a different authentication approach.

The spike findings were crystal clear:

- Standard API: Too slow for peak hours, would create 2-3 second delays
- Premium API: Handles peak volume, requires OAuth 2.0 setup instead of simple API key authentication
- Both options: Support real-time updates, but require webhook setup for order status

Instead of three more weeks of building toward different assumptions, they had concrete information to plan their next sprint.

That's the power of a good spike: it transforms "We think this might work" into "Here's exactly how to make it work."

What Is a Spike?

First introduced in Extreme Programming (Beck, 2004), a spike is time-boxed research that answers specific questions about how to build something, without actually building the production version.

Think of it like scouting ahead on a hiking trail. You don't know if the path ahead is passable, so you send someone to check it out and report back. They're not building the final trail—they're figuring out what you'll need to cross it successfully.

Spikes come in two flavors:

Technical Spikes. They answer "Can we build this (this way)?"

- Can this API handle our expected load?
- Will this database design support the queries we need?
- Which payment gateway gives us the features we need?

Functional Spikes. They answer "What exactly should we build?"

- How do customers actually want to customize their orders?
- What information do delivery drivers need to see?
- Which notification triggers matter most to restaurant owners?

Most spikes blend both types. You're usually figuring out what to build and how to build it at the same time.

The key insight: spikes don't deliver customer value directly. They clear the path so your user stories can deliver value successfully.

When Your Team Needs a Spike

You know you need a spike when:

A user story feels too risky to estimate. "As a customer, I want to pay with my preferred method so checkout is fast" sounds simple until you realize you don't know which payment methods to support or how to handle failed transactions.

Technical constraints are murky. "Will our current database handle 10x more orders?" You could guess, or you could spend a day load-testing and know for sure.

Multiple solutions need evaluation. "Should we build our own notification system or use a third-party service?" A spike can test both approaches with real data.

Customer needs require validation. "Do customers actually want voice ordering?" Before building speech recognition, spend a day interviewing customers and testing low-fi prototypes.

The restaurant team used spikes throughout their app development:

- Before building loyalty points: Interviewed 15 customers to understand what rewards actually motivated them
- Before implementing search: Tested three different filtering approaches to see which felt fastest
- Before integrating delivery tracking: Prototyped with different GPS update frequencies to balance accuracy and battery life

Each spike saved them weeks of building the wrong solution.

How to Write a Spike That Actually Works

Follow this simple approach to turn your uncertainties into focused research:

Step 1: Name the uncertainty. Get specific about what you don't know. Instead of "Payment integration might be tricky," write "We don't know if the payment API can handle 500 concurrent transactions during dinner rush."

Step 2: Define the learning goal. What decision will this research help you make? Use the VERB + NOUN format from Chapter 2:

- Test API performance limits
- Compare notification platforms
- Validate customer preferences

Step 3: Set a time-box. Spikes should take 1-2 days max. Any longer and you're probably trying to solve too many questions at once.

Step 4: Write clear acceptance criteria. What specific information do you need to move forward? Be concrete:

- Confirm API can handle 500 requests per minute with <2 second response time
- Identify which notification triggers customers find most valuable
- Document integration steps and potential gotchas

Step 5: Plan your follow-up. How will spike findings turn into user stories? This keeps your research connected to actual delivery.

Step 6: Choose your spike format. Here are the syntax formats that work (Fuqua, 2016):

- In order to <achieve a goal>, <a system or persona> needs to <action>
- In order to <make a decision>, <a system or persona> needs <information>

Examples:

- In order to handle dinner rush traffic, our payment system needs to process 500 concurrent transactions with sub-2-second response times
- In order to reduce customer support tickets, our notification system needs to send timely order status updates
- In order to choose the right payment processor, the development team needs performance benchmarking data under peak load conditions
- In order to decide on notification timing, the product team needs customer preference data on order update frequency

Notice how each spike connects directly to a business outcome and makes the research purpose crystal clear. Your spike should read like a hypothesis you can actually test, not a vague exploration.

Making Spikes Work in Your Team Workflow

Spikes aren't just a tool—they're a mindset shift toward tackling uncertainty systematically:

During backlog refinement. When you hit a user story that makes people go "Hmm, how would we actually do that?", write a spike instead of guessing or arguing.

Before sprint planning. Use spikes to de-risk user stories so your sprint commitments are based on knowledge, not hope.

When estimates are all over the map. If developers estimate the same user story anywhere from 2 points to 13 points, that's a signal you may need a spike to understand the work better.

During Example Mapping. When your Example Mapping session uncovers assumptions or unknowns (Chapter 13), capture them as potential spikes.

One team we worked with keeps a "spike backlog" alongside their product backlog. During refinement, they ask: "What would we need to know to estimate this confidently?" Those unknowns become spike candidates.

Try This Right Now

Look at your backlog and find a user story that feels uncertain or hard to estimate. Maybe it's an integration, a new feature area, or something that's been sitting in the backlog because nobody knows how to approach it.

Now write a spike for it:

1. **Identify the uncertainty:** What specific thing don't you know?

2. **Define the goal:** What research would help you move forward? (Use VERB + NOUN)

3. **Set a time-box:** How much time would it take to get the information you need?

4. **Write acceptance criteria:** What specific findings would help you write user stories?

5. **Plan the follow-up:** How will you turn those findings into buildable user stories?

Share it with your team and ask: "Would completing this spike give us enough information to estimate and build the original user story confidently?"

The magic happens when you realize how much time you've been spending arguing about unknowns instead of just researching them.

Making Spikes a Team Habit

To make spikes more than a one-off experiment:

Start small. Pick obvious uncertainty candidates—integrations, new technologies, unclear requirements. Build confidence with easy wins.

Keep them visible. Track spikes in the same system as user stories so they don't get forgotten or lose priority.

Document findings clearly. Create a simple template for spike outcomes: What we learned, what we decided, what user stories come next.

Review regularly. In retrospectives, ask: "What uncertainties slowed us down? Could spikes have helped?"

Pair with other techniques. Use spikes alongside Example Mapping to surface unknowns and with user story splitting to break down complex requirements.

The restaurant app team now starts every epic with a "spike planning" session. They ask: "What don't we know about this feature area? What assumptions are we making? What research would give us confidence to commit to user stories?"

It takes 30 minutes and saves them weeks of building in the wrong direction.

What's Next

Chapter 18 dives into **sub-tasking user stories**, where you'll take your now-clear, de-risked user stories and break them down into specific development tasks. You'll learn how to bridge the gap between "what we're building" and "exactly how we're building it" so your team can execute smoothly within sprints.

Sub-Tasking User Stories

Tactical Planning for Delivery

What You'll Learn

- How to break user stories into bite-sized sub-tasks that your team can actually tackle in a day or two
- Why sub-tasking is where the real collaboration magic happens (and where many teams miss the boat)
- A practical process for turning "As a customer, I want . . ." into "Here's exactly what I'm doing today"

The Day Everything Ground to a Halt

The restaurant app team was pumped about their upcoming sprint. They'd written beautiful user stories, estimated them carefully, and committed to what felt like a reasonable workload. The user story that had everyone excited was simple enough: "As a customer, I want to re-order my last meal quickly, so I don't have to browse the menu again."

Day one of the sprint: Sarah the developer opens her laptop, stares at the user story, and realizes she has no idea where to start. Does she need to change the database? Update the API? What about the mobile app interface? She spends two hours just figuring out what code she needs to look at.

Meanwhile, Mike the designer is working on the reorder button, but he doesn't know how the backend will work, so he's making assumptions about what data will be available. And Jessica the tester? She's waiting for something to test, but nobody knows what "done" actually looks like yet.

By day three, they're behind schedule and frustrated. The user story that seemed so clear in planning has become a messy tangle of assumptions, dependencies, and "I thought you were handling that" conversations.

Sound familiar? This is exactly why our Structured Conversations Manifesto emphasizes *Clear language sparks action.* A user story by itself isn't clear enough to spark action—it's just a destination. Sub-tasking is how you create the step-by-step directions to get there.

Tasks vs. Sub-Tasks: Getting Our Terms Straight

Before we dive in, let's clarify what we mean by "sub-tasking." If you're using tools like Jira, you might be familiar with a hierarchy that looks like this:

- Epic (big initiative)
- User Story (deliverable slice of value)
- Task (specific work item)

In this chapter, when we say "sub-tasking," we mean breaking a user story down into the specific, actionable work items that different team members will tackle. Whether your tool calls these "tasks," "sub-tasks," "work items," or "to-dos" doesn't matter—the principle is the same.

The key distinction: a user story describes value for the customer ("As a customer, I want to reorder . . ."), while sub-tasks describe work for the team ("Create reorder button component," "Update orders API").

Where This Fits

You've written solid user stories (Chapter 15), split them into deliverable slices (Chapter 16), and used spikes to tackle the unknowns (Chapter 17). Now you need to bridge the gap between "what we're building" and "what I'm doing today."

This connects directly to your Example Mapping work from Chapter 13—you're taking those acceptance criteria and turning them into concrete sub-tasks that different team members can work on simultaneously.

Why Sub-Tasking Actually Matters (Beyond Just Breaking Things Down)

Many teams think sub-tasking is just about making big things small. But the real value happens during the conversation where you break the user story down together.

Here's what actually happens when you sub-task well:

You catch the invisible work early. Every user story has hidden sub-tasks that only surface when you start building: testing, error handling, documentation updates, integration work. Sub-tasking conversations are where these surface before they derail your sprint.

You align everyone's mental model. Sarah the developer, Mike the designer, and Jessica the tester all have different pictures in their heads of how this user story will work. Sub-tasking is where those different movies become one shared vision.

You create natural collaboration points. Instead of everyone working in isolation and hoping it fits together, you identify exactly where handoffs happen and what each person needs from the others. This is why the most productive standups focus less on the classic three questions ("What did you do yesterday? What will you do today? Any blockers?") and more on "What do you need from me to move forward?" When you've sub-tasked well, everyone knows exactly who they're waiting for and what they need to deliver to others.

You make the work feel manageable. "Implement reorder functionality" feels overwhelming. "Update the orders API to include a reorder endpoint" feels like something you can knock out this afternoon.

You spot dependencies before they bite you. You realize that Mike's UI design depends on what data Sarah's API returns, which depends on how the database stores order history. Better to figure that out now than on Thursday when everything's supposed to integrate.

The key insight from teams that do this well: sub-tasking isn't just planning—it's the most important collaborative conversation you'll have about any user story. (Yes, we can hear you groaning through the internet. No, we will not be taking questions at this time).

What Makes a Good Sub-Task

Before we dive into the process, let's be clear about what we're creating. A good sub-task is:

Specific enough that someone can start immediately. "Update the UI" is not specific enough. "Add a 'Reorder Last Meal' button to the order history screen" is.

Small enough to finish in a day or two. If a sub-task takes more than 6 hours, it's probably hiding smaller sub-tasks inside it.

Owned by one person. Shared ownership usually means no ownership. Each sub-task should have a clear owner, even if multiple people contribute.

Testable. You should be able to tell when it's done. "Update API" is vague. "Add reorder endpoint that returns order confirmation" is testable.

Connected to the bigger picture. Each sub-task should clearly contribute to the user story's acceptance criteria.

The Sub-Tasking Process That Actually Works

Here's the step-by-step process our best teams use. Download our free template (Fig. 28) from structured-conversations.com to follow along:

Step 1: Get the right people in the room. You need the people who will actually do the work: developers, designers, testers—anyone who touches this user story. Don't do this as a solo planning exercise.

Step 2: Start with the acceptance criteria. Pull up your acceptance criteria from Example Mapping (Chapter 13). These are your definition of done. Every sub-task should connect to getting one of these criteria working.

Step 3: Walk through the customer's journey. Trace through what the customer will actually do, step by step: "First, they open their order history . . ." "Then they see their last order with a reorder button . . ." "When they tap it, the system checks if all items are still available . . ." "Then it adds everything to their cart and takes them to checkout . . ."

Step 4: Map the technical flow. For each customer step, identify what needs to happen behind the scenes: "To show order history, we need to query the orders database . . ." "The reorder button needs to call a new API endpoint . . ." "The availability check requires calling the restaurant's inventory system . . ."

Step 5: Identify all the layers. Make sure you're thinking about:

- **Frontend/UI**: What customers see and interact with
- **Backend/API**: Server-side logic and data processing
- **Database**: Data storage and retrieval changes
- **Integration**: Calls to external services
- **Testing**: Unit tests, integration tests, test automation, manual testing
- **DevOps**: Deployment, monitoring, configuration changes

Step 6: Write the sub-tasks using action language. Use the VERB + NOUN pattern from Chapter 2. Each sub-task should start with a clear action:

- Create reorder button component
- Implement reorder API endpoint
- Update order database schema
- Write integration tests for reorder flow

Step 7: Size and assign. Each sub-task should be 2-6 hours of work. If it's bigger, break it down further. Assign a clear owner for each sub-task.

Real Example: Breaking Down the Reorder User Story

Let's see this in action with our restaurant app story: As a customer, I want to reorder my last meal quickly, so I don't have to browse the menu again.

Acceptance Criteria (from Example Mapping):

- Order history shows "Reorder" button for past orders
- Reorder adds all items to cart with original customizations
- System checks item and ingredient availability and handles unavailable items gracefully
- User sees confirmation before checkout, including order date and restaurant name
- Reorder is blocked if the restaurant is closed or inactive
- Reorder events are logged for analytics and usage tracking

Sub-Tasks:

Frontend:

- Add "Reorder" button to order history item component (Mike, 3 hours)
- Create unavailable items dialog for when some items can't be reordered (Mike, 4 hours)
- Update cart screen to show reordered items with source order reference (Sarah, 3 hours)

- Display error messages gracefully for partially unavailable items (Mike, 2 hours)
- Show order date and restaurant name in reorder confirmation screen (Mike, 2 hours)
- Coordinate with backend to align on API contract and data model changes (Mike & Sarah, 1 hour)

Backend:

- Build the system that checks if items and ingredients are still available when customers reorder (Sarah, 5 hours)
- Add check for restaurant availability before reorder is allowed (Sarah, 2 hours)
- Update cart service to handle bulk item additions with customizations (Sarah, 4 hours)
- Add error handling for partially unavailable orders (Sarah, 3 hours)
- Update reorder API to include source order reference and customization metadata (Sarah, 2 hours)
- Emit reorder events for analytics tracking (Sarah, 2 hours)

Testing:

- Write unit tests for reorder API endpoint (Jessica, 3 hours)
- Create automated UI tests for reorder flow (Jessica, 4 hours)
- Test reorder flow with unavailable items (Jessica, 2 hours)
- Verify reorder preserves all original customizations (Jessica, 2 hours)
- Perform regression testing on cart and checkout flows (Jessica, 2 hours)

Integration:

- Update mobile app to call new reorder endpoint (Mike, 2 hours)
- Mid-sprint integration checkpoint to validate frontend/backend alignment (Team sync, 1 hour)
- Test end-to-end reorder flow on staging environment (Jessica, 3 hours)

Design & Review:

- UX review of reorder button placement, unavailable item dialog, and confirmation screen clarity (Team sync, 1 hour)

Notice how each sub-task is specific, actionable, and clearly owned. The total adds up to about 55 hours of work, which feels right for a large-sized user story that three people can tackle in a sprint.

(Note: This is a simplified example for illustration. Real-world estimates may vary based on team size, tech stack, legacy constraints, and unexpected edge cases.)

The Magic Happens in the Conversation

The real value isn't in the final list of sub-tasks—it's in the conversation that creates them. This is where Sarah realizes she needs to handle partial availability ("What if the restaurant ran out of one ingredient?"). Where Mike discovers he needs to show which order the items came from ("Customers might reorder the wrong meal if they don't see the date"). Where Jessica identifies edge cases nobody thought of ("What if they try to reorder from a restaurant that's now closed?").

These insights only surface when you walk through the work together, step by step.

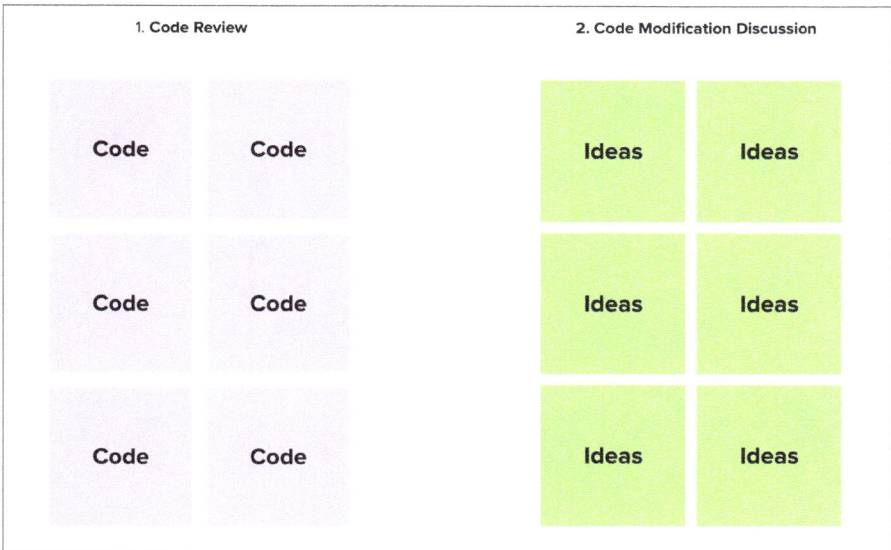

Fig. 28: Sub-Tasking Template

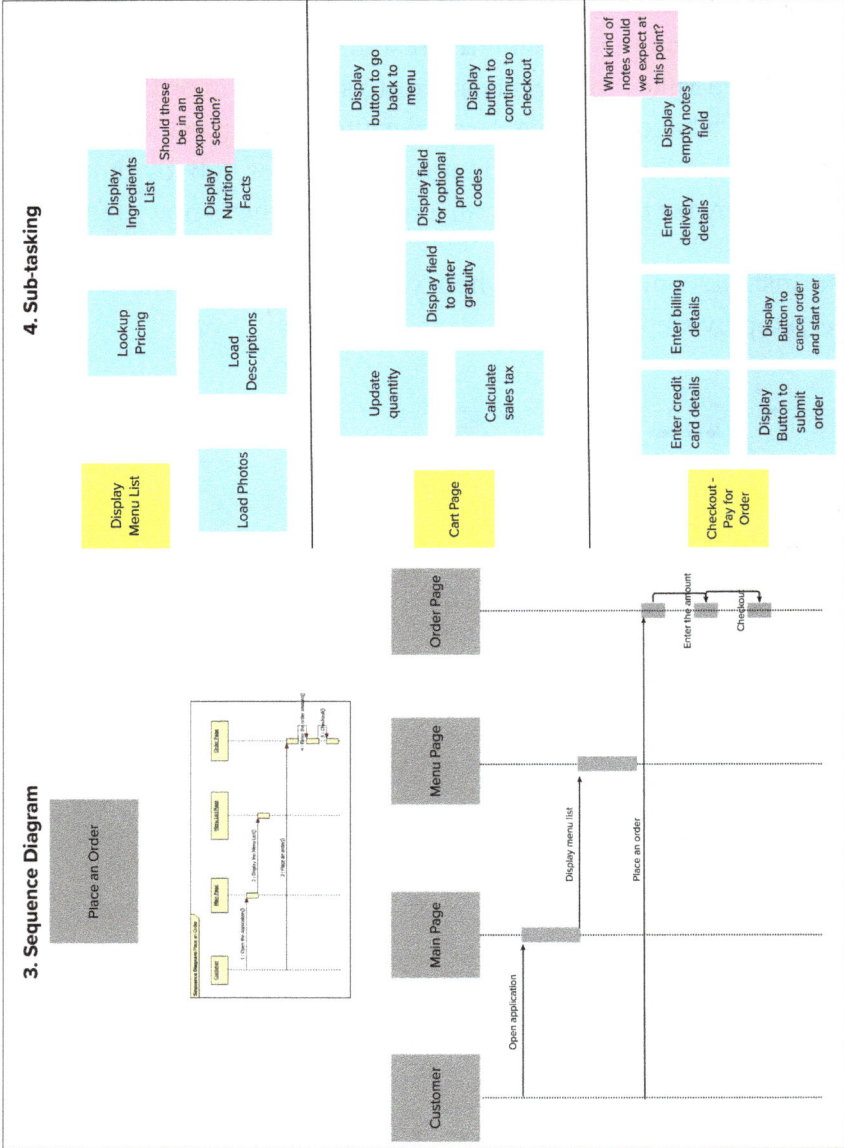

Fig. 28: Sub-Tasking Template

Try This Right Now

Pick a user story your team is planning to work on soon. Gather the key players (developer, designer, tester) and spend 30 minutes sub-tasking it together:

1. Write the user story and its acceptance criteria on a whiteboard

2. Walk through the customer journey step by step

3. For each step, ask: "What needs to happen behind the scenes?"

4. Write sub-tasks using VERB + NOUN format

5. Size each sub-task (2-6 hours) and assign an owner

6. Review: Do these sub-tasks add up to completing all the acceptance criteria?

Pay attention to what questions come up during the conversation. Those questions are pure gold—they're the assumptions and unknowns that would have caused problems later.

Common Sub-Tasking Pitfalls (and How to Avoid Them)

Pitfall 1: Sub-tasking in isolation. Some teams have one person (usually a tech lead) break down user stories alone. This misses the whole point. The conversation is where alignment happens.

Pitfall 2: Tasks that are too big. "Implement reorder functionality" isn't a sub-task—it's just restating the user story. If a sub-task can't be finished in a day or two, keep breaking it down.

Pitfall 3: Forgetting the testing layer. Many teams sub-task the building but forget the testing. Every user story needs explicit testing sub-tasks, not just "we'll test it when it's done."

Pitfall 4: No clear ownership. Tasks like "Frontend and backend integration" with no clear owner often fall through the cracks. Each sub-task needs one person who feels responsible for getting it done.

Pitfall 5: Losing sight of the user story. It's easy to get caught up in technical details and create sub-tasks that don't actually serve the user story. Keep asking: "How does this sub-task help us meet the acceptance criteria?"

Making Sub-Tasking a Team Habit

To make this a natural part of your workflow:

Address the "micromanagement" concern. Some developers initially resist sub-tasking, worried it feels like micromanagement or exposes their uncertainty about approaching a problem. This re-action is understandable—nobody wants to feel like they're being watched or that admitting "I'm not sure how to tackle this yet" is a sign of weakness.

Here's how to reframe it: sub-tasking isn't about monitoring what people do hour by hour. It's about making the invisible work visible so the team can help each other succeed. When Sarah says "I need to update the API but I'm not sure about the data structure yet," that's not weakness—that's exactly the kind of uncertainty that de-rails sprints when it stays hidden.

The best teams treat sub-tasking as collaborative problem-solving, not task assignment. Instead of "Here's your list of things to do," it becomes "Let's figure out together what needs to happen, and who's best positioned to handle each piece."

Sub-task during sprint planning, not before. You want the people doing the work to be part of breaking it down.

Use your Example Mapping sessions as input. The rules and examples you identified become the foundation for your sub-tasks.

Keep sub-tasks visible during the sprint. Whether it's on a physical board or in your digital tool, everyone should see what needs to happen.

Update the board daily. As sub-tasks get completed, move them forward. When new sub-tasks emerge (they will), add them and discuss with the team.

Reflect in retrospectives. What sub-tasks took longer than expected? What did we miss? How can we get better at estimating and breaking down work?

One team we worked with has a simple rule: if you can't finish a sub-task in one day, you have to break it down further and ask for help. This keeps work flowing and prevents anyone from getting stuck in isolation.

What's Next

In Chapter 19, we'll tackle what happens when things don't go as planned—how to **document and communicate defects** in a way that helps your team learn and improve, rather than just track what's broken. You've got the planning pieces in place. Now let's talk about handling the inevitable bumps in the road.

Documenting Defects

Ensuring Clarity for Swift Resolution

What You'll Learn

- How to write defect reports that actually help your team fix problems fast (instead of creating more confusion)
- Why the way you document defects determines whether they get fixed in hours or drag on for days
- A simple process that turns "something's broken" into actionable information that developers can use

The Monday Morning Fire Drill

It's 9 AM on Monday, and the restaurant app team's Slack is blowing up. Customers can't complete their orders—the checkout page isn't showing delivery fees, so people don't know what they're actually paying. The CEO is asking for updates every 20 minutes.

Sarah the developer jumps on the issue, but the defect report in their system just says: "Checkout broken—delivery fee missing. URGENT!!!"

She starts digging. What device? What version of the app? Which restaurants? What exactly did the customer do before this happened? She spends two hours just trying to reproduce the problem, then another hour figuring out it only happens on iOS devices when customers enter addresses with apartment numbers.

By the time she fixes it, customers have been frustrated for half a day, and the team has burned a whole morning on detective work that could have been avoided with a better defect report.

Meanwhile, Mike the QA tester is feeling defensive because everyone's asking why this wasn't caught before release. And the product manager is trying to figure out how many customers were affected so she can assess the damage.

This is exactly why our Structured Conversations Manifesto says "*Clear language sparks action.*" When something breaks in production, you don't have time for guesswork. You need information that lets your team act immediately.

Where This Fits

You've built your features using user stories (Chapter 15), broken them into sub-tasks (Chapter 18), and shipped them to customers. Now you're in the real world, where things sometimes don't work as expected.

This chapter builds directly on your Example Mapping work (Chapter 13)—those acceptance criteria you defined become your baseline for what "working correctly" looks like. And it sets you up perfectly for Chapter 20 on Gherkin scenarios, where you'll formalize testing to catch issues before they reach customers.

Why Many Defect Reports Are Terrible (And Why It Matters)

Let's be honest—many defect reports fall short. They're often written in the heat of frustration and read by developers who lack the full context of what happened.

Here's what usually goes wrong:

Vague titles that tell you nothing. "App is broken" or "Payment doesn't work"—these could mean literally anything.

Missing context. What device? What browser? What version? What were you trying to do? Without this, developers are shooting in the dark.

Unreproducible steps. "I clicked some buttons and then it broke" doesn't help anyone fix anything.

Emotional language instead of facts. "This stupid feature never works" might express frustration, but it doesn't help identify the root cause.

No clear impact assessment. Is this blocking all customers or just affecting edge cases? The response urgency depends on the answer.

The result? Your developers spend more time figuring out what's broken than fixing it. Your customers stay frustrated longer. And your team starts dreading defect reports because they're more puzzle than problem statement.

But when you get defect documentation right, everything changes. Problems get fixed in hours instead of days. Your team can prioritize based on actual impact. And you start catching patterns that help prevent future issues.

What Makes a Defect Report Actually Useful

Before we dive into the process, let's be clear about what we're aiming for. A good defect report is like a GPS route to the problem—it tells the developer exactly where to go and what they'll find when they get there.

Here's what that looks like:

Specific enough to reproduce immediately. A developer should be able to follow your steps and see the exact same problem within minutes.

Complete enough to understand impact. How many people are affected? What can't they do? How urgent is this really?

Factual, not emotional. Stick to what happened, not how you feel about it. "Checkout button doesn't respond" is better than "This checkout is completely broken."

Connected to customer value. What user story or feature is failing? This helps prioritize and provides context for the fix.

Actionable from day one. Don't make developers hunt for missing information. Give them everything they need to start working.

The key insight: a defect report isn't just documentation—it's the starting point for a conversation between the person who found the problem and the person who needs to fix it.

The Defect Documentation Process That Actually Works

Here's the step-by-step approach that helps our best teams turn chaos into clarity. You can grab our template at structured-conversations. com to follow along:

Step 1: Write a title that actually means something. Use the VERB + NOUN pattern from Chapter 2, but focus on what's failing, not what you wanted to happen.

- **Bad**: Delivery fee issue
- **Good**: Missing delivery fee from checkout summary

The title should be specific enough that someone can understand the problem without reading the description.

Step 2: Describe the impact in plain English. Start with 2-3 sentences that explain what's broken and why it matters: "Customers can't see delivery fees during checkout, so they don't know their total cost until after they've entered payment info. This is causing cart abandonment and customer service complaints."

Step 3: Capture the environment details. This is the boring but crucial stuff:

- Device type and OS version (iPhone 14 Pro Max, iOS 26.0.1)
- Browser (if it's a web app)
- App version (v2.3.1)
- Environment (production, staging, etc.)

Step 4: Write steps to reproduce (the most important part).

This is where many defect reports fail. Write numbered steps that anyone can follow:

1. Open the restaurant app on iOS

2. Add any menu item to cart

3. Tap "Checkout"

4. Enter delivery address with apartment number (e.g., "123 Main St, Apt 4B")

5. Observe that delivery fee is missing from order summary

The golden rule: if a developer can't reproduce the issue using your steps, your steps aren't good enough.

Step 5: Define what should happen instead. Be specific about expected behavior: The checkout summary should display the delivery fee below the subtotal, showing both the fee amount and total including tax.

Step 6: Assess severity and priority. Use your team's agreed-upon scale, but here's a simple framework:

- **Critical:** System down, no workaround, blocks core customer flows
- **High:** Major feature broken, workaround exists, affects many customers
- **Medium:** Minor feature broken, affects some customers
- **Low:** Cosmetic issues, edge cases, nice-to-have improvements

Step 7: Add helpful context. Include anything that might speed up the fix:

- When did this start happening?
- Does it happen for all customers or specific conditions?
- Are there any workarounds?
- Related user stories or recent changes?

Real Example: A Defect Report that Actually Helps

Let's see this in action with our restaurant app checkout issue:

Title: Missing delivery fee from checkout summary on iOS with apartment addresses

Impact: Customers entering apartment numbers in their delivery address don't see delivery fees during checkout, causing confusion about final cost and increased cart abandonment.

Environment:

- Device: iPhone 14 Pro Max, iOS 26.0.1
- App: Restaurant App v2.3.1
- Environment: Production

Steps to Reproduce:

1. Open Restaurant App on iOS device
2. Browse menu and add any item to cart
3. Tap "Checkout"
4. Enter delivery address including apartment number (e.g., "456 Oak St, Apt 2C, New York, NY 10001")

5. Proceed to order summary

6. Observe delivery fee is missing from cost breakdown

Expected Result: Delivery fee should appear in order summary below subtotal, showing fee amount and updated total.

Actual Result: Order summary shows only subtotal and tax, no delivery fee listed.

Severity: High—affects checkout flow, impacts revenue. Priority: Urgent—customer-facing, blocking conversions.

Additional Notes:

- Issue doesn't occur with addresses without apartment numbers
- Started happening after v2.3.1 release on Friday
- Workaround: Customers can see total fee after entering payment info, but many abandon before then
- Related to user story: "As a customer, I want to see all costs upfront so I can make informed ordering decisions"

Notice how this report gives a developer everything they need to start working immediately? They know exactly how to reproduce it, understand the business impact, and have context about when it started.

The Magic Is in the Details (But Not Too Many Details)

The best defect reports walk a fine line—enough detail to be actionable, but not so much that the important stuff gets buried.

Here's what to include:

- Exact steps that reproduce the problem every time
- Specific environment details that might matter
- Clear expected vs. actual behavior
- Business impact and urgency level
- Context that might speed up the fix

Here's what to skip:

- Long emotional rants about how broken everything is
- Technical speculation about what might be causing it (unless you're sure)
- Screenshots of things that are better described in words
- Duplicate information that's already captured elsewhere

One team we worked with has a simple rule: if someone who wasn't involved can't reproduce the issue using your defect report, it's not ready to submit.

Try This Right Now

Think about the last defect your team encountered. If you don't have one handy, create a hypothetical issue like "customers can't save their delivery preferences."

Spend 20 minutes writing a defect report using the format below:

1. Write a specific title using VERB + NOUN
2. Describe the impact in 2-3 sentences
3. Capture the environment details
4. List the exact steps to reproduce

5. Define what should happen instead

6. Assess severity and priority

Then ask someone else on your team: "If you got this defect report, would you know exactly what to do next?"

Pay attention to what questions they ask—those gaps are where your report needs more detail.

Common Defect Documentation Mistakes (And How to Fix Them)

Mistake 1: Writing for yourself instead of for the fixer. You know what you were trying to do, but the developer doesn't. Write for someone with no context.

Mistake 2: Combining multiple issues into one report. "The app crashes and also the buttons are the wrong color" should be two separate reports. Mixed issues are hard to prioritize and fix.

Mistake 3: Reporting every variation as a separate bug. If the delivery fee is missing on both iPhone and Android, that's probably one underlying issue, not two separate defects.

Mistake 4: No clear reproduction steps. "It happens sometimes when I do stuff" isn't reproducible. Find the exact sequence that triggers the problem.

Mistake 5: Missing the user story connection. Always link back to what customer value is being impacted. This helps with prioritization and provides context for the fix.

Making Defect Documentation a Team Habit

To make this a natural part of your workflow:

Agree on your template during team setup. Everyone should use the same format so people know what to expect.

Include it in your definition of done. Before marking a user story complete, think about how you'd document issues if they arise.

Practice during retrospectives. Look at recent defect reports and ask: "What would have made this faster to resolve?"

Connect to your user stories. Every defect should trace back to a user story that's not working as expected. This provides context and helps with prioritization.

Make it safe to report issues. The person who finds the defect shouldn't feel blamed for it. Focus on fixing, not finger-pointing.

One team we worked with reviews their defect reports in weekly team meetings, not to assign blame, but to ask: "What can we learn from this? How can we catch similar issues earlier?"

Building Quality Feedback Loops

The best teams don't just fix defects—they use defect reports as learning opportunities:

Pattern recognition. Are you seeing the same types of issues repeatedly? Maybe there's a deeper problem with how you're building or testing.

Process improvement. Are defects coming from areas you thought you had covered in testing? Time to adjust your testing approach.

Empathy. What do defect reports tell you about how customers actually use your product versus how you think they use it?

Team communication. Are some types of issues consistently under-documented? Maybe certain team members need more support with defect reporting.

Remember: every defect report is data about how your product works in the real world. Use that data to build better products and better processes.

What's Next

In Chapter 20, we'll flip the script from reactive defect fixing to proactive quality building. You'll learn about **Gherkin Scenarios**—a way to formalize your acceptance criteria so that expected behavior is testable from day one. Instead of documenting what went wrong after the fact, you'll be defining what "right" looks like before you build, making it much less likely that things will go wrong in the first place.

CHAPTER 20

Writing Gherkin Scenarios

Defining Behavior for Clarity and Automation

What You'll Learn

- How to turn vague acceptance criteria into crystal-clear, testable scenarios that everyone can understand
- Why writing scenarios before writing code prevents most of the arguments your team has about what features should do
- A simple format that bridges the gap between business requirements and automated testing

The Great Discount Disaster of Sprint 23

The restaurant app team was excited about their new customer discount feature. It seemed straightforward enough: give first-time customers 10% off their order to encourage them to try the service.

Sarah, the developer, built it based on the user story: As a first-time customer, I want a discount on my order so that I'm incentivized to try the service. She implemented logic to detect new accounts and apply a 10% reduction to the total—specifically, she checked whether the customer had any orders with a "completed" status in the database.

Mike, the designer, created a cheerful badge that appeared in the cart: "New Customer Discount Applied!" His design documentation noted that the badge should appear "for first-time users within their first 30 days," based on his assumption that the goal was to create urgency.

Jessica, the tester, wrote test cases covering the basic flow: a new customer creates an account, adds items, the discount appears, the order total is reduced. Since the user story didn't mention edge cases, she focused on the happy path, ignoring scenarios like failed payments, or older accounts.

David, the product manager, reviewed the implementation and assumed the 10% applied only to the food subtotal—not taxes or delivery fees—since that's how a key competitor handled it.

Marketing, meanwhile, launched an email campaign that said: "Use your first-time discount code on your next order." Customer service therefore expected customers to enter a promo code manually.

They shipped it on Friday feeling good about the work.

By Monday morning, customer service was flooded with complaints. Some customers got their discounts; others didn't. Those who had created accounts weeks earlier to browse menus weren't eligible anymore because the 30-day window had expired. The finance team was panicking because the discount was applying to the entire order total, not just the food subtotal. And customer service was overwhelmed with calls from confused customers asking "Where do I enter my first-time discount code?"

What went wrong?

Everyone had a different interpretation of what "first-time customer" meant:

- Sarah thought it meant anyone who had never placed a completed order
- Mike assumed it referred to anyone within their first 30 days of account creation
- Jessica tested only brand-new accounts placing immediate successful orders
- David believed the discount applied only to the food subtotal, not the full order total
- Customer service expected a promo code flow, not automatic application

No one set out to be wrong. Each assumption was reasonable in isolation—but together, they created a feature built on conflicting interpretations. Reasonable isn't enough when you're building software. You need to be precise.

This is exactly why our Structured Conversations Manifesto emphasizes *"Intentional syntax surpasses accidental semantics."* Gherkin scenarios give you that intentional syntax for defining exactly what your features should do, in language that everyone—developers, testers, product managers, even customer service—can understand and agree on.

Where This Fits

You've written user stories (Chapter 15), broken them down into sub-tasks (Chapter 18), and you know how to document problems when they arise (Chapter 19). Now you need a way to prevent those problems by being crystal clear about what "working correctly" means before anyone writes code.

This builds directly on your Example Mapping work from Chapter 13. Remember those rules and examples you identified? Gherkin scenarios are how you turn those into precise, testable specifications.

Why Most Teams Skip This (And Why They Shouldn't)

Let's be honest—writing Gherkin scenarios feels like extra work. You've got user stories. You've got acceptance criteria. You've got smart people who can figure out what makes sense. Why do you need another layer of documentation?

Here's why teams that skip this step end up regretting it:

Everyone's mental model is different. Even with good user stories, people fill in gaps with their own assumptions. The discount user story seemed clear to everyone—until they had five different interpretations of "first-time customer."

Edge cases hide in plain sight. When you force yourself to write specific examples, you discover scenarios nobody thought about.

Testing becomes guesswork. Without clear specifications, testers either miss important scenarios or waste time testing things that don't actually matter to the business.

Defects become arguments. When something doesn't work as expected, you end up debating what "expected" means instead of just fixing the problem.

Automation is impossible. You can't automate tests for behavior that isn't clearly defined. And manual testing of unclear requirements is just expensive guessing.

But when you get Gherkin scenarios right, everything changes. Developers know exactly what to build. Testers know exactly what to verify. Product managers can spot gaps in the requirements before they become defects. And when you do find issues, you can trace them back to specific scenarios instead of arguing about intentions.

What Makes Gherkin Special

Gherkin isn't just another documentation format—it's designed to bridge the gap between human conversation and automated testing.

Here's what makes it work:

It's structured but readable. The Given-When-Then format forces you to be specific, but it reads like natural language that anyone can understand.

It focuses on behavior, not implementation. You describe what the system should do, not how it should do it. This keeps scenarios stable even when the underlying code changes.

It's testable by design. Every scenario describes a specific situation you can set up, an action you can take, and an outcome you can verify.

It bridges roles—but only if written together. Business people might draft the initial scenarios. Developers can implement them. Testers can automate them. But if each role writes in isolation, assumptions creep in. Gherkin works best when scenarios are co-created—collaboratively refined in structured conversations that surface edge cases, clarify intent, and align expectations.

It becomes Living Documentation (Chapter 21). When scenarios are automated, they prove that the system actually works the way the documentation says it does.

The key insight: Gherkin scenarios aren't just about testing—they're about achieving shared understanding before you start building.

Understanding the Given-When-Then Structure

Before we dive into writing scenarios, let's break down the three parts:

Given sets up the context—the state the world needs to be in before the behavior can happen. This includes data setup, user state, system configuration—anything that needs to be true as a precondition.

When describes the action or event that triggers the behavior you're testing. This should be a single, specific action from the customer's perspective.

Then states the expected outcome—what should be different in the world after the When action happens. This needs to be something observable and verifiable.

You can add **And** or **But** to the Given or Then sections when you need multiple conditions or outcomes, but keep it focused—if you need too many And/But statements, you might be trying to test too much in one scenario.

Writing Gherkin Scenarios That Actually Help

Here's the step-by-step process our most successful teams use:

Step 1: Start with a user story and its examples. Pull up a user story from your backlog and the examples you created during Example Mapping (Chapter 13). These examples become the foundation for your scenarios.

For our discount story: As a first-time customer, I want a discount on my order so that I'm incentivized to try the service.

Examples from Example Mapping:

- New customer creates account and places first order → gets 10% off
- Customer with failed first payment tries again → still gets discount
- Customer who got discount tries to order again → no discount on second order

Step 2: Write one scenario for each example. Each distinct example becomes its own scenario. Don't try to cover everything in one mega-scenario.

Step 3: Use descriptive scenario titles. Give each scenario a title that clearly describes the behavior being tested. Use the VERB + NOUN pattern from Chapter 2 when possible.

- **Good**: Apply first-time customer discount to food total
- **Bad**: Test discount feature

Step 4: Structure with Given-When-Then. For each scenario:

- **Given** describes the starting state
- **When** describes what the customer does
- **Then** describes what should happen

Step 5: Keep it at the right level of detail. This is where many teams struggle. Too vague, and the scenario doesn't provide clarity. Too specific, and it becomes brittle and hard to maintain.

Focus on *what* happens, not *how* it happens:

- **Good**: When the customer adds items to their cart
- **Bad**: When the customer clicks the 'Add to Cart' button on the menu page
- **Good**: Then a 10% discount is applied to the food total
- **Bad**: Then the discount amount is calculated and displayed in the cart summary section

Step 6: Make each scenario independent. Every scenario should be able to run on its own, in any order. Don't create dependencies between scenarios—it makes testing fragile and debugging harder.

Real Examples: Restaurant App Discount Scenarios

Let's see how this works with our discount feature:

Scenario: Apply first-time customer discount
    Given a first-time customer has created an account
    But never completed an order
    And they have added food items totaling $25 to their cart
    When they view their cart
    Then a 10% discount is applied to the food subtotal
    And the discount amount is $2.50

And the total shows the discounted price

Scenario: No discount for returning customers
    Given a returning customer has previously completed an order
    And they have added food items to their cart
    When they view their cart
    Then no discount is applied
    And they see the regular total

Scenario: Discount applies after failed payment
    Given a first-time customer's order attempt failed due to payment issues
    And they have added food items totaling $30 to their cart
    When they view their cart
    Then a 10% discount is still applied
    And the discount amount is $3.00

Scenario: Discount excludes taxes and fees
    Given a first-time customer has added food items totaling $20 to their cart
    And delivery fee is $2.99
    And tax is $1.80
    When they view their cart
    Then the 10% discount applies only to the $20 food subtotal
    And the discount amount is $2.00
    And the final total includes undiscounted delivery fee and tax

Notice how each scenario is specific, testable, and focuses on one particular aspect of the discount behavior. A developer reading these scenarios knows exactly what to implement. A tester knows exactly what to verify. And a product manager can spot if any important cases are missing.

Common Gherkin Mistakes (And How to Avoid Them)

Mistake 1: Writing scenarios that are too implementation-specific.

- **Bad**: When the customer clicks the submit button and the system calls the payment API
- **Good**: When the customer completes their order

Keep scenarios focused on customer behavior, not system internals.

Mistake 2: Trying to test everything in one scenario.

- **Bad**: A single scenario that tests login, adding items, applying discounts, and completing checkout
- **Good**: Separate scenarios for each behavior

Each scenario should have one clear purpose.

Mistake 3: Vague or unmeasurable Then statements.

- **Bad**: Then the customer is happy
- **Good**: Then the confirmation page displays the order number

Every Then should describe something specific and verifiable.

Mistake 4: Creating dependencies between scenarios.

- **Bad**: Given the customer completed the scenario from the previous test
- **Good**: Given the customer has a completed order in their history

Each scenario should set up its own preconditions.

Mistake 5: Writing novels.

If your scenario needs more than seven lines, you're probably trying to test too much. Break it into smaller, focused scenarios.

Try This Right Now

Pick a user story your team is working on (or about to work on). Something with clear business rules that could have multiple interpretations.

Spend 20 minutes writing Gherkin scenarios:

1. List 3-4 specific examples of the behavior from your Example Mapping work

2. Turn each example into a scenario with a descriptive name

3. Write Given-When-Then for each, keeping it focused on customer behavior

4. Read each scenario out loud—does it make sense to someone who wasn't involved in writing it?

Share the scenarios with your team and ask:

- Do these scenarios capture what we agreed the feature should do?
- Are there any important cases we're missing?
- Could a developer implement this feature based solely on these scenarios?
- Could a tester verify the feature works based on these scenarios?

The conversations that come up during this exercise are pure gold—they reveal the misaligned assumptions and overlooked edge cases that would have turned into defects later.

Making Gherkin Scenarios a Team Habit

To make Gherkin scenario writing a natural part of your workflow:

Start in backlog refinement sessions. Don't wait until sprint planning. Write scenarios when you're discussing and estimating user stories.

Make it collaborative. The product manager shouldn't write scenarios alone, then hand them off. Get developers and testers involved in the conversation.

Connect to your Example Mapping. Those rules and examples you identified in Chapter 13? They become your Gherkin scenarios.

Keep scenarios with the user stories. Don't hide them in a separate document. Make them part of your user story definition.

Automate the scenarios that matter. Not every scenario needs automation, but the core business rules should always be covered by automated tests.

Review and refine. As you learn more about customer behavior and edge cases, update your scenarios. Keep them current and valuable.

One team we worked with has a simple rule: no user story goes into a sprint without at least one Gherkin scenario that everyone agrees captures the core behavior. This simple practice has cut their defect count by more than half.

When Gherkin Gets You More Than Just Testing

Here's something interesting that happens when teams start writing good Gherkin scenarios: they realize they're not just defining tests—they're creating a shared vocabulary for talking about their product.

Those scenarios become:

- **Examples for customer support** when customers have questions about how features work
- **Specification for new team members** who need to understand what the system does
- **Documentation that stays current** because it's tied to automated tests
- **Input for user training materials** and help documentation
- **Reference for business stakeholders** who want to understand what was actually built

The best teams find that their Gherkin scenarios become the most reliable documentation they have, because unlike other documentation, these scenarios are automatically verified to be accurate every time the tests run.

What's Next

In Chapter 21, we'll explore how to turn your Gherkin scenarios into **Living Documentation**—a system where your specifications, your tests, and your actual product behavior stay perfectly synchronized. You'll learn how to create documentation that never gets out of date because it's automatically generated from your working software. No more wondering if the documentation matches reality. No more outdated specifications that confuse new team members. Just reliable, current information about how your product actually works.

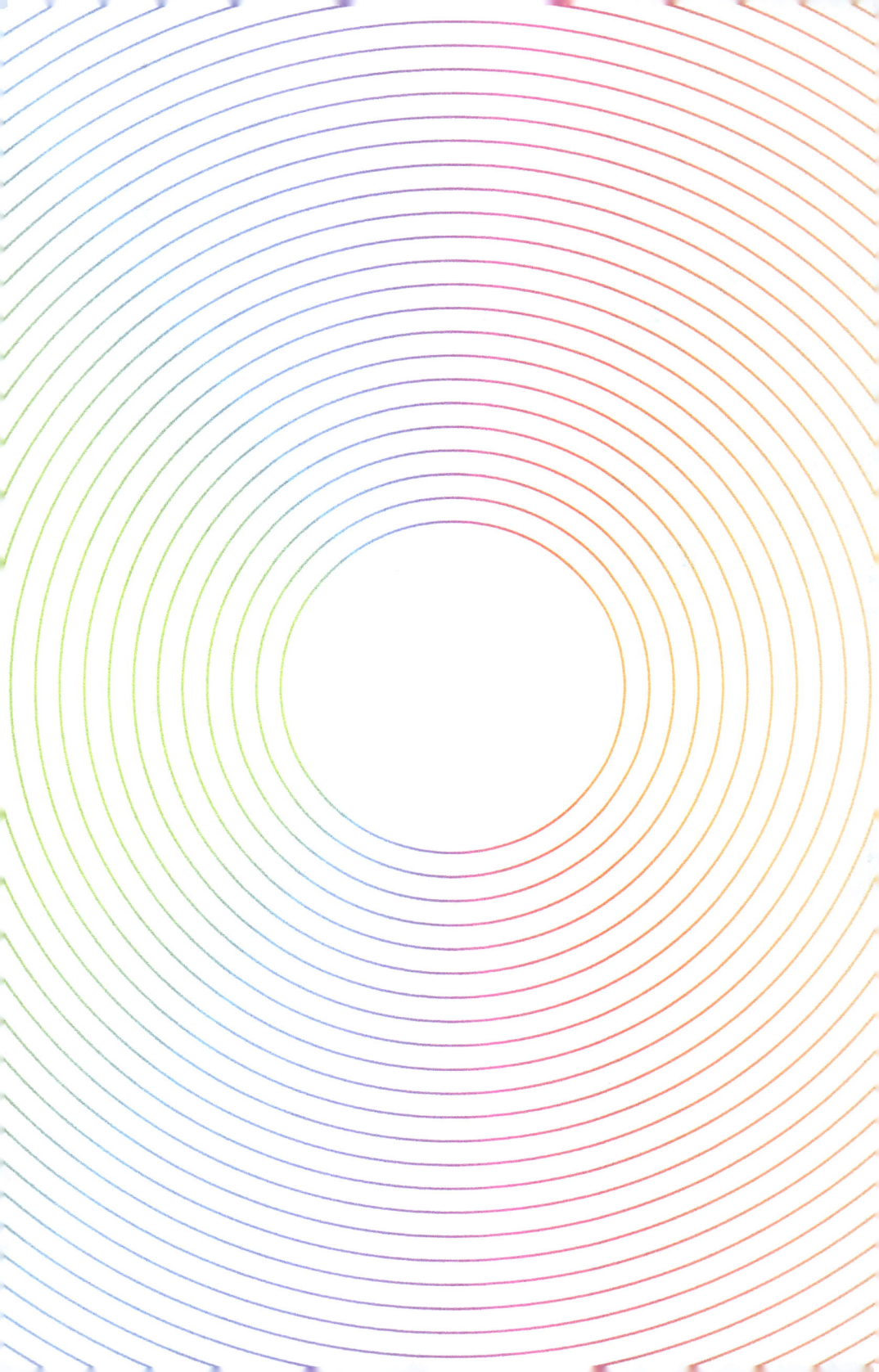

PART 4

STRATEGIC OUTCOMES

CHAPTER 21

Living Documentation

When Your Documentation Actually Tells the Truth

What You'll Learn

- How to create documentation that automatically stays current with your product (instead of becoming a beautiful lie)
- Why most documentation fails teams when they need it most, and what to do about it
- A practical approach to building documentation that actually helps people understand and maintain your product

The Day the Documentation Lied

It was 6 AM on a Tuesday when Sarah got the alert: critical payment processing error in production. A critical payment processing defect had surfaced, and Sarah the developer was frantically trying to understand how the discount system was supposed to work so she could fix it without breaking anything else.

She pulled up the team's documentation—a lovingly crafted Confluence space with detailed flowcharts, comprehensive API specifications, and step-by-step customer journeys. It looked professional and thorough.

But as Sarah dug deeper into the code, she realized the documentation was describing a system that no longer existed. The discount logic had been refactored six months ago. The API endpoints had changed. The customer flow had been simplified. None of it matched what the documentation claimed the system did.

By the time she figured out how the system actually worked, it was 9 AM, and customers had been unable to place orders for hours, and she'd introduced two new defects while fixing the original one.

The worst part? The documentation wasn't malicious or lazy—it was just outdated. Someone had spent days creating those beautiful flowcharts and detailed specifications. But as the product evolved, the documentation fell behind. And when the team needed it the most, it didn't just fall short—it pointed the team in the wrong direction.

This is exactly why our Structured Conversations Manifesto emphasizes *"Clear language sparks action."* Documentation that doesn't reflect reality can't spark the right action. It sends people down the wrong path when they're already under pressure.

Living Documentation solves this by making your documentation prove itself. Instead of hoping someone remembers to update the documentation when the code changes, you create documentation that automatically breaks when it's wrong.

Where This Fits

You've written Gherkin scenarios (Chapter 20) that define exactly what your features should do. Now you're going to turn those scenarios into documentation that stays current because it's constantly being verified against your actual product.

This builds on all the mapping and specification work you've done— your user stories (Chapter 15), Example Mapping (Chapter 13), even your Product Elevator Pitch (Chapter 10). But instead of letting that knowledge decay in static documents, you're going to make it live and breathe with your product.

Why Most Documentation Dies (And Takes Teams With It)

Let's be brutally honest about documentation in many software teams: it's terrible. Not because people don't care, but because traditional documentation goes stale the moment you write it.

Here's what usually happens:

Phase 1: The golden age. Someone (usually a well-intentioned product manager or tech lead) creates comprehensive documentation. It's beautiful. It's detailed. It perfectly describes the system as it exists today.

Phase 2: The subtle drift. Development continues. Small changes get made. Defect fixes alter behavior slightly. New features are added. Each change is tiny, and updating the documentation feels like it can wait until later.

Phase 3: The growing gap. Months pass. The gap between documentation and reality grows. New team members join and get confused by discrepancies. Existing team members stop trusting the documentation and rely on tribal knowledge instead.

Phase 4: The death spiral. Someone finally tries to update the documentation, but it's so far out of date that fixing it would require rewriting everything. The effort seems overwhelming, so they give up. The documentation becomes a museum piece—preserved perfectly, completely useless, and occasionally glanced at with pity.

Phase 5: The crisis. Something breaks at 2 AM. Someone needs to understand how the system works. The documentation lies. Chaos ensues.

This cycle is so common that many developers have learned to ignore documentation entirely. They read the code, experiment in development environments, or ask around for tribal knowledge. This works until the person with the knowledge leaves, or there's an emergency and no one has time for detective work.

But it doesn't have to be this way.

What Makes Documentation "Living"

Living Documentation flips the traditional model. Instead of writing documentation that you hope stays current, you create documentation that proves it's current.

Here's how it works:

Your documentation becomes executable. The scenarios you write don't just describe what the system should do—they actually test that it does it.

When the system changes, the documentation automatically breaks. If someone modifies the discount logic but doesn't update the scenarios, the automated tests fail. The broken documentation becomes immediately obvious.

Fixing the system means fixing the documentation. You can't just patch the code and leave the documentation behind. To make the tests pass, you have to make sure the documented behavior matches the actual behavior.

The documentation is always current. If the tests are passing, you know the documentation accurately describes what the system actually does right now.

The key insight: instead of documentation that describes the system, you create documentation that validates the system.

Building Living Documentation That Actually Works

Here's the step-by-step process for creating documentation that stays alive:

Step 1: Start with your Gherkin scenarios. Those scenarios you wrote in Chapter 20? They're the foundation of your Living Documentation. Each scenario describes a specific behavior in language that both humans and computers can understand.

Example from our restaurant app:

Scenario: First-time customer receives discount
   Given a first-time customer has never placed an order before
   And they add $25 worth of food to their cart
   When they proceed to checkout
   Then they see a 10% discount applied
   And their total is $22.50 plus tax and fees

Step 2: Organize scenarios by feature. Group related scenarios into feature files. Each feature file tells the story of one part of your product:

features/
    ordering/
    first_time_discount.feature
    reorder_last_meal.feature
    special_dietary_requests.feature
payments/
    credit_card_processing.feature
    refund_handling.feature
    failed_payment_retry.feature

Step 3: Connect scenarios to automation. This is where the magic happens. Use tools like Cucumber, SpecFlow, or Behave to turn your human-readable scenarios into automated tests.

When you run the tests, each scenario either passes (proving the documentation is accurate) or fails (revealing that something has changed).

Step 4: Add context and business rules. Your scenarios tell the story of what happens, but sometimes you need to explain why. Add comments or separate documentation sections that explain the business reasoning:

Business Rule: First-time discounts encourage trial usage

The discount applies to food subtotal only, not taxes or delivery fees

This feature was added in response to customer feedback about high perceived costs

Scenario: First-time customer receives 10% discount
 Given a first-time customer has never placed an order before
 # "Never placed an order" means no successful payments,
 # even if they've created accounts or added items to cart before
 When they proceed to checkout
 Then they see a 10% discount applied to the food subtotal

Step 5: Keep everything in version control. Your Living Documentation should live right alongside your code. When someone makes a change that affects behavior, they should update both the code and the scenarios in the same commit.

This creates a natural coupling between implementation and documentation that traditional documentation can never achieve.

Step 6: Generate human-readable reports. Most automation tools can generate readable reports from your scenarios. These become your user-facing documentation—guides that customer support can reference, specifications that new developers can learn from, and requirements that stakeholders can validate.

The beautiful thing? These reports are automatically generated from tests that prove the system works as described.

Real Example: Restaurant App Living Documentation

Let's see what this looks like in practice with our reorder feature:

Feature: Reorder last meal
 As a returning customer
 I want to quickly reorder my previous meal
 So I can skip browsing the menu when I want the same thing

Background:

Given the customer "sarah@example.com" exists

And she has previously ordered:

Item	Customizations	Price
Chicken Caesar Wrap	No croutons, extra sauce	$12.99
Diet Coke	None	$2.49

Scenario: Customer reorders exact previous meal

Given Sarah is logged into the app

When she taps "Reorder Last Meal"

Then her previous order is added to the cart

And the cart shows "Chicken Caesar Wrap—No croutons, extra sauce"

And the cart shows "Diet Coke"

And the total is $15.48

Scenario: Handle unavailable items gracefully

Given Sarah is logged into the app

And the "Chicken Caesar Wrap" is temporarily unavailable

When she taps "Reorder Last Meal"

Then she sees a message "Some items from your last order are unavailable"

And the available items are added to her cart

And she can choose replacements for unavailable items

Scenario: No reorder option for first-time customers

Given Sarah has never placed an order

When she views the main menu

Then the "Reorder Last Meal" option is not displayed

Notice how this documentation tells a complete story. A new developer can read it and understand not just what the reorder feature does, but why it exists and how it handles edge cases. A customer support person can reference it when helping confused customers. A product manager can validate that the implementation matches the intended behavior.

And because it's automated, everyone knows this documentation is accurate right now, not six months ago.

The Power of Always-Current Documentation

Here's what happens when your team starts using Living Documentation:

New team members onboard faster. Instead of outdated wikis and tribal knowledge, they have current, verified examples of how everything works.

Defects get caught earlier. When someone changes behavior without updating the scenarios, the tests fail immediately. No more "working on my machine" surprises.

Product discussions become more concrete. Instead of abstract conversations about requirements, you're discussing specific, testable scenarios.

Regression testing becomes automatic. Every time you run your test suite, you're verifying that existing features still work as documented.

Knowledge gets preserved. When team members leave, their understanding of the system stays behind in the Living Documentation.

Stakeholder confidence increases. Business people can read the scenarios and know exactly what the system does, verified by passing tests.

Common Living Documentation Pitfalls (And How to Avoid Them)

Pitfall 1: Writing scenarios that are too UI-specific

- **Bad**: When the customer clicks the 'Submit Order' button in the bottom right corner
- **Good**: When the customer confirms their order

Keep scenarios focused on behavior, not interface details. UI changes shouldn't break your documentation.

Pitfall 2: Trying to document everything. You don't need Living Documentation for every single feature. Start with your core business logic—the stuff that would cause real problems if it broke.

Pitfall 3: Making scenarios too complex. If a scenario takes 10 steps to set up and has 15 different assertions, it's trying to test too much. Break complex scenarios into simpler, focused ones.

Pitfall 4: Not maintaining the automation. Living Documentation only works if the tests actually run regularly. Make sure they're part of your continuous integration pipeline.

Pitfall 5: Writing for robots instead of humans. Remember that humans need to read and understand these scenarios too. Write for clarity, not just test automation.

Try This Right Now

Pick one feature your team built recently—something with clear business rules that you want to make sure keeps working.

Spend 30 minutes creating Living Documentation for it:

1. Write 2-3 Gherkin scenarios that cover the main behaviors

2. Include both the happy path and at least one edge case

3. Add comments explaining any business rules that aren't obvious

4. Show it to someone else on your team and ask: "Does this clearly explain how this feature works?"

If you have automation tools available, try connecting one scenario to an actual test. The goal isn't perfection—it's to experience the difference between static documentation and documentation that can prove itself.

Making Living Documentation a Team Habit

To make this a natural part of your workflow:

Start small. Pick one important feature and create Living Documentation for it. Learn what works before scaling up.

Make it part of your definition of done. New features should include scenarios that document their behavior.

Run the tests regularly. Living Documentation only works if you actually validate it. Make scenario testing part of your CI/CD pipeline.

Keep it readable. These scenarios should be clear to product managers, customer support, and new developers, not just the person who wrote them.

Update scenarios with behavior changes. When you modify how something works, update the scenarios in the same commit as the code changes.

Generate reports for stakeholders. Use the output from your test runs to create readable documentation for people who don't want to read raw scenarios.

One team we worked with reviews their Living Documentation during retrospectives, asking: "What scenarios helped us this sprint? What scenarios are we missing? What documentation do we wish we had?"

The Long-Term Payoff

Here's something beautiful that happens when teams stick with Living Documentation: they stop having arguments about what the system is supposed to do (Martraire, 2019).

When there's a defect, instead of debating whether the current behavior is correct, you look at the scenarios. Either the system matches the documented behavior (and you need to decide if the documented behavior is right), or it doesn't (and you have a clear defect to fix).

When someone wants to change how a feature works, you update the scenarios first, then implement the change. This forces you to think through the implications and edge cases before you start coding.

When a new team member joins, they can read the Living Documentation and trust that it accurately describes the system they'll be working on.

Your scenarios become a shared language between developers, testers, product managers, and stakeholders. Everyone can read them, everyone can contribute to them, and everyone can trust them.

What's Next

In Chapter 22, we'll shift from documenting what you've built to planning what you'll build next. You'll learn about **Goal-Oriented Roadmapping**—how to create product roadmaps that stay connected to real customer value instead of drifting into feature factories. You've got the tools to build features right and document them well. Now let's talk about how to choose the right features to build in the first place.

CHAPTER 22

Goal-Oriented Roadmapping

Charting a Path to Customer Value

What You'll Learn

- How to build roadmaps that focus on customer outcomes instead of just shipping features on time
- Why traditional timeline roadmaps set teams up to build the wrong things (and what to do instead)
- A practical approach for creating roadmaps that actually help teams make better decisions

The Roadmap That Led Nowhere

The restaurant app team had what looked like a perfect roadmap. Beautiful Gantt charts showed exactly when each feature would be delivered. Q1 would bring the loyalty program. Q2 would add social sharing. Q3 would introduce voice ordering. Every stakeholder had signed off on the timeline.

Six months later, they were right on schedule and completely off track.

The loyalty program launched exactly when promised, but customers found it confusing and rarely used it. Social sharing shipped in Q2, but it turned out customers didn't actually want to broadcast their food orders. The voice ordering project was proceeding smoothly toward its Q3 deadline, even though early testing showed customers tried it once out of curiosity but then reverted to browsing—they preferred seeing all their options and customizations laid out visually.

Meanwhile, their biggest customer problem—checkout taking too long and causing cart abandonment—remained unfixed because it wasn't on the roadmap.

The team was hitting every milestone and missing every outcome that mattered.

This is exactly why our Structured Conversations Manifesto says *"Visual maps show the path."* But not all maps lead to the right destination. Timeline roadmaps show the path to shipping features on schedule. Goal-oriented roadmaps show the path to delivering value that customers actually care about.

Where This Fits

You've built your foundation with customer research and mapping (Chapters 5-9), defined what you're building with user stories and scenarios (Chapters 15-20), and created Living Documentation to keep everyone aligned (Chapter 21). Now you need to step back and ask the big questions: What should we build next? How do we know we're working on the right things?

This chapter builds directly on your Impact Mapping work from Chapter 6. Remember those customer behaviors you wanted to influence? Those become the goals that drive your roadmap decisions.

Why Many Roadmaps Become Feature Factories

Let's talk about what went wrong with that restaurant app roadmap—because it's a pattern that plays out on almost every product team.

Traditional roadmaps are built around deliverables and dates. They answer questions like:

- When will the loyalty program be done?
- What features are we shipping this quarter?
- How do we communicate our delivery timeline to stakeholders?

These seem like reasonable questions, but they're focused on the wrong things. They're about output (what we're building) rather than outcomes (what change we're trying to create in the world).

Here's what happens when roadmaps focus on deliverables:

Teams optimize for shipping, not for impact. Success means hitting deadlines, not helping customers. So teams cut corners on customer research, skip validation, and ship features that technically meet the requirements but don't solve real problems.

Learning gets deprioritized. When you've committed to specific features by specific dates, there's no room to pivot based on what you learn. Customer feedback that contradicts the roadmap becomes a threat to the timeline instead of valuable input.

Stakeholder conversations become about scope and dates. Instead of discussing whether you're solving the right problems, meetings focus on whether features will be delivered on time and what to cut if they won't be.

Innovation happens by accident. The roadmap becomes a conveyor belt of predetermined features. There's no space for the unexpected insights or market changes that could lead to breakthrough improvements.

Customer value becomes secondary. Teams measure success by whether they delivered what was planned, not by whether customers' lives got better.

The result? You end up with teams that are highly efficient at building things customers don't want.

What Makes a Roadmap Goal-Oriented

Goal-oriented roadmaps flip the script. Instead of starting with features and deadlines, they start with customer outcomes and business goals (Pichler, 2022).

Here's the fundamental difference:

Traditional roadmap. We will ship a loyalty program in Q2 so customers can earn points on their orders.

Goal-oriented roadmap. We will increase customer retention by 25% this quarter by giving frequent customers a compelling reason to order from us instead of competitors.

Notice the difference? The goal-oriented version:

- Starts with a measurable outcome (25% retention increase)
- Explains why it matters (customer choice and business impact)
- Leaves room for different solutions (maybe loyalty points, maybe something else entirely)
- Creates a clear success metric (retention, not just "loyalty program shipped")

This changes everything about how teams work. Instead of asking "How do we build this feature?" they ask "How do we achieve this outcome?" Instead of measuring progress by features completed, they measure by customer behavior changed.

The Now-Next-Later Format (That Actually Works)

The most effective goal-oriented roadmaps use a simple format: *Now-Next-Later* (Bastow, 2019). But the secret isn't in the format—it's in what you put in each section.

Now (1-3 months): Clear commitments. These are the bets you're making right now. You have high confidence that these initiatives will drive the outcomes you care about. You've done the research, you understand the problem, and you're ready to execute.

Next (3-6 months): Validated directions. These are initiatives you're reasonably confident about, but you want to learn more before fully committing. Maybe you need to validate demand, test technical feasibility, or understand the competitive landscape better.

Later (6+ months): Emerging opportunities. These are areas you're keeping an eye on. Market trends, customer feedback patterns, or technical possibilities that might become important but aren't ready for investment yet.

The key insight: each section represents a different level of confidence and commitment, not just different time periods (Pereira, 2024).

Building Your Goal-Oriented Roadmap (Step by Step)

Here's the process our most successful teams use:

Step 1: Start with strategic goals. What customer behavior or business outcome are you trying to influence? Use the VERB + NOUN pattern from Chapter 2 to make it specific:

- **Good**: Increase weeknight order frequency by 30%
- **Bad**: Improve customer engagement
- **Good**: Reduce checkout abandonment to under 5%
- **Bad**: Make checkout better

Step 2: Connect goals to customer value. For each goal, use your Impact Mapping work from Chapter 6 to identify:

- Which customers you're targeting (busy parents, office workers, etc.)
- What behavior change you want to see (order more often, complete more purchases)
- Why this matters to them (save time, reduce decision fatigue, feel confident in their choice)

Step 3: Brainstorm potential solutions. Now—and only now— start thinking about what you might build. Use your empathy maps (Chapter 5) and customer research to generate ideas that could drive the behavior changes you want.

Don't worry about feasibility or timeline yet. Just get all the possibilities on the table.

Step 4: Organize by confidence level. For each potential solution, ask:

- How confident are we that this will drive the outcome we want?
- How much do we need to learn before we can commit resources?
- What evidence would we need to see to move forward?

High confidence + clear evidence = **Now**
Medium confidence + some unknowns = **Next**
Interesting but uncertain = **Later**

Step 5: Define success metrics. For everything in your Now and Next sections, be specific about what success looks like:

- What customer behavior will change?
- How will you measure it?
- What would convince you that the initiative is working?

Step 6: Make it visual and collaborative. Create a simple visual representation that your whole team can understand and contribute to. This isn't about fancy tools—a template or simple table works fine.

Real Example: Restaurant App Goal-Oriented Roadmap

Let's see what this looks like for our restaurant app team after they learned from their feature factory mistakes:

Strategic Goal: Increase weeknight order frequency for families by 40% in the next 6 months

NOW (Building this quarter).

Initiative: Simplify weeknight ordering for repeat customers

- **Why**: Parents at 6 PM don't want to browse menus—they want dinner solved quickly
- **What**: One-tap reordering of family favorites with smart suggestions
- **Success metric**: 60% of repeat family customers use reorder feature within 30 days
- **Evidence**: User interviews showed menu browsing is the #1 friction point for families

Initiative: Introduce weeknight family meal deals

- **Why**: Price predictability reduces decision stress for budget-conscious parents
- **What**: "4 meals for $20" promotion on weeknight staples
- **Success metric**: 25% of family orders include the meal deal, average order value stays stable
- **Evidence**: Competitor analysis shows bundling drives frequency without hurting margins

NEXT (Exploring this quarter, building next).

Initiative: Smart dietary restriction filtering

- **Why**: Families with allergies/preferences spend extra time checking ingredients
- **What**: Profile-based filtering that remembers dietary needs and highlights safe options
- **Success metric**: 30% reduction in time-to-order for families with dietary restrictions
- **Learn more**: Need to validate how many families this actually affects

Initiative: Group ordering for family decisions

- **Why**: Parents often need to coordinate with kids/spouse on meal choices
- **What**: Shareable cart where family members can add their preferences
- **Success metric**: 40% of group orders convert vs. 25% of individual decision-making
- **Learn more**: Validate demand through prototype testing

LATER (Keeping an eye on).

Initiative: Voice ordering integration

- **Why**: Could eliminate screen interaction while driving
- **What**: Integration with smart speakers or car systems
- **Learn more**: Technical feasibility, customer demand in noisy environments

Initiative: Predictive ordering based on weather/events

- **Why**: Could automate routine decisions ("Order our usual rainy day comfort food")
- **What**: Smart suggestions based on external factors + order history
- **Learn more**: Machine learning capabilities, customer comfort with automation

Notice how each initiative starts with why it matters to customers, defines what success looks like, and acknowledges what the team still needs to learn.

Using Your Roadmap to Make Better Decisions

A good goal-oriented roadmap isn't just a planning document—it's a decision-making tool. Here's how to use it:

When stakeholders ask for new features. Check if they align with your strategic goals. If not, they go in Later (or off the roadmap entirely) unless the goals need to change.

When customer feedback suggests pivots. Ask if the pivot would better serve your strategic goals. If yes, it might bump something from Next to Now.

When technical constraints emerge. Focus on the outcomes, not the specific solutions. Maybe you can't build exactly what you planned, but can you achieve the same customer outcome a different way?

When you discover new opportunities. Assess them against your confidence level. High-confidence opportunities might jump into Next. Interesting but uncertain ones go in Later.

When reporting progress. Talk about customer behavior changes and metric improvements, not just feature delivery status.

A good roadmap does three things: it communicates a vision for what the product should become, provides direction like a compass, and guides the team's journey (Mee, 2021).

Download our free template (Fig. 29) from structured-conversations. com to craft a goal-oriented roadmap that is clear, collaborative and outcome-driven.

Restaurant Menu Expansion

	Now	Next
Goal	Increase weeknight order frequency for families by 40% in 6 months	
Initiative	**Simplify weeknight ordering** for repeat customers **Why**: Parents at 6 PM don't want to browse menus **What**: One-tap reordering of family favorites with smart suggestions **Evidence**: Menu browsing is #1 friction point for families **Weeknight family meal deals** **Why:** Price predictability reduces decision stress **What**: "4 meals for $20" promotion on weeknight stables **Evidence**: Bundling drives frequency without hurting margins	**Smart dietary restriction filtering** **Why**: Families with allergies spend extra time checking ingredients **What**: Profile-based filtering that remembers dietary needs **Learn more**: Validate how many families this actually affects **Group ordering for family decisions** **Why**: Parents need to coordinate with kids/spouse on meals **What**: Shareable cart for family member preferences **Learn more**: Validate demand through prototype testing

Fig. 29: Goal-Oriented Roadmap Template

Last Revised: May 4, 2025

Later	Product Outcomes
	60% of repeat family customers user reorder feature 25% of family orders include meal deal 30% reduction in time-to-order for families with dietary restrictions

Voice ordering integration

Why: Could eliminate phone/screen interaction while cooking/driving

What: Integration with smart speakers or car systems

Learn more: Technical feasibility, customer demand in noisy environments

Predictive ordering based on weather/events

Why: Could automate routine decisions ("Order usual rainy day food")

What: Smart suggestions based on external factors + order history

Learn more: ML capabilities, customer comfort with automation

Customer Needs (Outcomes)

Parents don't want to browse menus at 6pm

Quick dinner solution
Price predictability
Reduce decision stress

Families need to accommodate dietary restrictions

Save time checking ingredients
Coordinate family preferences

Eliminate manual ordering friction

Hands-free ordering
Automate routine decisions

Try It Now

Pick one area where your product isn't performing as well as you'd like. Maybe it's customer retention, feature adoption, customer satisfaction, or conversion rates.

Spend 30 minutes creating a mini goal-oriented roadmap:

1. Define a specific, measurable goal using VERB + NOUN format

2. Identify which customers you're targeting and what behavior you want to change

3. Brainstorm 4-6 potential initiatives that might drive that change

4. Sort them into Now-Next-Later based on your confidence level

5. Define success metrics for your Now items

Share it with your team and ask:

- Does this goal align with our bigger product strategy?
- Are we confident enough in our Now items to start working on them?
- What would we need to learn to move Next items into Now?
- Are there important initiatives missing from this roadmap?

Pay attention to what questions come up—they're probably questions worth answering before you commit resources.

Common Roadmapping Mistakes (And How to Avoid Them)

Mistake 1: Putting too much in Now. Teams often try to pack their Now section with everything they think is important. But if everything is a priority, nothing is. Keep Now focused on 2-3 major initiatives you can actually execute well.

Mistake 2: Making Next too specific. Next isn't just "Now but later"—it's for things you need to learn more about. Don't over-specify Next items before you have the evidence to support them.

Mistake 3: Ignoring Later. Later isn't a dumping ground for ideas you don't want to say no to. It's for genuinely promising opportunities that aren't ready yet. Review and prune it regularly.

Mistake 4: Focusing on features instead of outcomes. It's easy to slip back into "ship the loyalty program" thinking. Keep bringing the conversation back to customer behavior and business results.

Mistake 5: Not updating the roadmap as you learn. Goal-oriented roadmaps should evolve as you get new information. If you're not moving things between sections or changing your approach based on results, you're probably not learning fast enough.

Making Goal-Oriented Roadmapping a Team Habit

To make this a natural part of how your team works:

Review monthly, refresh quarterly. Check your progress on Now items monthly. Do a full roadmap refresh every quarter based on what you've learned.

Make it visible. Keep your roadmap somewhere everyone can see and reference it. Use it in sprint planning to connect daily work to bigger goals.

Connect to your other artifacts. Your user stories should trace back to roadmap initiatives. Your Gherkin scenarios should test the behaviors your roadmap is trying to influence.

Include the whole team. Don't make roadmapping a product management solo activity. Get input from designers, developers, customer support—anyone who touches customers or understands the technical constraints.

Use it in stakeholder conversations. Instead of promising features by dates, talk about the customer outcomes you're working toward and how you'll measure success.

One team we worked with starts every sprint planning session by reviewing their Now section: "Are we still confident in these bets? What have we learned that might change our approach?"

The Long-Term Benefits of Goal-Oriented Roadmapping

When teams stick with goal-oriented roadmapping, something interesting happens: they get better at building the right things.

They stop shipping features that customers ignore because they validate demand before building. They catch themselves when they're optimizing for the wrong metrics. They have more productive conversations with stakeholders because everyone's aligned on outcomes, not just outputs.

Most importantly, they build products that actually improve people's lives instead of just adding more stuff to an already cluttered interface.

Your roadmap becomes a tool for saying no to good ideas that don't serve your goals, and yes to unexpected opportunities that could drive even better outcomes.

What's Next

In Chapter 23, we'll dive into **Hypothesis-Driven Development**—how to turn your roadmap initiatives into testable experiments that help you learn fast and build confidence in your approach. You've got a roadmap that focuses on the right outcomes. Now let's talk about how to validate that you're on the right track before you invest too heavily in any particular solution.

Formulating Hypotheses

Validating Ideas for Impactful Outcomes

What You'll Learn

- How to turn your roadmap assumptions into testable hypotheses that save you from building the wrong things
- Why most product decisions are really just expensive guesses (and how to make cheaper, smarter bets instead)
- A simple approach for designing experiments that actually answer the questions you need answered

The $50,000 Loyalty Program Nobody Wanted

The restaurant app team was convinced they had a winner. Customer surveys showed people wanted "more rewards for ordering frequently." Competitive analysis revealed that every major food delivery app had some form of loyalty program. The business case was solid: increase customer lifetime value by giving frequent orderers points they could redeem for free meals.

They spent three months building it. Beautiful point-tracking animations. Sophisticated tier systems. Push notifications celebrating milestone achievements. The CEO loved the demo. Marketing prepared a big launch campaign.

Two weeks after launch, the usage stats were brutal. Less than 8% of customers had even opened the loyalty section. Of those who did, most never progressed past viewing their point balance. The feature that was supposed to drive repeat orders was being completely ignored.

In the post-mortem, the team discovered something painful: they'd built an entire feature based on assumptions they never tested. Sure, people said they wanted rewards in surveys—but saying you want something and actually using it are very different things. The competitive analysis missed the fact that most loyalty programs have terrible engagement rates. And the business case assumed customers would change their behavior in ways they'd never validated.

They'd spent three months and $50,000 building a solution to a problem that may not have existed in the way they thought it did.

This is exactly why our Structured Conversations Manifesto emphasizes *"Visual maps show the path"*—but you need to know you're mapping the right territory. Hypothesis-Driven Development (HDD) is how you test whether your map matches the actual landscape before you commit to the journey.

Where This Fits

You've built a goal-oriented roadmap (Chapter 22) that focuses on customer outcomes instead of just feature delivery. But your roadmap is still full of assumptions: assumptions about what customers want, what will change their behavior, what problems are worth solving, and what solutions will actually work.

HDD is how you test those assumptions before you bet big on them. It builds directly on all your research and mapping work—your empathy maps (Chapter 5), impact maps (Chapter 6), and customer journey maps (Chapter 7)—all have helped you identify problems and opportunities. Now you need to validate that your solutions will actually address them.

Why Product Decisions Without Hypotheses Are Just Expensive Guesses

Let's be honest about how many product decisions get made. Someone (a product manager, a designer, an executive, a customer) has an idea about what would make the product better. The idea sounds reasonable. Maybe there's some supporting evidence—customer feedback, competitive analysis, survey data. The team discusses it, decides it's worth building, and starts development.

But here's what's usually missing: **a hypothesis**—a clear, testable prediction about what will happen when you build it

Without that prediction, you're not making a decision—you're making a guess. And guess-driven development is expensive:

You discover problems after you've built the solution. By the time you realize the loyalty program isn't engaging, you've already spent months building it.

You can't tell if your solution is working. Without a clear prediction, how do you know if the feature is successful? Lower engagement than expected might still be "good enough," or it might be a sign of fundamental problems.

You can't improve systematically. When something doesn't work as expected, you don't know which assumptions were wrong, so you can't fix them strategically.

You build features, not outcomes. Teams measure success by whether they shipped what they planned, not by whether they achieved the customer or business outcomes they were aiming for.

Learning happens accidentally. Important insights about customers and markets only surface when things go wrong, and even then, they often get buried in the rush to fix problems.

HDD changes this by making your assumptions explicit and testable before you commit significant resources.

What Makes a Good Hypothesis

A hypothesis isn't just an idea about what might work—it's a specific, testable prediction about what will happen if you're right.

Here's the difference:

Idea. Customers want a loyalty program.

Hypothesis. If we offer points for repeat orders, then frequent customers (3+ orders per month) will increase their order frequency by at least 20% within 30 days.

The hypothesis is better because:

- It's specific about who it affects (frequent customers)
- It predicts a measurable behavior change (20% increase in order frequency)
- It has a timeline for evaluation (30 days)
- It can be proven wrong (if frequency doesn't increase, the hypothesis fails)

A good hypothesis also connects to your bigger goals. It's not just "this feature will work"—it's "this feature will work in a way that drives the customer outcome we care about."

The Hypothesis Framework That Actually Works

Here's the step-by-step process our most successful teams use to turn roadmap ideas into testable hypotheses:

Step 1: Identify your core assumption. Look at something on your roadmap and ask: What would have to be true for this to create the outcome we want?

For the loyalty program example:

- **Assumption 1**: Customers want to be rewarded for frequent ordering
- **Assumption 2**: Point-based rewards will motivate behavior change
- **Assumption 3**: Frequent orderers will engage with a points system
- **Assumption 4**: Increased engagement will lead to more orders

Step 2: Pick the riskiest assumption to test first. Don't try to test everything at once. Find the assumption that, if wrong, would make your entire initiative pointless.

For loyalty programs, the riskiest assumption is probably #3: Will frequent orderers actually engage with a points system? If they don't engage, nothing else matters.

Step 3: Write a clear, testable hypothesis. Use this structure: "We believe that [action] for [customer] will result in [measurable outcome] because [underlying assumption]."

Example: We believe that showing point balances and redemption options for customers who've ordered 3+ times will result in 60% of them checking their points at least once per week because frequent customers are motivated by progress toward rewards.

Step 4: Design the smallest possible test. Don't build the full feature to test the hypothesis. Design the minimum experiment that could prove or disprove your prediction.

For the loyalty hypothesis, you might:

- Create a "points balance" screen for frequent customers
- Track how many people click on it
- Survey those who engage to understand their motivation
- Measure if engagement correlates with ordering behavior

Step 5: Define success criteria up front. Be specific about what results would make you confident in the hypothesis versus what would make you reject it.

Example:
- **Strong validation**: 70%+ of frequent customers check points, and those who do order 25%+ more often
- **Weak validation**: 40-60% engagement, 10-20% ordering increase
- **Rejection**: <30% engagement or no ordering behavior change

Step 6: Run the test and learn. Execute your experiment, collect data, and honestly evaluate the results against your success criteria.

Download our free template (Fig. 30) from structured-conversations. com for collaboration.

Formulating Hypotheses

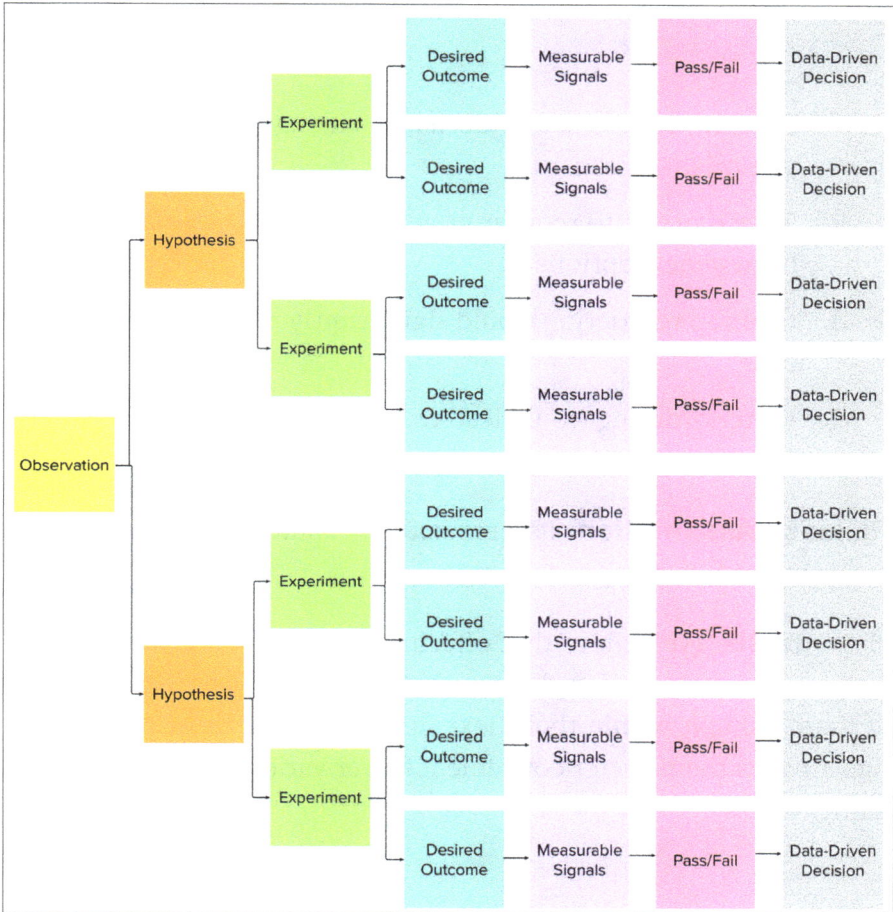

Fig. 30 Hypotheses Template

Real Example: Restaurant App Hypothesis Testing

Let's see how this worked for our restaurant app team after their loyalty program disappointment:

New Initiative: Simplify weeknight ordering for busy families

Core Assumptions:

1. Parents are stressed by decision-making during weeknight dinner rush

2. They'd prefer to reorder previous meals rather than browse new options

3. One-tap reordering would significantly reduce ordering time

4. Faster ordering would lead to more frequent weeknight orders

Riskiest Assumption: Parents actually want to reorder previous meals instead of trying new things

Hypothesis: We believe that offering a 'Reorder Last Meal' button for parents who've ordered dinner between 5-7 PM will result in 40% of them using it within their next three orders because decision fatigue makes them prefer convenience over variety during weeknight dinner stress.

Minimal Test:

- Add a simple "Reorder Last Meal" button for customers who fit the parent profile and have ordered during dinner hours
- Track button usage and time-to-order completion
- Survey customers about their experience and motivation

Success Criteria:

- **Strong validation**: 50%+ use reorder button, average order time drops 30%+
- **Weak validation**: 25-40% usage, 15-25% time reduction
- **Rejection**: <20% usage or minimal time savings

Results: 65% of targeted parents used the reorder button at least once, and those who did completed orders 45% faster on average. Strong validation—time to build the full feature.

This approach lets them test their core assumption for the cost of a few days of development work instead of months.

Syntax Options

Here are three proven formats for writing hypotheses—choose the one that works best for your team:

Option 1 (Classic HDD)

We believe that <this capability>
Will result in <this outcome>
We will know we have succeeded when <we see a measurable signal>

Option 2 (Sandy, 2020)

We know that <data or observation>
And believe that <need or issue>
Through delivering/testing <concept>
For <target user>
We expect <measurable outcome>

Option 3 (Gotthelf & Seiden, 2021)

> **We believe**
> **We will achieve** <outcome>
> **When** <these people>
> **Attain** <this benefit>
> **With** <this feature/product>

Common Hypothesis Mistakes (And How to Avoid Them)

Mistake 1: Testing multiple assumptions at once.

- **Bad**: Customers will engage with loyalty points and it will increase orders and improve satisfaction
- **Good**: Frequent customers will check their point balance at least weekly

Test one thing at a time so you know which assumptions are right or wrong.

Mistake 2: Making hypotheses too vague to disprove.

- **Bad**: Customers will like the new feature
- **Good**: 60% of trial customers will use the feature more than twice in their first week

If you can't imagine what would prove your hypothesis wrong, it's not testable.

Mistake 3: Designing tests that can't change your mind.

If your test is so small or limited that negative results wouldn't actually stop you from building the feature, it's not a real test.

Mistake 4: Ignoring results that don't match expectations.

It's tempting to rationalize weak results ("engagement was low, but that's probably because . . ."). Be honest about what the data tells you.

Mistake 5: Testing implementation details instead of customer value.

- **Bad**: Customers will click the loyalty points button
- **Good**: Customers will increase their order frequency when they can track progress toward rewards

Test whether your solution creates the outcome you care about, not just whether people use the feature.

Try It Now

Pick something from your current roadmap—a feature you're planning to build or a problem you're thinking about solving.

Spend 20 minutes applying the hypothesis framework:

1. List 3-4 core assumptions behind why you think this initiative will succeed

2. Identify which assumption is riskiest (which one, if wrong, would make the whole thing pointless)

3. Write a clear hypothesis for that assumption

4. Design the smallest possible test to validate or disprove the hypothesis

5. Define what results would make you confident vs. what would make you pivot

Share it with your team and ask:

- Is this hypothesis clear and testable?
- Would this test actually change our decision about whether to proceed?
- What are we assuming about our test design itself?

The conversations that come up are usually more valuable than the hypothesis itself.

Building a Hypothesis-Driven Culture

To make this a natural part of how your team works:

Start small. Pick one roadmap item per quarter to test with hypotheses. Build the skill before scaling the practice.

Make assumptions explicit. In roadmap discussions, always ask: "What would have to be true for this to work?" Write those assumptions down.

Design cheap tests. The goal isn't perfect validation—it's learning enough to make better decisions with less risk.

Celebrate learning, not just validation. When a hypothesis fails, that's valuable information that saved you from building the wrong thing.

Connect to your goals. Every hypothesis should tie back to the customer outcomes or business metrics you're trying to influence.

Update your roadmap based on results. If tests invalidate key assumptions, be willing to pivot your plans.

One team we worked with has a simple rule: nothing moves from "Next" to "Now" on their roadmap without at least one validated hypothesis supporting it.

When Hypothesis-Driven Development Really Pays Off

Here's what happens when teams get good at hypothesis-driven development: they stop building features that nobody uses.

They catch bad ideas early, when pivoting is cheap. They build confidence in good ideas before committing major resources. They have better conversations with stakeholders because they can explain not just what they're building, but why they believe it will work.

Most importantly, they get better at understanding their customers. Each hypothesis test is a small experiment in customer behavior. Over time, these experiments build a deep understanding of what actually motivates people to change how they use your product.

The teams that master this approach don't just ship features faster—they ship better features that actually solve real problems.

What's Next?

In Chapter 24, we'll explore how to connect all this hypothesis testing to your broader business goals using **OKRs** (Objectives and Key Results). You'll learn how to measure whether your validated experiments are actually driving the outcomes that matter to your organization.

Objectives and Key Results (OKRs)

Driving Impacts and Outcomes with Focused Goals

What You'll Learn

- How to create OKRs that actually align your team instead of becoming another layer of bureaucracy
- Why most goal-setting frameworks fail teams (and what makes OKRs different when done right)
- A practical approach to connecting your daily work to outcomes that matter to customers and the business
- The component that often gets overlooked (and why it might be time to call them OKRIs)

Before we dive in, here's a question that might sound silly at first: Are OKRs missing a letter? While everyone talks about objectives and key results, the most successful implementations we see actually have three components—with initiatives as the often overlooked 'I' that completes the picture. Maybe it should really be OKRIs, following that natural flow from vision to measurement to action (Vellore, 2023). It's not just a cute observation—this missing piece explains why so many teams nail the goal-setting and metrics but then find themselves asking, 'Okay, so what do we actually do now?

The Quarter When Everything Pulled in Different Directions

The restaurant app team started Q2 with the best of intentions. Everyone agreed on the high-level goal: increase weeknight orders to drive revenue growth. The leadership team was excited, stakeholders were aligned, and the team was ready to execute.

But then reality hit.

Marketing launched an aggressive discount campaign to drive immediate order volume. Engineering focused on optimizing checkout speed because slow performance was hurting conversion rates. The product team prioritized a loyalty program because customer feedback suggested people wanted rewards for frequent ordering. Design worked on improving the browsing experience because customer research showed people struggled to find what they wanted.

Each initiative made perfect sense in isolation. Each group had data supporting their approach. Each team was working hard on something that could theoretically increase weeknight orders.

Three months later, the results were disappointing. Order volume had increased slightly, but not nearly enough to justify the effort. Worse, the team felt scattered and frustrated. Marketing's discounts had attracted price-sensitive customers who didn't stick around. The faster checkout helped, but only marginally. The loyalty program launched but had low engagement. The browsing improvements were well-received but didn't translate to more orders.

In the post-mortem, someone finally asked the obvious question: "We all agreed on increasing weeknight orders, and we even tracked the right metrics. But did anyone actually plan what we'd *do* to achieve this?" The room went quiet. They'd spent hours debating what success looked like but almost no time planning how to get there. They'd fallen into the classic OKR trap—the missing 'I' problem.

The painful truth emerged: everyone had been optimizing for different definitions of success. Marketing measured immediate order volume. Engineering measured page load times. Product measured loyalty program sign-ups. Design measured customer satisfaction scores.

They'd all been working toward "increase weeknight orders," but they'd never defined what that actually meant or how they'd measure it together.

This is exactly why our Structured Conversations Manifesto says *"Outcomes define success."* But outcomes only define success if everyone agrees on what the outcomes are and how to measure them. OKRs (Objectives and Key Results) give teams a shared language for turning vague goals into specific, measurable targets that everyone can work toward together.

Where This Fits

You've built hypotheses to test your assumptions (Chapter 23), created goal-oriented roadmaps that focus on outcomes (Chapter 22), and developed all the research and mapping techniques to understand what customers need (Chapters 5-21). Now you need to connect all that work to the bigger goals that matter to your organization.

OKRs are the bridge between your day-to-day product work and your company's strategic objectives. They help you answer the question: "If we execute all these features and experiments perfectly, will we actually achieve the business outcomes we care about?"

Why Goal-Setting Approaches Often Fall Apart

Before we dive into what makes OKRs work, let's talk about why goal-setting approaches can fail teams.

Problem 1: Goals are too vague to guide decisions. "Increase customer satisfaction" or "improve customer engagement" sound important, but they don't help teams choose between competing priorities. When everything can contribute to a vague goal, nothing is clearly more important than anything else.

Problem 2: Success metrics are misaligned across teams. Different functions naturally focus on different metrics. Marketing cares about acquisition, product cares about engagement, engineering cares about performance, support cares about ticket volume. Without shared success criteria, teams optimize for their own metrics at the expense of overall outcomes.

Problem 3: Goals are set once and forgotten. Many teams do annual or quarterly goal-setting exercises, then file the results away and get back to their regular work. The goals become decorative rather than functional—they look good in presentations but don't actually influence daily decisions.

Problem 4: No clear connection between daily work and strategic goals. Individual contributors often can't explain how their current tasks connect to the company's bigger objectives. This leads to disengagement and work that feels pointless, even when it's strategically important.

Problem 5: Goals focus on activities instead of outcomes.
"Launch the loyalty program" is an activity. "Increase customer retention by 20%" is an outcome. When goals focus on shipping features rather than changing customer behavior, teams can succeed at building things while failing to create value.

Problem 6: Framework theater over genuine progress.
Teams implement OKRs perfectly on paper—writing inspiring objectives, setting measurable key results, conducting quarterly reviews—but still struggle to connect their daily work to meaningful business outcomes. They're trapped in what Herbig (2025) calls "Alibi Progress"—prioritizing the correctness of the framework over the value it should create. The OKRs look impressive in presentations but don't actually drive the strategic alignment and focused decision-making they promise.

What Makes OKRs Actually Work

OKRs aren't magic—they're just a structured way to answer two fundamental questions:

1. **What do we want to achieve?** (Objective)
2. **How will we know if we're succeeding?** (Key Results)

But the structure matters because it forces clarity and alignment:

Objectives are qualitative and inspirational. They describe what you want to accomplish in language that gets people excited about the work.

Key results are quantitative and specific. They define exactly what success looks like with numbers that can't be interpreted in different ways.

Time-bound focus. OKRs typically run for a few quarters, creating urgency and enabling regular recalibration.

Limited number. Many teams set 1-3 objectives with 2-3 key results each, forcing prioritization.

Transparent and shared. Everyone can see what everyone else is working toward, creating natural coordination.

Outcome-focused. Key results measure changes in customer or business metrics, not just feature delivery. As Seiden (2019) emphasizes in *Outcomes Over Output*, the key metric for business success isn't what we ship, but how customer behavior changes as a result. OKRs force this shift from measuring outputs (features completed) to measuring outcomes (value created).

The key insight: OKRs create a shared definition of success that's specific enough to guide daily decisions and broad enough to allow creative problem-solving.

The Mystery of the Missing "I"

That missing letter we talked about? It's not just a theoretical problem—it's the reason many OKR implementations feel like setting intentions without making plans. Teams end up with inspiring objectives and measurable key results, but find themselves in that familiar spot of asking "Now what?"

The most successful teams we work with solve this by quietly adding initiatives back into their process—they just don't rebrand it as "OKRIs" because, well, everyone still calls it OKRs. Though honestly, OKRIs just sounds better anyway—more vowels, easier to pronounce.

The Missing Piece: Why Initiatives Matter More Than the Acronym Suggests

We've established that initiatives deserve to be the 'I' added to OKRs—but why does this matter beyond just expanding the acronym?

Think of initiatives as the GPS navigation between your starting point and destination. Objectives tell you where you want to go ("Become the preferred dinner choice"). Key results tell you what arrival looks like ("30% increase in orders"). But without initiatives, you're standing at the starting line with a clear destination and no directions. Initiatives are your turn-by-turn navigation—the specific actions that transform aspiration into achievement.

Here's what changes when you add initiatives to the mix:

Clarity in chaos. Instead of teams staring at ambitious objectives wondering "where do we even start?", initiatives provide concrete next steps that anyone can understand and act on.

Manageable momentum. Complex objectives become less overwhelming when broken into specific, actionable pieces. It's the difference between "climb Mount Everest" and "complete base camp training by March."

Accountability that works. When someone owns a specific initiative, progress gets tracked and problems get solved. Ownership of vague objectives often leads to everyone assuming someone else is handling it.

Organizational alignment. When teams can see not just what everyone is trying to achieve, but how they're going about it, coordination becomes natural rather than forced.

Built-in adaptability. Objectives might stay constant, but initiatives can shift as you learn what's working. This keeps your strategy responsive without losing sight of your goals.

The Anatomy of OKRs (Actually OKRIs)

Now that we've established why that missing "I" matters, let's break down how all three components work together:

- **Objective.** Your ambitious, inspirational destination. It answers: "Where do we want to go?"
- **Key Result.** Your measurable outcomes that show you're on track. It answers: "How will we know we're making progress?"
- **Initiative.** Your core activities that drive progress. It answers: "What exactly are we going to do?"

Think of it as the complete journey: Objectives set your destination, key results track your progress along the way, and initiatives are your step-by-step directions for actually getting there.

This three-part structure ensures you're not just setting inspiring goals or measuring progress in isolation—you're creating a complete system that connects vision to action. When teams have all three elements working together, they spend less time wondering what to do next and more time actually making progress (Vellore, 2023).

Building OKRIs That Actually Drive Alignment

Here's the step-by-step process our most successful teams use:

Step 1: Start with customer or business outcomes you want to influence. Don't start with features or initiatives. Start with the change you want to create in the world. This customer-centric approach, as detailed by Gothelf and Seiden (2024), ensures your OKRIs drive real value rather than just internal efficiency. Use your Impact Mapping work (Chapter 6) and goal-oriented roadmap (Chapter 22) as input.

Examples:

- More busy families choose us for weeknight dinners
- Existing customers order more frequently
- New customers have a great first experience and come back

Step 2: Turn outcomes into inspirational objectives. Write your objective as a qualitative statement that describes what you want to achieve. Use the VERB + NOUN pattern from Chapter 2, but focus on the change you want to create, not just the metric you want to move.

- **Good**: Become the go-to solution for busy families' weeknight dinners
- **Better**: Make weeknight dinner ordering effortless for busy families

The objective should be something the team feels excited about accomplishing.

Step 3: Define 2-3 key results that prove you've achieved the objective. For each objective, identify the specific, measurable signals that would indicate success. These should be outcome metrics (customer behavior changes, business results) rather than output metrics (features shipped, tasks completed).

For "Make weeknight dinner ordering effortless for busy families":

- **KR1**: Monday-Thursday order volume increases by 25% within 90 days
- **KR2**: Average time-to-order for repeat family customers falls below 2 minutes
- **KR3**: Weeknight ordering satisfaction score reaches 7.5/10

Step 4: Connect key results to your hypotheses and experiments. Each key result should connect to testable hypotheses from Chapter 23. This ensures your OKRIs aren't just wishful thinking—they're grounded in specific theories about what will drive the outcomes you want.

For "Monday-Thursday order volume increases by 25%":

- **Hypothesis**: One-tap reordering will increase order frequency for repeat customers
- **Hypothesis**: Family meal deals will attract price-conscious parents
- **Hypothesis**: Faster checkout will reduce abandonment during dinner rush

Step 5: Add the missing "I"—Identify initiatives that could drive the key results. This is where we complete the OKRI sequence. Now—and only now—start thinking about what you might build. These initiatives should be directly connected to your hypotheses and designed to move specific key results. If OKRIs were a recipe, initiatives would be the actual cooking instructions, not just the list of ingredients and the photo of the finished dish.

- Build one-tap reorder feature (targets KR1 and KR2)
- Launch "4 meals for $20" weeknight promotion (targets KR1)
- Optimize checkout flow for mobile customers (targets KR2 and KR3)

Step 6: Make it visual and collaborative. Create a simple visual representation that shows the connection between your strategic objective, the key results that define success, and the initiatives that will drive those results.

Download our free template (Fig. 31) from structured-conversations.com to follow along.

Real Example: Restaurant App OKRIs

Let's see what this looks like for our restaurant app team's revised approach:

Objective: Make weeknight dinner ordering effortless for busy families

Key Results:

- **KR1**: Monday-Thursday order volume increases by 25% within 90 days
- **KR2**: Average time-to-order for repeat family customers falls below 2 minutes
- **KR3**: Weeknight ordering satisfaction score reaches 7.5/10

Supporting Initiatives:

- Build one-tap reorder functionality based on order history
- Launch "Family Night Special"—4 entrees for $20 on weeknights
- Optimize mobile checkout flow for speed and clarity
- Create family-friendly menu filtering and recommendations

Connected Hypotheses:

- Families will reorder previous meals rather than browsing when time-pressed
- Price predictability will reduce decision stress for budget-conscious parents
- Faster ordering will lead to more frequent impulse orders during dinner rush

Notice how this OKRI creates a clear thread from making weeknight ordering effortless for busy families through measurable success criteria (25% volume increase, sub-2-minute ordering, 7.5/10 satisfaction) to specific initiatives that can drive those results.

Most importantly, everyone on the team can now answer the question: "How does my work this week connect to our bigger goals?"

Using OKRIs to Make Better Decisions

A good OKRI isn't just a measurement framework—it's a decision-making tool. Here's how to use it:

When stakeholders request new features. Ask how the request connects to your key results. If it doesn't clearly drive one of your success metrics, it either needs strong justification or should wait until the next OKRI cycle.

When prioritizing between competing initiatives. Choose the one more likely to move your key results. This gives you an objective framework for difficult trade-off decisions.

When experiments don't work as expected. Focus on the key result you're trying to achieve, not the specific initiative that failed. Maybe one approach didn't work, but there are other ways to drive the same outcome.

When reporting progress. Talk about key result movement, not just initiative completion. "We shipped the reorder feature" is less important than "Reorder feature increased repeat ordering by 15%."

When planning the next quarter. Evaluate whether you achieved your key results, not just whether you completed your planned initiatives. Use that learning to inform your next set of OKRIs.

Objectives and Key Results (OKRs)

	Objectives	Key Results	Initiatives
	An ambitious goal that provides inspiration and direction	We will measure the success of this objective by using the following key result(s)	We will reach the key results (outcomes) by doing the following initiatives:
Company level	Become the fastest-growing restaurant chain in the US	Surpass our competition by 1.5x more locations / Increase sales by 20% Year-Over-Year for 3 years	Open 50 more locations in the fastest-growing cities / Create national franchise marketing program
Regional Level	Achieve profitability of all stores	Reduce expenses by 10% / Increase regional sales by 35%	Create regional delivery service app / Implement national marketing program
Store Level	Increase weeknight business	Receive repeat orders from 25% of csutomers 2x/ week / Increase weeknight revenues by 50% / Receive 2x # orders for weeknight special vs a la carte items	Sign up for delivery app service / Create weeknight specials
	Goal that inspires and sets direction (where do we need to go?)	2 - 3 desired outcomes that gauge progress toward achieving an objective (How do we know we're getting getting or not?)	The action(s) necessary to propel advancement towards fulfilling the key results and achieving the desired outcomes (What will we do to get there?)

Fig. 31: OKRI Template

Syntax Options

Choose between two syntax options depending on whether you want to emphasize measurement or include implementation details upfront:

Option 1 (Concise Format): We will achieve <objective> as measured by <key results>

Option 2 (Narrative Format): We will achieve <objective> as measured by <key results> by doing <initiatives>

OKRs vs. KPIs

OKRs push you toward ambitious goals; KPIs tell you if you're maintaining standards.

OKRs	KPIs
Drive desired change (e.g., "Increase orders by 20%")	Monitor current state (e.g., "Track order volume")
Time-bound, tied to strategy	Long-term performance indicators
Fuel hypotheses and experiments	Focus on thresholds and stability
Reviewed quarterly	Monitored continuously

Integrating OKRIs with User Story Mapping

User Story Mapping (Chapter 9) acts as a compass: it links customer goals to prioritized user stories. Combined with OKRIs, the effect multiplies. User stories show what customers need (e.g., "Reorder dinner quickly"), while OKRIs anchor those user stories to strategic outcomes (e.g., "Increase weeknight orders by 20%").

This synergy keeps teams aligned from user story to epic to initiative. For example, mapping "Add one-tap reorder" to the OKRI's key result "20% more weeknight orders" ensures development effort drives measurable impact. Frequent feedback loops in User Story Mapping complement OKRI's quarterly cadence, enabling adaptability and continuous improvement (Gothelf, 2023).

Connecting OKRIs to Hypotheses

OKRIs amplify impact when paired with Hypothesis-Driven Development (Chapter 23). Each key result acts as a measurable signal for a hypothesis, while initiatives become testable experiments (Murphy, 2019). For example:

- **Objective**: Increase weeknight orders
- **Key Result**: 20% increase in Monday-Thursday orders
- **Hypothesis**: *We believe that launching a 4-for-$20 special for busy parents will result in higher weeknight order volume. We'll know this when orders increase by 20% in 30 days*
- **Initiative**: Launch "Family Night Special"—4 entrees for $20 on weeknights

This integration ties objectives to experiments with shared syntax and clear metrics.

Try It Now

Pick an area where your product or team needs to improve. Maybe it's customer retention, feature adoption, customer satisfaction, or business growth.

Spend 30 minutes creating a draft OKRI:

1. Write an inspirational objective that describes the change you want to create (not just the metric you want to move)

2. Define 2-3 key results that would prove you've achieved that objective

3. Connect each key result to a hypothesis about what will drive that outcome

4. Identify 1-2 initiatives that could test those hypotheses

5. Ask: If we achieved all these key results, would we consider this objective accomplished?

Share it with your team and ask:

- Does this objective inspire you? Is it clear what success looks like?
- Are the key results actually measuring the outcomes we care about?
- Do our proposed initiatives have a realistic chance of driving these results?
- What are we assuming about our ability to influence these metrics?

Common OKRI Mistakes (And How to Avoid Them)

Mistake 1: Making objectives too operational.

- **Bad**: Ship the loyalty program feature
- **Good**: Increase customer lifetime value through better retention

Objectives should describe the impact you want to create, not the work you want to complete.

Mistake 2: Key results that measure activity instead of outcomes.

- **Bad**: Complete user research on 3 customer segments
- **Good**: Increase conversion rate for new customers by 20%

Key results should measure changes in customer or business metrics, not just task completion.

Mistake 3: Too many OKRIs.

Most teams can only focus effectively on 1-2 objectives per quarter. More than that and you lose the focusing benefit that makes OKRIs valuable.

Mistake 4: Key results that aren't actually measurable.

- **Bad**: Improve user experience significantly
- **Good**: Achieve NPS score of 70+ for new customer onboarding

If you can't measure it objectively, it's not a good key result.

Mistake 5: Not connecting OKRIs to daily work.

OKRIs that live in PowerPoint presentations but don't influence sprint planning, feature prioritization, or resource allocation are just bureaucracy.

Mistake 6: Forgetting the missing "I"

- **Bad:** Setting OKRIs in a planning meeting, then starting the next sprint with "So what should we build first?"
- **Good:** Walking out of OKRI planning with clear initiatives that everyone understands and is excited to execute

The most common OKRI failure isn't setting bad objectives or un-measurable key results—it's treating goal-setting as separate from execution planning.

Making OKRIs a Team Habit

To make this a natural part of how your team works:

Set them collaboratively. Don't let one person write OKRIs and impose them on the team. The conversation about what to measure and why is where alignment happens.

Review progress weekly. Check key results movement in your regular team meetings. This keeps OKRIs visible and actionable.

Connect to your existing workflow. Reference OKRIs in sprint planning, use them to prioritize features, and connect user stories back to key results.

Celebrate key result movement, not just completion. If you're 80% of the way to a key result, that's success worth celebrating, even if you didn't hit 100%.

Learn from what doesn't work. When key results don't move as expected, treat it as valuable learning about your customers, your product, or your assumptions.

Review quarterly. Use what you learned in the previous quarter to adjust key results and set better initiatives for the next one.

One team we worked with starts every sprint planning session with a simple question: "Which of our key results will move forward if we execute this sprint successfully?"

The Long-Term Impact of Good OKRIs

Here's what happens when teams get good at OKRIs: they stop having arguments about priorities.

When everyone agrees on what success looks like and how to measure it, decisions become clearer. Features that don't drive key results get deprioritized. Experiments that could move multiple key results get fast-tracked. Resources flow toward the work most likely to create the outcomes everyone cares about.

Teams also get better at connecting their daily work to customer value. Instead of just shipping features, they're solving customer problems in measurable ways. Instead of just completing tasks, they're creating business outcomes.

Most importantly, they build products that actually matter—products that change customer behavior in positive ways and drive business results that justify the investment.

What's Next

You've reached the end of our journey through Structured Conversations. In the **Epilogue**, we'll reflect on how all these techniques work together to transform the way product teams communicate, align, and deliver value.

From Empathy Mapping through OKRIs, you now have a complete toolkit for turning messy conversations into clear action, scattered efforts into focused outcomes, and good intentions into measurable results.

The question isn't whether these techniques work—it's whether you'll use them to build something that matters.

Your Conversations Shape the Future

You've just finished reading about 20 different techniques for improving how product teams communicate, align, and deliver value. If you're feeling a bit overwhelmed, that's completely normal. Looking at everything from VERB + NOUN syntax to OKRIs can feel like a lot to absorb.

But here's the thing: you don't need to implement all of these techniques tomorrow. The real power of Structured Conversations isn't in using every technique—it's in changing how you think about the conversations your team has every day.

The Conversation That Started It All

Remember the restaurant app team from Chapter 1? They were stuck in the same cycle that traps many product teams: lots of meetings, lots of good intentions, lots of hard work, but frustratingly little progress toward outcomes that actually mattered to customers.

Their breakthrough didn't come from adopting a new project management tool or hiring more people. It came from recognizing that their biggest problem wasn't execution—it was communication. Specifically, it was the gap between what they thought they were all agreeing on and what they were actually agreeing on.

When they said "improve the customer experience," everyone nodded. But Sarah, the developer, was thinking about page load times. Mike, the designer, was thinking about visual hierarchy. Jessica, the product manager, was thinking about conversion rates. They all supported "improving UX," but they were working toward completely different definitions of improvement.

The techniques in this book show up in project management, product management, agile delivery, and product strategy—but at their core, they're about closing the gap between what we think we're saying and what we're actually communicating.

What Actually Changes When Teams Master This

Time and again, we see a consistent pattern when teams get good at structured conversations:

The arguing stops. Not because people agree about everything, but because disagreements become productive. When someone says "we should improve the checkout flow," the team automatically asks "what specific customer behavior are we trying to change?" Arguments about opinions turn into discussions about evidence.

Planning becomes faster and more accurate. Teams that used to spend days in planning meetings start making decisions in hours. When everyone understands the same techniques for breaking down problems, the conversation moves quickly from "what should we build?" to "how should we build it?"

New team members contribute faster. Instead of spending months learning tribal knowledge and unspoken assumptions, new hires can read user stories, scenarios, and roadmaps that actually explain how the product works and why decisions were made.

Stakeholder conversations become easier. Instead of defending feature decisions with "our customers want this," teams can point to specific research, clear hypotheses, and measurable outcomes. Executive conversations shift from asking only "when will it be done?" to also asking "how will we know if it's working?" and "what would cause us to change direction?"

Customer value becomes the default filter. Teams stop building features because they seem cool or because competitors have them. Every conversation starts with "how does this help our customers accomplish their goals?"

Most importantly, work becomes more meaningful. When everyone understands how their daily tasks connect to customer outcomes and business results, the work feels purposeful instead of arbitrary.

Where to Start
(Because You Don't Need to Boil the Ocean)

If you're leading a team, don't try to implement everything at once. Pick one technique that addresses your biggest current pain point:

If your team struggles with vague goals and priorities, start with VERB + NOUN syntax (Chapter 2) and Goal-Oriented Roadmapping (Chapter 22). Spend one meeting turning "improve customer engagement" into "increase daily active customers by 25% in Q2."

If your planning meetings feel endless and unproductive, try Example Mapping (Chapter 13) for your next user story. Watch how quickly the team aligns when you're discussing concrete examples instead of abstract requirements.

If your team builds features that customers don't use, start with Empathy Mapping (Chapter 5) or Customer Journey Mapping (Chapter 7). Understanding what customers actually think and feel changes everything about what you choose to build.

If your product feels like a random collection of features, try Impact Mapping (Chapter 6) to connect your work to specific customer behavior changes you want to influence.

If your team has good ideas but struggles to validate them, experiment with Hypothesis-Driven Development (Chapter 23) on your next initiative. Turn assumptions into testable predictions before you commit resources.

The key is to pick one technique, try it for a few weeks, and let the team experience the difference. Once they see how much clearer and more productive conversations become, they'll naturally want to try more.

The Ripple Effect

Here's something interesting that happens when teams master structured conversations: the techniques start spreading beyond the immediate team.

Customer support starts using the same format to communicate defects and feature requests. Sales teams reference the same customer journey maps when talking to prospects. Executives start asking for OKRIs instead of just project timelines.

The shared vocabulary becomes a competitive advantage. When everyone in the organization can communicate precisely about customer problems, customer needs, and business outcomes, the entire company becomes more aligned and more agile.

A Different Kind of Meeting

Imagine walking into your next sprint planning meeting and hearing conversations like this:

The user story says 'As a busy parent, I want to reorder my last meal so I can skip menu browsing during dinner stress.' Our Gherkin scenario tests whether families actually use the reorder button at least once in their first week. Our hypothesis is that this will reduce order time by 30% and increase weeknight order frequency by 20%. If we're right, it moves us toward our OKRI of making weeknight ordering effortless for families.

Instead of: We should build a reorder feature because customers have been asking for it.

That's the difference structured conversations make. Not longer meetings with more documentation, but shorter meetings with clearer outcomes.

Your Next Conversation

You don't need to wait for organizational change or team training to start applying these techniques. You can start in your very next conversation:

- When someone proposes a vague goal, ask "what specific customer behavior are we trying to change?"
- When the team debates feature priorities, suggest sketching a quick impact map to see which options best serve your strategic objectives
- When requirements feel unclear, try Example Mapping to surface concrete examples
- When you're not sure if an idea will work, frame it as a testable hypothesis

Every conversation is an opportunity to move from vague to specific, from assumptions to evidence, from outputs to outcomes.

The Future You're Building

The techniques in this book aren't just about building better products—they're about building better teams. Teams that communicate clearly, align around shared goals, and deliver value that customers actually care about.

In a world where misalignment is expensive and clarity is rare, structured conversations are a competitive advantage. They help teams avoid building the wrong thing, solve the right problems, and spend their energy on what matters.

Your next conversation could be the one that changes everything. The question isn't whether you've mastered Example Mapping or can write perfect Gherkin scenarios. The question is whether you're ready to help your team move from talking past each other to talking toward something meaningful.

What will your next conversation change?

Visit structured-conversations.com for free templates to help you implement these techniques with your team.

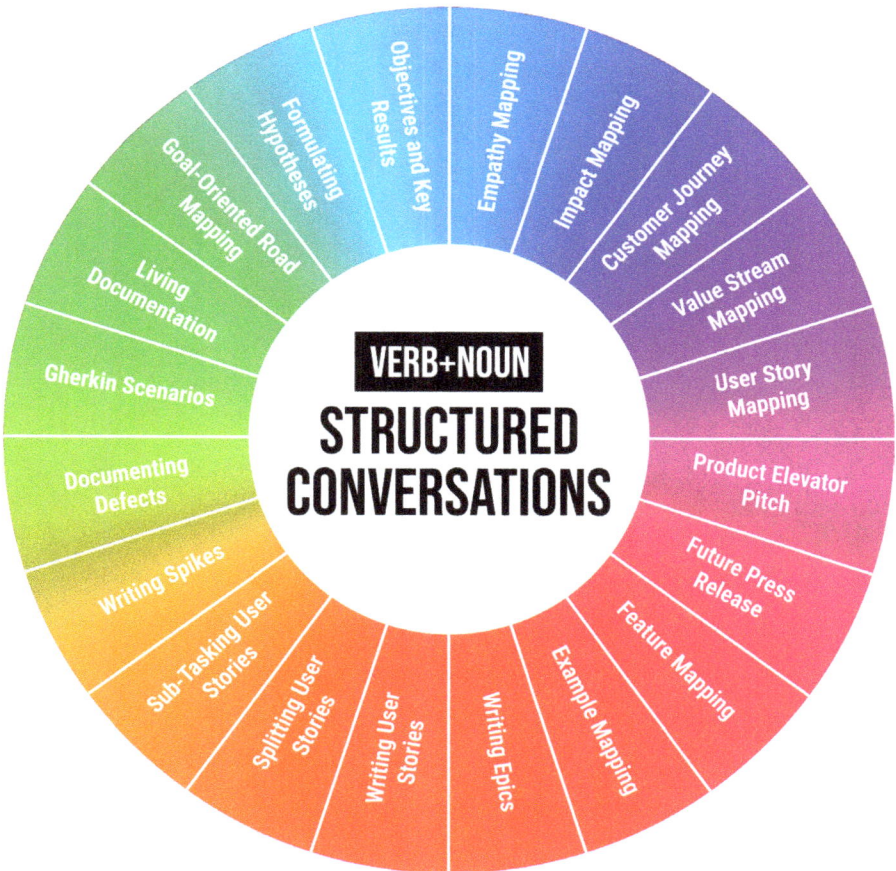

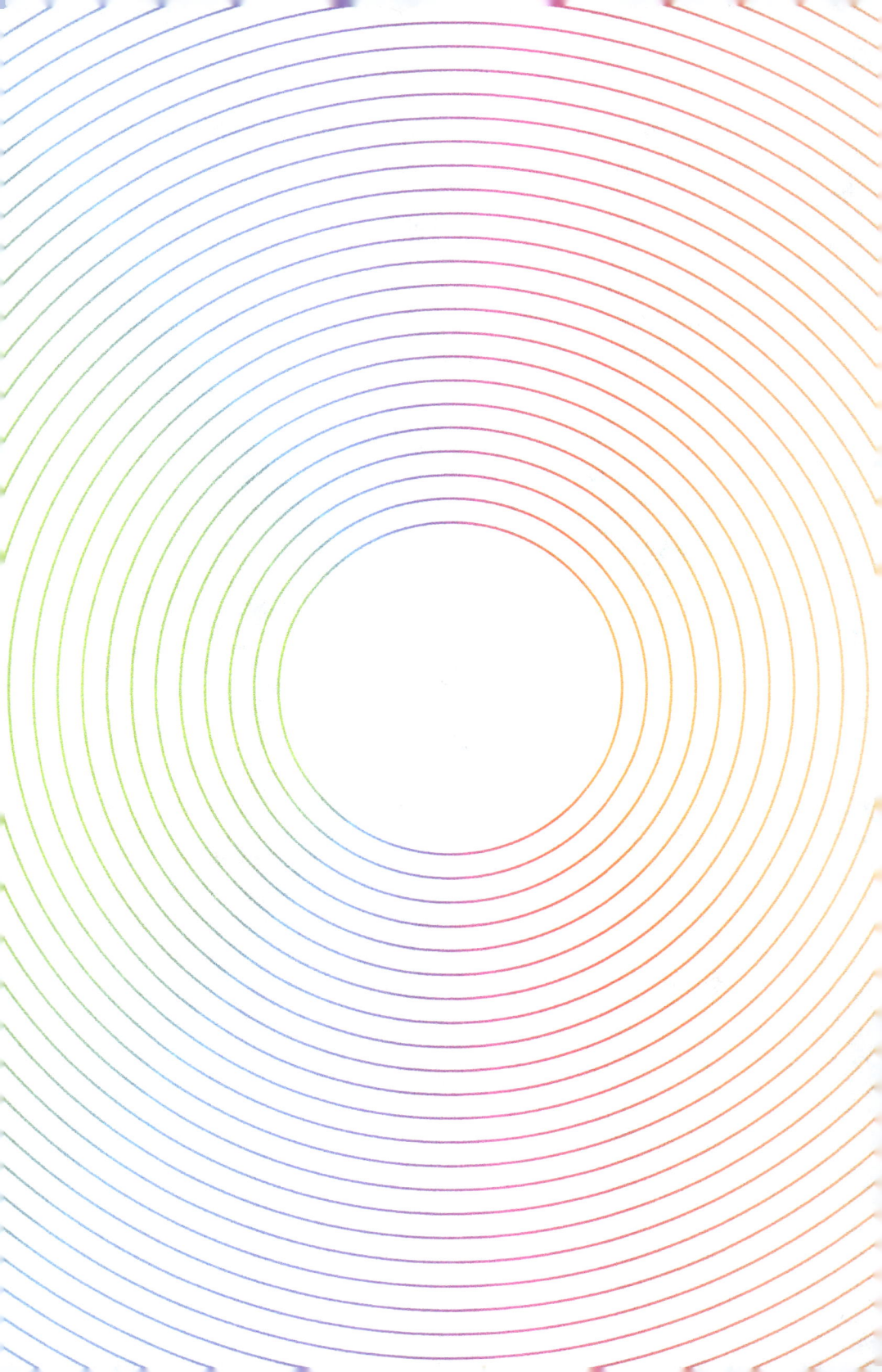

Templates

Find free templates online at structured-conversations.com.

Chapter 22 — Goal-Oriented Roadmapping

Chapter 23 — Formulating Hypotheses

Chapter 24 — Objectives and Key Results (OKRs)

Bibliography

Adzic, Gojko. *Impact Mapping: Making a Big Impact with Software Products and Projects*. Provoking Thoughts, 2012.

Adzic, Gojko. "Splitting user stories—the hamburger method." *Gojko's Blog*, 23 Jan. 2012, gojko.net/2012/01/23/splitting-user -stories-the-hamburger-method.

Adzic, Gojko, et. al. "Getting the most out of impact mapping." *InfoQ*, 8 Nov. 2014, infoq.com/articles/most-impact-mapping.

Adzic, Gojko and David Evans. *Fifty Quick Ideas to Improve Your User Stories*. Neuri Consulting LLP, 2014.

Bastow, Janna. "Free Your Product Roadmap and Ditch the Time-line." *Mind the Product*, 1 Oct. 2019, mindtheproduct.com/free -your-product-roadmap-and-ditch-the-timeline.

Beck, Kent, and Cynthia Andres. *Extreme Programming Explained: Embrace Change, 2nd Edition (The XP Series)*. Addison-Wesley, 2004.

Brower, Tracy. "Empathy Is The Most Important Leadership Skill According To Research." *Forbes*, 19 Sep. 2021, forbes.com/sites /tracybrower/2021/09/19/empathy-is-the-most-important -leadership-skill-according-to-research/?sh=7f2111e53dc5.

Bryar, Colin, and Bill Carr. *Working Backwards: Insights, Stories, and Secrets from Inside Amazon*. St. Martin's Press, 2021.

Cohn, Mike. "Not Everything Needs To Be a User Story: Using FDD Features." *Mountain Goat Software*, 21 Jul. 2015, mountaingoatsoftware.com/blog/not-everything-needs-to-be -a-user-story-using-fdd-features.

Cohn, Mike. "Five Simple but Powerful Ways to Split User Stories." *Mountain Goat Software*, 16 Mar. 2017, mountaingoatsoftware .com/blog/five-simple-but-powerful-ways-to-split-user-stories.

Cohn, Mike. "Job Stories Offer A Viable Alternative to User Stories." *Mountain Goat Software*, 29 Oct. 2019, mountaingoatsoftware .com/blog/job-stories-offer-a-viable-alternative-to-user-stories.

Curedale, Robert. *Mapping Methods 2: Step-by-step guide*. Design Community College Inc., 2018.

Fuqua, Andrew. "Agile Spike, Who Should Enter It, And How To Word It." *LeadingAgile*, Sep. 2016, leadingagile.com/2016/09/whats -an-agile-spike-who-should-enter-it-how-to-word-it.

Gallo, Carmine. "Jeff Bezos Banned PowerPoint in Meetings. His Replacement is Brilliant: Narrative memos have replaced PowerPoint presentations at Amazon. Here are 3 reasons." *Inc.*, 25 Apr. 2018, inc.com/carmine-gallo/jeff-bezos-bans-powerpoint -in-meetings-his-replacement-is-brilliant.html.

Gilad, Itamar. *Evidence-Guided: Creating High Impact Products in the Face of Uncertainty*. 2023.

Gilad, Itamar. "Why you should stop using product roadmaps and try the GIST Framework." *Itamar Gilad*, itamargilad.com/gist -framework.

Gilad, Itamar. "The GIST Board and OTHER GIST Tools." *Itamar Gilad*, itamargilad.com/the-gist-board-and-other-gist-tools.

Gothelf, Jeff, and Josh Seiden. *Lean UX: Designing Great Products with Agile Teams, 3rd Edition*. O'Reilly Media, 2021.

Gothelf, Jeff. "OKRs and User Story Mapping." *Jeff Gothelf*, 24 Apr. 2023, jeffgothelf.com/blog/okr-and-user-story-mapping

Gothelf, Jeff. "How to Combine OKRs and User Story Mapping." *Continuous Learning*, 27 Aug. 2023, continuouslearning.beehiiv .com/p/how-to-combine-okrs-and-user-story-mapping

Gothelf, Jeff, and Josh Seiden. *Who Does What By How Much? A Practical Guide to Customer-Centric OKRs*. Sense & Respond Press, 2024.

Grandin, Temple. *Visual Thinking: The Hidden Gifts of People Who Think in Pictures, Patterns, and Abstractions*. Riverhead Books, 2022.

Gray, Dave. "Updated Empathy Map Canvas." *Medium*, 15 Jul. 2017, medium.com/@davegray/updated-empathy-map-canvas -46df22df3c8a.

Herbig, Tim. *Real Progress: How to Connect the Dots of Product Strategy, OKRs, and Discovery*. Herbig.co, 2025.

Jeffries, Ron. "Essential XP: Card, Conversation, Confirmation." *Ron Jeffries*, 30 Aug. 2001, ronjeffries.com/xprog/articles /expcardconversationconfirmation.

Kaplan, Kate. "When and How to Create Customer Journey Maps." *Nielsen Norman Group: UX Training Consulting & Research*, 31 Jul. 2016, nngroup.com/articles/customer-journey-mapping.

Lawrence, Richard, and Peter Green. "The Humanizing Work Guide to Splitting User Stories." *The Humanizing Work Company*, 20 Sep. 2023, humanizingwork.com/the-humanizing-work-guide -to-splitting-user-stories.

Martraire, Cyrille. *Living Documentation: Continuous Knowledge Sharing by Design*. Addison-Wesley Professional, 2019.

Mee, Chaz. "Why "Now" "Next" "Later" is one of the best frameworks for roadmapping." *Medium*, 1 Apr. 2021, medium.com /the-creative-strategist/why-now-next-later-is-one-of-the-best -frameworks-for-roadmapping-4d547a2f2692.

Moore, Geoffrey A. *Crossing the Chasm, 3rd Edition: Marketing and Selling Disruptive Products to Mainstream Customers*. Harper Business, 2014.

Murphy, Ant. "Alignment through OKRs and Hypotheses." *Product Coalition*, 26 Aug. 2019, productcoalition.com/alignment -through-okrs-and-hypotheses-4f2b9bf94499.

Nadella, Satya. "Microsoft CEO Satya Nadella: How Empathy Sparks Innovation." *Knowledge at Wharton*, 22 Feb. 2018, knowledge.wharton.upenn.edu/article/microsofts-ceo-on-how-empathy-sparks-innovation.

Nadella, Satya. *Hit Refresh: The Quest to Rediscover Microsoft's Soul and Imagine a Better Future for Everyone*. Harper Business, 2019.

Nadella, Satya. "How Empathy Helped Generate A $2 Trillion Company." *Forbes*, 18 Jul. 2021, www.forbes.com/sites/stevedenning/2021/07/18/how-empathy-helped-generate-a-two-trillion-dollar-company.

Onuta, Anca. "How Agile Spikes Help to Improve Your Agile Product Delivery?" *Medium*, 14 Jul. 2019, ancaonuta.medium.com/how-spikes-help-to-improve-your-agile-product-delivery-a0f104305911.

Onuta, Anca. "Hamburger technique to Split User Stories from Development team perspective." *Medium*, 7 Jul. 2019, ancaonuta.medium.com/hamburger-method-to-split-user-stories-from-dev-team-perspective-d17aba58be02.

O'Reilly, Barry. "How to Implement Hypothesis-Driven Development." *Barry O'Reilly*, 21 Oct. 2013, barryoreilly.com/explore/blog/how-to-implement-hypothesis-driven-development.

Patton, Jeff, and Peter Economy. *User Story Mapping: Discover the Whole Story, Build the Right Product*. O'Reilly Media, 2014.

Pereira, David. *Untrapping Product Teams: Simplify the Complexity of Creating Digital Products*. Addison-Wesley, 2024.

Pereira, Steve, and Andrew Davis. *Flow Engineering: From Value Stream Mapping to Effective Action*. IT Revolution, 2024.

Pichler, Roman. *Strategize: Product Strategy and Product Roadmap Practices for the Digital Age, 2nd Edition*. Pichler Consulting, 2022.

Rissen, Paul. *Experiment-Driven Product Development: How to Use a Data-Informed Approach to Learn, Iterate, and Succeed Faster*. Apress, 2019.

Sandy, Ken. *The Influential Product Manager: How to Lead and Launch Successful Technology Products*. Berrett-Koehler Publishers, 2020.

Seiden, Joshua. *Outcomes Over Output: Why customer behavior is the key metric for business success.* Sense & Respond Press, 2019.

Smart, John Ferguson. "Feature Mapping—a simpler path from stories to executable acceptance criteria." John Ferguson Smart, 25 Jan. 2017, johnfergusonsmart.com/feature-mapping-a-simpler-path-from-stories-to-executable-acceptance-criteria.

Smart, John Ferguson. "Feature Mapping—a lightweight requirements discovery practice for agile teams." *John Ferguson Smart*, 6 Nov. 2019, johnfergusonsmart.com/feature-mapping-a-lightweight-requirements-discovery-practice-for-agile-teams.

Smart, John Ferguson, and Jan Molak. *BDD in Action, Second Edition: Behavior-Driven Development for the whole software lifecycle.* Manning, 2023.

Squirrel, Douglas, and Jeffrey Fredrick. *Agile Conversations: Transform Your Conversations, Transform Your Culture.* IT Revolution Press, 2020.

Stillman, Daniel. *Good Talk: How To Design Conversations That Matter.* Management Impact Publishing, 2020.

Torres, Teresa. *Continuous Discovery Habits: Discover Products that Create Customer Value and Business Value.* Product Talk LLC, 2021.

Ulwick, Anthony W. *Jobs To Be Done: Theory to Practice.* Idea Bite Press, 2016.

Vellore, Vetri. *OKRs for All: Making Objectives and Key Results for your Entire Organization.* Wiley, 2022.

Walker, Stephen M. "PR/FAQ: the Amazon Working Backwards Framework for Product Innovation." *productstrategy.co*, 2 May 2024, productstrategy.co/working-backwards-the-amazon-prfaq-for-product-innovation.

Wynne, Matt. "Introducing Example Mapping." *Cucumber.io*, 8 Dec. 2015, cucumber.io/blog/bdd/example-mapping-introduction.

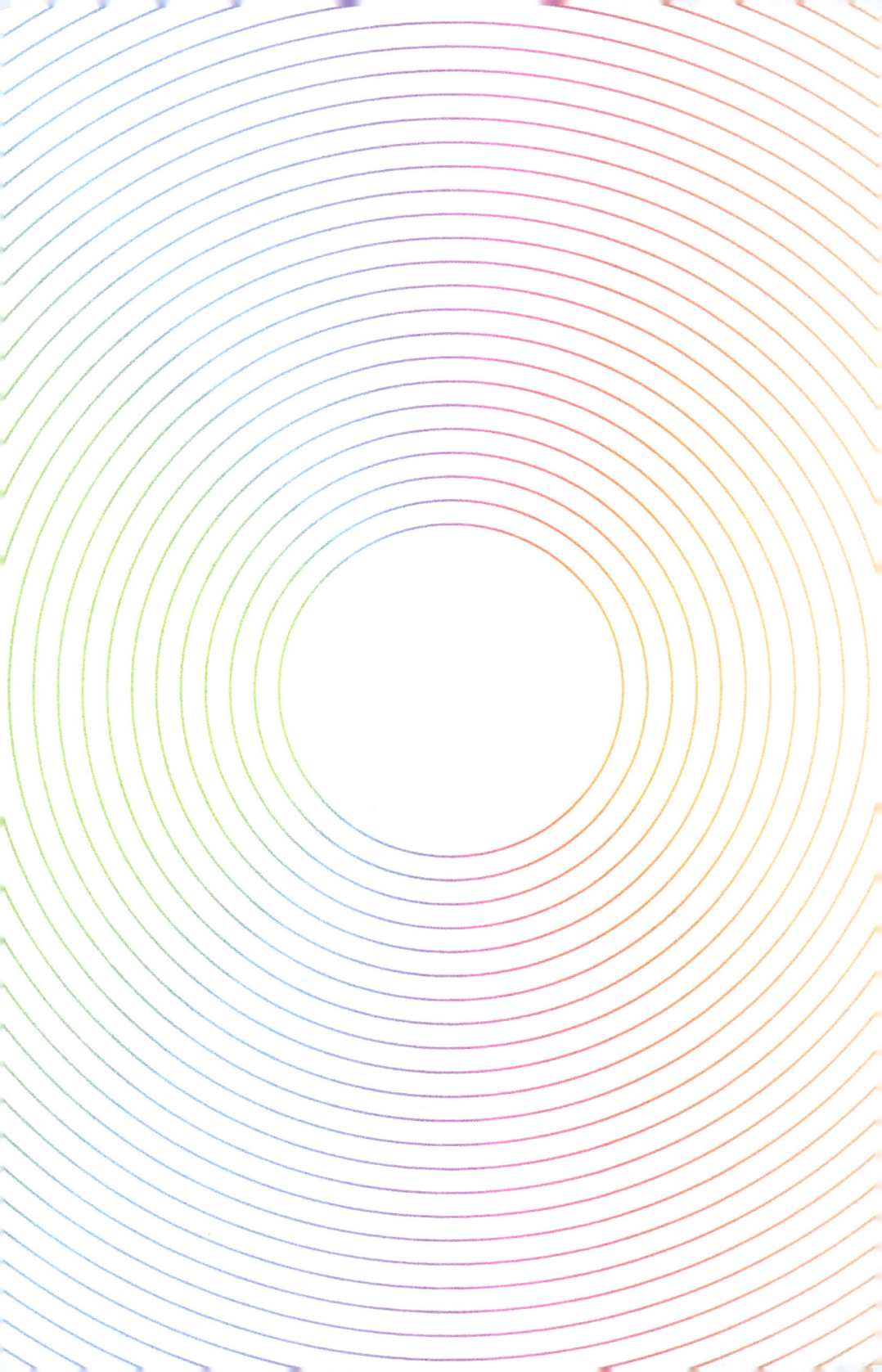

About the Authors

Claude Hanhart is a Product Strategist and Agile Coach with 10+ years of leadership experience in driving groundbreaking product strategies and agile transformations. His approach centers on fostering innovation rooted in business objectives, customer experience, and market leadership through tools such as Generative AI, OKRs, and Behavior-Driven Development (BDD).

Claude's unique academic background—with an MA in Ancient Near Eastern Archaeology and Languages from the University of Berne in Switzerland and an MA in Geography from the University of Minnesota—brings an interdisciplinary perspective to modern product challenges. His multilingual abilities in German, Swiss German, and French have proven invaluable in international collaborations.

Structured Conversations represents Claude's commitment to bridging strategic thinking with practical implementation. Currently based in New Jersey with his wife, Claude finds that their three energetic dogs serve as daily reminders about the importance of clear communication and patient guidance—principles that translate beautifully into his professional coaching work.

Rachel Collins is a seasoned business-strategy professional whose career has been built around turning complex challenges into clear, actionable solutions. With a track record of guiding organizations toward measurable impact, she blends rigorous, data-driven analysis with a human-centric mindset—always asking how people, processes, and technology can work together more effectively. Her practical, results-focused approach has helped teams align goals, streamline actions, and translate those actions into lasting outcomes.

Structured Conversations marks Rachel's first full-length publication, and she feels especially honored to have been invited by Claude to co-create this work. Rachel lives in North Carolina with her husband and their four rambunctious cats. When she isn't untangling business puzzles, you'll find her exploring the local arts scene, hiking and mountain biking, or enjoying a quiet evening of reading with her feline companions.

www.ingramcontent.com/pod-product-compliance
Lightning Source LLC
Chambersburg PA
CBHW071319210326
41597CB00015B/1276